ACCOUNTING

FOR LIBRARIES

&

Other Not-for-Profit Organizations

ACCOUNTING
FOR LIBRARIES
and
Other Not-for-Profit Organizations

SECOND EDITION

G. Stevenson Smith

AMERICAN LIBRARY ASSOCIATION
Chicago and London
1999

While extensive effort has gone into ensuring the reliability of information appearing in this book, the publisher makes no warranty, express or implied, on the accuracy or reliability of the information, and does not assume and hereby disclaims any liability to any person for any loss or damage caused by errors or omissions in this publication.

Project editor: Louise D. Howe
Cover design by Dianne M. Rooney
Text design by Lucy Lesiak

Printed on 50-pound white offset, a pH-neutral stock, and bound in B-grade Arrestox linen cloth by McNaughton & Gunn.

The paper used in this publication meets the minimum requirements of American National Standard for Information Sciences–Permanence of Paper for Printed Library Materials, ANSI Z39.48-1992.∞

Library of Congress Cataloging-in-Publication Data
Smith, G. Stevenson.
    Accounting for libraries and other not-for-profit organizations /
  G. Stevenson Smith. — 2nd ed.
      p. cm.
    Rev. ed. of: Accounting for librarians and other not-for-profit managers. 1983.
    Includes index.
    ISBN 0-8389-0758-X
    1. Libraries—United States—Accounting. 2. Nonprofit organizations—United States—Accounting. 3. Fund accounting—United States. I. Smith, G. Stevenson. Accounting for librarians and other not-for-profit managers. II. Title.
Z683.2.U6S65 1999
025.1'1—dc21   99-22476

Printed in the United States of America.

03 02 01 00 99   5 4 3 2 1

This book is dedicated to my mother, who told me "be an accountant" and to my wife, Carol, and our two children—all of whom, as a result, have to live with one.

CONTENTS

PREFACE

THE AMERICAN LIBRARY ASSOCIATION (ALA) has had a tradition in augmenting librarians' understanding of financial reporting for a number of years. For example, in 1943, the ALA published a book entitled *Public Library Finance and Accounting* by Edward A. Wight that outlined library accounting from costing to budgeting and financial reporting. In that tradition, this book discusses and explains the methods of *financial* accounting to be followed by small and medium-sized libraries and other not-for-profit organizations (NFO) that do not issue their own debt securities. It is a second edition. The first edition was published in 1983, forty years after Wight's book.

In an accounting sense, most libraries are considered to be component units of another governmental organization. Consequently, the accounting staff of the larger governmental organization often prepares the financial reports for the library. As a result, the report that is prepared may not provide all the information needed by library managers. This does not mean that these reports cannot be adjusted to be more meaningful to the library manager. It does mean that the library director and other staff members must clearly identify the financial information they need. This book is dedicated to helping the library manager get more useful financial reports.

Since Wight's publication, the methods of financial accounting have become more prescribed by the accounting profession. These accounting methods and their corresponding financial statements are illustrated throughout the book, but especially in part 2. Part 1 explains the basics of accounting and the models of accounting that are available. In part 1, it is apparent that the method of financial reporting prescribed for NFOs is not necessarily the best method that can be used in explaining the NFO's financial environment. But, the methods that are used and illustrated in the book are the ones that accounting policy bodies have prescribed for use.

Since the publication of the 1983 edition of this book, numerous accounting changes have occurred in NFO financial reporting. In fact since 1983, these new reporting requirements have changed the basic foundation on which library accounting is based. Readers with copies of the 1983 book can see many of these changes. These changes are set by the Government Accounting Standards Board (GASB), the Financial Accounting Standards Board (FASB), and influenced by the American Institute of Certified Public Accountants.

It should be noted that in the accounting standard setting process, at both the GASB and the FASB, *proposed* new accounting rules are issued in a preliminary form. At that time, comments about the new rules are requested especially from the organizations that are going to be affected by the proposed changes. If there are concerns about the changes, NFOs need to document their concerns to the accounting body considering the change. The manner in which the final rule is adopted is influenced by submitted comments, so NFOs can affect their accounting reporting requirements.

This manuscript was written in the days and evenings when I was not teaching, and it was not always fun. Therefore, as with every manuscript, thanks must be given to a number of individuals who encouraged me during the writing of this book. First, I would like to thank the ALA staff members who scanned my first book onto disks as well as Marlene Chamberlain for her support and help throughout the writing of the book. My thanks also go to Herb Bloom at ALA who gave me my chance to write the first edition. Thanks to my children, Scott and Jessie, and my wife Carol who let me work twelve-hour days. Finally, a thanks to Seth Stephens who sent me this e-mail message during the writing of the book and made me want to keep on writing.

> I am the Director of a small public library in northwest New Jersey. This is my first Directorship and your book *Accounting for Librarians* has been very helpful to me in organizing the library's finances. I would like to purchase a copy of this book, but it is out of print. I contacted ALA, and they do not have any copies available. Do you have suggestions on where I might be able to purchase a copy of this book? I value your book because of its relevancy to public libraries. I greatly appreciate your book and the much needed guidance it has provided.

Thanks, Seth, and here it is.

PART 1

The Foundations of Fund Accounting

The five chapters in part 1 provide an introduction into the basics of accounting and fund accounting for not for profit organizations. They examine the different methods of accounting that are used in not-for-profit organizations and provide the accounting foundation for the chapters in part 2.

1
Where Are
We Headed?

Because serious organizational consequences can result from misunderstanding accounting reports, this book seeks to provide assistance in understanding the accounting, financial statement presentations, and reports prepared by not-for-profit organizations (NFOs). Although the book specifically deals with accounting systems in medium-sized public libraries, it also provides guidance for other similar-sized NFOs such as museums, public broadcasting stations, performing arts associations, and zoological or botanical societies. The service objectives of such organizations differ, but their accounting transactions are very similar. Users' fees, donations, acquisitions of buildings and equipment, and payroll accounting are examples of similar accounting transactions, and there is little difference in accounting for donations at an art center or a library.

WHO SHOULD USE THIS BOOK?

Although the accounting applications in this book relate to all NFOs, the book is directly related to libraries. Within libraries, those individuals without an extensive accounting background who need to use the library's financial reports will find the book useful. The book is not directed at the professional accountant, but rather those library professionals who deal with the accountant. The director of an art center, museum, or library who is concerned about understanding the institution's accounting records and financial reports for decision-making purposes will find the book useful. Those members of the public who want to know the financial situation facing an NFO will also find the book useful.

The book contains numerous "nuts and bolts" examples of business transactions at a very practical level. For the administrator, professionally trained as a librarian or curator, overall explanations of fund accounting systems are provided. Further, the book furnishes insights into financial decision making for library administrators and can be used in university courses dealing with library financial management. In summary, the material is written to help the person with little background in accounting understand and make sound decisions based on the financial information prepared for an NFO.

In preparation for the writing of this book, a survey was sent to library directors and chairs to solicit their opinions about the usefulness of accounting information in their jobs with a series of open-ended questions. Their responses are placed throughout the book's chapters in sidebars called **From the Library Desk**, such as the one below.

From the Library Desk: I believe it would be in the best interest of the universities and library science programs that produce librarians/information specialists to incorporate a larger selection of classes that pertain to the area of accounting and business. These areas are of vital interest to any library and to have no knowledge of how to properly create a budget can only hinder the profession of librarianship. If you have a budget then you have a business and you must conduct that business properly so that your business will not be out of business!

Daniel J. Oates, Library Director, New York Medical College Affiliation, Lincoln Medical & Mental Health Center, Bronx, New York

---

The material in the book assumes the reader has a minimal knowledge of accounting and begins with the foundations of accounting: debits and credits. Those readers familiar with the basic debiting and crediting procedures, including the budgetary accounts, can omit chapters 2 and 4. The subsequent chapters build upon the introduction of debits and credits in chapter 2; therefore, it is important to be familiar with debit and credit procedures before proceeding to subsequent chapters. A reader who is not concerned with the mechanics of an NFO accounting system, but only with the results, can turn to the final chapter, which deals with production of the combined financial statements and their interpretations (chapter 10).

Completion of chapters 2 and 3, which deal with debiting and crediting procedures and the foundations of fund accounting, respectively, leads into the use of the budgetary accounts in chapter 4. Chapter 5 explains the year-end accounting procedures that affect certain accounts. Chapters 6 through 10 deal with specific funds, their financial statements, and the typical entries in these funds. These five chapters deal with the hypothetical "Harold Know Fines Library" and its accounting transactions. Chapter 10 provides an analysis of previously prepared financial statements.

WHY SET ACCOUNTING STANDARDS?

Why is it important that the same or similar accounting events be recorded consistently? If transactions are not recorded in a consistent manner, difficulties will arise for those who try to interpret or compare summarized financial reports. Rules are needed to establish accepted accounting practices. Thus, it is necessary to follow certain prescribed rules in recording NFOs' business transactions in order to understand the summarized results. For example, it would be difficult to make comparisons between baseball leagues if one league counted three strikes before a batter was struck out and another counted four strikes. The same problem arises, with more complexity, between organizations that use different accounting methods to record the same transaction.

Therefore, NFOs need to follow established accounting standards for correct analysis of their summarized results. In addition, certain basic principles are used in accounting, and the accounting methods used by NFOs are guided by these accepted standards. This book follows the standards currently recommended for NFOs by the official bodies that set accounting standards for NFOs.

WHO SETS ACCOUNTING STANDARDS FOR NFOS?

Accounting standards at the highest level in the United States are set by the Financial Accounting Standards Board (FASB) and the Government Accounting Standards Board (GASB). These accounting standard-setting boards are financially supported by professional organizations such as the American Institute of Certified Public Accountants (AICPA) and the Government Finance Officers Association (GFOA). Organizationally, both boards are overseen by the Financial Accounting Foundation. Offices for both boards are located in Norwalk, Connecticut. The FASB consists of seven full-time members, supported by a staff structure. There are five full-time members and a staff at the GASB. The objective of the two boards is to solve accounting problems through the establishment of accounting standards to be followed by the accounting profession. These standards are issued through series of "Statements" and "Interpretations," and they represent enforceable accounting practices.

In addition to the FASB and the GASB, the AICPA issues accounting guidelines to be followed through its "Statement of Position" (SOP), industry audit and accounting guides, and statements of auditing standards (SAS). These issuances are not as binding as Statements and Interpretations issued by the FASB or GASB, but they are considered representative of the best accounting practices.[1]

The standard-setting process may appear to create NFO accounting guidelines that are entirely comparable and consistent among all NFOs. This is not the case, however. Similar NFOs such as libraries may be considered to be "governmental" or "nongovernmental" NFOs. As a result, they will follow different methods of accounting. Even among "governmental" NFOs the methods of accounting may differ. An NFO designated as a governmental NFO meets one or more of the following characteristics:

a. Popular election of officers or appointment (or approval) of a controlling majority of the members of the organization's governing body by officials of one or more state or local governments;
b. The potential for unilateral dissolution by a government with the net assets reverting to a government; or
c. The power to enact and enforce a tax levy.[2]

The characteristic dealing with the appointment of a majority of board members by officials of a state or local government is the most significant factor in classifying an NFO as "governmental."

The AICPA publication *Not-for-Profit Organizations* recognizes the following twenty-two types of organizations as nongovernmental nonprofits.[3] Yet, at least nine categories can be identified as including both governmental (G) and nongovernmental (N) organizations.

Cemetery Organizations (G, N)
Civic and Community Organizations
Colleges and Universities (G, N)
Federated Fund-raising Organizations[4]
Fraternal Organizations
Labor Unions
Libraries (G, N)
Museums (G, N)
Performing Arts Organizations (G, N)
Political Action Committees
Political Parties
Private and Community Foundations (G, N)
Private Elementary and Secondary Schools
Professional Associations
Public Broadcasting Stations
Religious Organizations
Research and Scientific Organizations (G, N)
Social and Country Clubs
Trade Associations
Voluntary Health and Welfare Organizations (G, N)
Zoological and Botanical Societies (G, N)
Other Cultural Institutions

If one of the above organizations is considered governmental, there are two separate ways in which the financial statements and reports can be prepared.[5] Thus, there are currently three alternative accounting methods for use in preparing the financial reports for an organization like a library depending on whether it is a nongovernmental or governmental organization. Figure 1-1 outlines those choices as business accrual, not-for-profit accrual, and state and local government modified accrual. This book is concerned with the right side of figure 1-1 and with modified accrual, which is introduced in chapter 3 and discussed in detail in chapters 6 through 10.

As a result of these differences in accounting, the dollars expenditures between two libraries may not be comparable as they have not been accounted for in the same manner. In one recent article, it was estimated that 70 percent of the public libraries in one state were using the wrong model of accounting in preparing their financial statements.[6] These issues are dealt with in later chapters, but for now two factors should be noted. First, if one library's cost structure is compared with another's without understanding the underlying accounting methods, it could result in damaging and dangerous misinterpretations. Second, for the purposes of this book the governmental NFO model is used, and although there are two accounting methods acceptable for governmental NFOs, the more common method—modified accrual—is used here.

FIGURE 1-1   The Three Choices of Accounting Methods for NFOs

Nongovernment NFO (Business accrual)	Government NFO (Not-for-profit accrual)
	Government NFO (State and Local modified accrual)

WHAT IS FUND ACCOUNTING?

Recording business transactions within a series of separate funds is a common method of accounting for NFOs. This is the system that will be explained in this book. Within an NFO, fund accounting uses a system of accounts to separate fund groups that are more or less independent of one another.[7] If this accounting method were adopted by a family, separate checking accounts could exist for each family member. Each checking account would represent a separately balanced account, even though the family members together form one unit. It is assumed that the objectives of the money in each checking account are slightly different: Dad's checking account is used to support the family, and Junior's account is used for purchasing CDs, for example. In this way, each family member has his or her own fund (i.e., checking account) with slightly different objectives.

Expanding this concept within NFOs results in a fund accounting system. Such an accounting system exists when the books in an NFO contain several sets of separate, self-balancing account groups. Each of these separate, self-balancing account groups has different objectives and the monies in these funds are used to support those varied objectives.

At this point, a distinction should be made between the terms "fund" and "funds." A fund is a self-balancing set of accounts, and two sets of self-balancing accounts are considered to be two funds. Yet, in many cases, "funds" is a synonym for "monies." In this book, the term "funds" will not be used to mean money. Any reference to a "fund" or "funds" will refer to a self-balancing set of accounts in an NFO.

WHAT ABOUT AUDITS?

An audit is an annual review of an organization's financial records by an independent accountant to determine whether accepted accounting standards are being followed. One of the auditor's responsibilities is to ensure that the NFO is following the correct accounting model. Most NFOs are required to have an audit. In conjunction with the audit, an opinion is issued on the audit's results. This opinion should note any incorrectly applied accounting procedures or other matters of concern to the auditor. Audits are more fully described in chapter 3.

It should be pointed out that the AICPA has outlined the audit procedures at NFOs through its audit guides. Audit guides are issued for the benefit of the independent accountant who performs the audit. The accountant is required to justify any departures from an audit guide's procedures. As a result, audit guides and other auditing rules are likely to be closely followed. This can affect the way accounting functions are performed at an NFO because the accountant may suggest that changes be made in order to meet certain auditing standards.

SUMMARY

Readers who will find this book most useful are those whose accounting experience is limited and who work in organizations that can be classified as governmental organizations. Examples of those organizations have been given in the chapter. The financial reporting for these entities is the subject of this book. This book is not oriented toward cost analysis of projects or other managerial accounting questions. Those topics are covered in *Managerial Accounting for Libraries and Other Not-for-Profit Organizations* by G. Stevenson Smith.

FOR MORE INFORMATION

Addresses for accounting standard-setting bodies affecting NFOs:

American Institute of Certified Public Accountants, 1211 Avenue of the Americas, New York, New York 10036 (212-575-6434).

Government Accounting Standards Board and Financial Accounting Standards Board, 401 Merritt 7, Norwalk, CT 06150 (203-847-0700).

NOTES

1. American Institute of Certified Public Accountants, Statement on Auditing Standards No. 69, *The Meaning of "Fairly Present" in the Auditor's Report* (New York: AICPA, 1992). This SAS provides guidance in the hierarchy of accounting pronouncements for nongovernmental NFOs. The hierarchy of accounting standards for *governmental* NFOs begins with the Governmental Accounting Standards Board's statements and interpretations.

2. American Institute of Certified Public Accountants, *Not-for-Profit Organizations*, par. 1.03 (New York: AICPA, 1996).

3. A number of different terms have been used to describe NFOs. The AICPA has used the term "nonprofit." The FASB has referred to NFOs as "nonbusiness." In the accounting area, they have come to be called "not-for-profit organizations." The term NFO or NFOs will be used here as the abbreviation for nonprofit organizations.

4. American Institute of Certified Public Accountants, *Not-for-Profit Organizations*, par. 1.02 (New York: AICPA, 1996).

5. Government Accounting Standards Board, Statement No. 29, *The Use of Not-for-Profit Accounting and Financial Reporting Principles by Governmental Entities* (Norwalk, Conn.: GASB, 1995).

6. Craig D. Shoulders and Robert J. Freeman, "Which GAAP Should NFOs Apply?" *Journal of Accountancy*, 180(November 1995):77–84.

7. NFOs that are *not* defined as "governmental" and thus are subject to FASB rules do not use fund accounting systems as part of their financial reporting model for the public. They may, however, optionally use funds for internal reporting purposes.

2

Those Pesky Debits and Credits

THE PREPARATION OF FINANCIAL reports for NFOs begins with analysis of transactions that affect the organization. A transaction is an event, initially occurring inside or outside the organization, which requires a change in the NFO accounting records. A simple example is the receipt of cash by the organization. The process of analyzing and recording this transaction, referred to as *transaction analysis,* involves analysis of a cash receipt for its accounting effect on the organization. The analysis begins with recording debits and credits, but before this is considered, several introductory terms and concepts must be explained and the fund accounting cycle described.

An account, such as "Cash," summarizes all the dollar changes affecting a specific accounting category. This summarization is an easy way to determine the total dollar amount in an account category. For example, the "Cash account" summarizes all the changes, known as debits and credits, affecting "Cash." Thus, a specific account summarization is provided for the "Cash account," and we determine the total dollar amount, or balance, in this account. For cash, this tells us "how much cash we have left."

Through transaction analysis, the correct cash balance in the Cash account can be determined. Transaction analysis relates to the procedures used to investigate business events that have affected a specific NFO and the accounts of that NFO. In this analysis, the accounting meaning of the term *entity* is important in setting limitations on the transactions analyzed. Entity defines the territorial division or boundary between one accounting system and another accounting system. For example, John Smith's personal accounting system is a separate entity from Tom Brown's. If John Smith owns a business, the business accounting system is separate from his personal records. Therefore, when John Smith buys his wife a mink coat, this transaction should not appear on the books of his business. Although this may appear simple, NFOs' boundaries are sometimes not clearly distinguishable. This could occur when a number of different business activities, loaning books and bookstore sales, or organizational objectives, servicing the community or a specific group under a grant, exist within one organization unit. The same problem may arise when government authority overlaps the same geographical area with state, regional, and local NFOs interacting on the same program. The boundaries of a particular transaction can become more uncertain in this situation.

In fund accounting, the entity concept applies to separate NFOs (i.e., a city library and an art center). Yet, in addition to external divisions, the entity concept applies to divisions within an NFO. An NFO's accounting system consists of separate self-balancing account groups called *funds*. These funds separate accounting transactions for different organizational activities, almost as if they themselves were separate organizational entities. One fund may represent the activities of the NFO's general operations or unrestricted resources of the organization, and this fund is accounted for separately from a fund representing restricted grant resources, for example. Therefore, the entity concept applies to individual funds within an NFO also.

At this point, one additional introductory consideration remains: the fund accounting cycle, which outlines the sequence of accounting procedures in the order they should be performed in a fund accounting system. Performance of these accounting steps in this sequence ensures the proper recording and functioning of the fund accounting system. They are outlined here to provide a guide for subsequent material in which these steps are applied.

1. *Analyzing transactions.* An analysis of source documents, such as invoices and purchase orders, to determine the proper accounts to debit and credit. This procedure also involves the accounting analysis of approved budget spending set by the governing board responsible for the fiscal activities of the NFO.
2. *Journalizing transactions.* These procedures involve the recording of debits and credits in the journal, usually the general journal, but in some cases a special journal is used. A journal shows a listing of transactions in debit and credit format by date of occurrence. Journalizing of transactions occurs after the source documents have been analyzed (step 1). The "journalization" of a transaction is its entry point into the accounting system.

3. *Posting.* Posting transfers entries from the journals listed by date to the accounts in the ledger. The ledgers are a summarized listing of each account such as Cash, Equipment, etc., showing current balances or amounts in each account.

4. *Adjusting entries and posting.* There are certain accounting activities that record adjustments at the end of the fiscal year. These adjustments may be "catch ups" to current changes or they may be adjustments that are necessary to correct for missing or inaccurately recorded journal entries. Once they are recorded, they are posted to the ledger.

5. *Preparing the trial balance.* The trial balance is a summation of all the balances in the accounts contained in the ledger to ensure that the debits are equal to the credits. The trial balance is prepared prior to completing the financial statements to be certain that the debits and credits in the accounts correctly balance.

6. *Preparing the financial statements.* The monthly schedules and year-end financial statements that are prepared provide the governing board and the management of the NFO with information about its performance. These reports are important for decision making and for making comparisons with prior periods as well as for making predictions about future performance.

7. *Journalizing and posting the closing entries.* The balances in certain accounts need to be "zeroed out" or closed at the end of the fiscal year because they are temporary accounts that relate only to the current time period. These accounts are the expense (or expenditures), revenue, and budgetary accounts. Their balances do not continue to accumulate beyond the current year's results.

8. *Preparing a final closing trial balance.* Preparing a year-end trial balance after the final or closing entries have been posted to the ledger accounts is the last step in the fund accounting cycle. This trial balance is prepared to ensure that the debits and credits in remaining open accounts are in balance.

This eight-point fund accounting cycle outlines the sequence to be periodically followed in any fund accounting system. The cycle is introduced here to show the procedures that will be covered in later chapters. There are a number of new terms in the cycle, but unfamiliarity with these terms should not be a concern as they will be explained in later chapters. It should also be noted that with today's accounting software packages some of these steps automatically occur when the initial debit and credit entry is made.

The first two steps in the cycle occur more frequently than the others, and the beginning chapters will concentrate on these procedures. The occurrence of the other steps will vary depending on the size of the accounting system and whether it is computerized. After analyzing and journalizing transactions, the most frequently performed accounting activity is posting to accounts and preparing trial balances. Although the financial statements may be prepared on a quarterly basis in a summarized form, the year-end financial statements are the major financial documents prepared for public distribution by the NFO.

WHAT'S AN ASSET?

The fund accounting cycle lists the fundamental procedures in an accounting system, but basic to the cycle is the analysis of debits and credits, and major portions of this chapter are devoted to understanding the debiting and crediting of journal entries. (Readers who are already familiar with these procedures may wish to skip this chapter.)

In analyzing accounts to determine how debits and credits affect them, the first step is to understand the distinction between assets, liabilities, and the Fund Balance. Assets, liabilities, and the Fund Balance represent the major classifications into which transactions are categorized. To understand debits and credits and changes in account amounts, the reader must become familiar with the parts of a transaction that affect assets, liabilities, or the Fund Balance.

As a first step in separating a transaction into its asset, liability, and Fund Balance components, it is necessary to define these terms. This analysis begins with assets. The term *asset* describes any portion of a transaction that results in a future benefit to the entity. For example, Cash is an asset, and its future benefit arises when the entity uses cash to reduce amounts owed to others or to make purchases. Another example of an asset is a truck or a car. In this case, the future benefit to the organization arises from the use of the vehicle.

There is yet another stipulation with regard to assets beyond the provision of a future benefit. Specifically, the organization must legally own the asset. For example, your personal car is your asset, but your neighbor's car is not your asset, even if you have a right to use it whenever you wish to. Therefore, two criteria exist for classifying an account as an asset: (1) it has to provide a future benefit to the organization and (2) legal ownership must exist.

Common examples of assets normally encountered in NFOs are:

Cash	Equipment
Accounts Receivable	Grants Receivable
Pledges Receivable	Prepaid Assets
Inventories	Due from Employees
Investments	Due from Other Governments
Land	Petty Cash
Buildings	

It is likely that not all these asset accounts are found in every NFO. Most accounting systems have the more common assets, such as Cash, Inventories,

Land, Buildings, and Equipment. Along with the more common assets, some type of receivable would likely appear in this list of assets. Five common receivables are included in the list above.

The term *receivable* represents a sum of money that is due to the entity. The reason for the sum being owed to the entity can vary. Accounts Receivable represent a sum of money owed to an entity because a service was provided or goods were transferred to another entity, and instead of receiving cash a claim was received. The dollar amount of this claim is shown in Accounts Receivable. As another example consider Pledges Receivable, a promise of money, as yet uncollected, made to the entity by an outside party. In such a case, the outside party asks for nothing tangible in return. Grants Receivable indicates that grants from another organization have been awarded to the entity but not yet received. Usually a "grant" represents a definite dollar amount, and requires that these monies be spent in a specific manner. An example of a grant is funding awarded by (but as yet uncollected from), say, the federal government to a library to start a program for handicapped persons.

Two other types of receivables are Due from Employees and Due from Other Governments. As an example of the use of a Due from Other Governments account, assume that the Town of Morgan lends the Morgan City Library $5,000. When the town transfers the monies to the library, two accounts are affected. The town recognizes a reduction of its cash account and, at the same time, a receivable is recognized on the town's books. The receivable is called "Due from Morgan City Library," and is an example of the use of the Due from Other Governments account. An account such as Due from Employees might be needed in an organization where employees make personal purchases through the organization's purchasing officer. In such a situation, the employee owes the organization the purchase price, and that purchase price is considered a receivable.

Prepaid Assets, also in the list, are an account classification that may not occur as often in NFOs. A prepaid asset is an expense that has been paid for before the organization uses it, and a common example is the prepayment of rent, insurance, or supplies. As time passes, the prepaid asset becomes an expense and the asset is reduced. The final asset listed is Petty Cash. Petty Cash acts as a subdivision of cash, and it is accounted for separately from the Cash account. Its purpose is to pay for small, miscellaneous charges such as C.O.D. deliveries. The accounting procedures for using this account are explained in chapter 7.

WHAT'S A LIABILITY?

The next major account classification is *liabilities*. Very simply defined, liabilities are the amounts owed to others outside the specific organization or a specific fund. Liabilities exist as legitimate claims against the assets of an entity and usually occur between an NFO and an external organization. In addition, a liability can exist between funds in the same NFO when one fund owes monies to another fund. The reason for liabilities among the funds of one NFO relates to the entity concept mentioned earlier; that is, each fund acts as a separate accounting entity.

In our personal finances, liabilities occur as claims of others against us. For example, a bank can have a claim on our assets equal to the amount we owe on our home mortgage. An NFO also can owe monies to others outside the organization, but, in addition, the NFO's fund groups may have liabilities among themselves. For example, assume there are two funds, Fund A and Fund B, in the same NFO. On May 1, Fund A borrows $100 from Fund B. As of that date, Fund A recognizes a liability on its books, and Fund B has a claim on the assets of Fund A. This $100 liability remains on A's books until a $100 repayment is made to Fund B.

Typical examples of liabilities that might be found in an NFO are the following:

Accounts Payable
Loans Payable
Deferred Restricted Contributions
Due to Other Funds
Taxes Payable.

Remember, not all the listed accounts occur in every NFO. Whether all these listed liabilities occur in a fund accounting system depends on basic decisions about the accounting system in use. (These decisions will have to await discussion in chapter 3.)

A commonly encountered liability account is *Accounts Payable,* representing amounts owed to those outside the organization from whom purchases of supplies, books, inventories, or services have been made. Normally, Accounts Payable are paid within one year. Loans Payable, which act as a form of temporary financing, are also repayable within a year. Loans payable usually indicate that lending institutions, such as commercial banks, have made short-term monies available to the NFO. Another form of financing is Long-Term Debt, but usually only large NFOs have a Long-Term Debt account.[1] Long-Term Debt's distinguishing characteristic is its longer period of repayment in comparison to other payables.

The liability *Deferred Restricted Contributions* occurs when monies are advanced to an organization in anticipation of some service the organization will perform in the future, such as the receipt of grant monies prior to the performance of grant activities. The organization accepts the monies with the knowledge that it must perform the service, but the performance itself has been delayed or "deferred." Once the monies have been accepted, the organization has an obligation to provide the service, and that obligation for performance is a liability. Upon completion of the service, the liability is removed from the books.

As an example of a deferred liability, assume that money is received by the Brooks City Library from Colonel Chesty Hammer, U.S. Army, ret., for the purchase of books on military history only. Once the monies are accepted by the library, it has an obligation to purchase books on military history only. This obligation is a liability that requires recognition on the books. Utilization of the monies received for purposes other than the purchase of military history books can result in Col. Hammer or his heirs requesting the return of his money. Usually a legal right exists for this type of action. The Brooks City Library has not fulfilled its obligation until it has purchased books on military history up to the full extent of the monies made available by the colonel.[2]

Another type of account in the list of liabilities is called "Due to Other Funds." This liability, previously discussed with the example of Fund A and Fund B, occurs between separate funds within one NFO. Continuing the example of Fund A and B, we assume the $100 that Fund A borrowed from Fund B is recognized on Fund A's books. In such a case, a liability account, called "Due to Fund B," appears in Fund A's accounts, showing that Fund A owes Fund B $100. Monetary transfers between funds are fairly common.

The final liability account in the list is Taxes Payable. Actually, this account represents a number of different types of taxes that are payable to local, state, or federal government. This group of accounts can include Sales Taxes, Federal Income Taxes Payable, and Employer's FICA Taxes Payable. The latter liability is more commonly known as "Social Security taxes." In chapter 7, the material on payroll accounting includes explanations of how to account for these latter two taxes.

WHAT'S THE FUND BALANCE?

Of the three major account classifications now under consideration, the last one is the Fund Balance. A residual account, it develops because of the difference between assets and liabilities. The Fund Balance functions as both a residual between the assets and liabilities and the account where the summarization of each year's difference between the inflows of resources[3] and expenses occurs.[4] For the moment, expenses can be considered as the outflow of resources.

If any funding balances exist in the Fund Balance, the NFO can usually use these amounts for its operational expenses.[5] When expenses during a year are higher than resource inflows, a decrease in the Fund Balance occurs. Conversely, resource inflows that are larger than expenses (during a year) cause an increase to occur. In effect, the Fund Balance provides a place for recording the difference between resource inflows and expenses. The concept of the Fund Balance as a residual account is further developed in the following section.[6]

THE ACCOUNTING EQUATION

Although the relationship between assets, liabilities, and the Fund Balance has been hinted at in the previous explanations, the *accounting equation* explicitly sets forth that relationship. The equation is presented in figure 2-1 and, as illustrated, it can be used in three different formats.

FIGURE 2-1   The Three Forms of the Accounting Equation

A. Assets	=	Liabilities	+	Fund Balance
B. Fund Balance	=	Assets	−	Liabilities
C. Liabilities	=	Assets	−	Fund Balance

The equation usually appears in the form of equation A. Equation B illustrates the concept of the Fund Balance as a residual between the assets and liabilities as well as the importance of an agreed-upon definition for assets and liabilities. In equation B, it can be seen that if the liabilities were larger than the assets, the Fund Balance would have a negative balance; that is, it would be "in the hole." A negative balance in the Fund Balance could result in questions about the continuing financial viability of the NFO.

The equations illustrate the importance of reaching a correct balance in the account classification and the problems that arise from an "out-of-balance" account. Asset totals have to equal the total of liabilities and the Fund Balance for the books to be in balance. For example, if the assets are equal to $100,000 and the Fund Balance is equal to $25,000, the liabilities should be equal to $75,000.[7] The problems in exercise 2-1 continue this example (working these problems will facilitate familiarity with the accounting equation). Answers to the exercises appear in a separate answer section at the end of the book.

EXERCISE 2-1   The Accounting Equation

1. The Sweetwater Library has liabilities of $35,000 and a current Fund Balance equal to $40,000. How much does it have in assets?
2. The director of the Henry County Art Center wants to know how much is available in its fund balance. It has assets of $45,000 and liabilities of $45,000. Determine the amount in the Fund Balance.
3. The Maryland Tulip Society has assets of $55,000 and a Fund Balance equal to $15,000. Determine the amount of liabilities.
4. The Fayetteville Cultural Center has assets of $15,000 and liabilities of $17,500. What is the amount in the Fund Balance? What does this balance mean?

(Continued)

EXERCISE 2-1   The Accounting Equation   *(Continued)*

5. Assume that the assets and liabilities of the Sexton City Library have been certified to be $25,000 and $15,000 respectively. Further assume the bookkeeper is unsure of the amount that is supposed to be in the Fund Balance. The records show the Fund Balance is equal to $8,000. Is this the correct balance?

Another use of the accounting equation is to introduce the concept of debits and credits and the manner in which they affect the assets, liabilities, and the Fund Balance. It is very important to understand how to debit and credit accounts, before additional accounting procedures can be appreciated.

ANALYZING DEBIT AND CREDIT CHANGES IN ASSETS AND LIABILITIES

There is a retold story about an accounting instructor who, in exasperation from trying to explain debits and credits to his students, finally told them that debits appear on the left side of the classroom, by the door, and credits appear on the right side, by the windows. In the following explanation of debits and credits, the accounting equation and "T accounts" will serve in place of windows and doors.

The T account is used for illustrative purposes, to represent a ledger account. It receives its name from the form it takes, the shape of a T. The debits, abbreviated "Dr.," appear under the left part of the T, and the credits, abbreviated "Cr.," on the right side. The name of the account appears across the top of the T. Figure 2-2 is an illustration of a T account for Cash.

FIGURE 2-2   The T Account

Cash

Debit	Credit
(Dr.)	(Cr.)

Before we use the T account, the term *balance* needs to be defined. The term is used to describe the "balance in an account." The balance is found by subtracting the sum of one side of the T account from the sum of the other. If the account is an asset, as shown in figure 2-3, a debit addition increases the balance in the account and a credit addition decreases the balance. With the Fund Balance or a liability, a debit entry decreases the balance and a credit entry increases it. This relationship is illustrated in figure 2-3.

In working with accounts, it is common practice to refer to the "normal balance," which refers to the balance usually found in an asset, liability, or the

Fund Balance account. (The normal balances have been marked with an asterisk in figure 2-3.) In figure 2-3, the normal balance for assets is a debit balance, whereas the normal balance for liabilities and the Fund Balance are credit balances.

FIGURE 2-3   Summary of Effect of Debits and Credits on Assets, Liabilities, and Fund Balance

Effect of	Assets*	=	Liabilities†	+	Fund Balance†
Debits	+		−		−
Credits	−		+		+

* "Normal" balance is a debit.
† "Normal" balance is a credit.

The relationship in figure 2-3 is not difficult to remember. If the effect of debits and credits on assets is kept in mind, the effect on liabilities and the Fund Balance occurs in the reverse order. The more difficult part of this analysis relates to understanding the effect of transactions on the accounting system. (As previously stated, this is described as "transaction analysis.")

USING TRANSACTION ANALYSIS WITH ASSETS AND LIABILITIES

Two transactions will be analyzed to trace the effect of debits and credits on assets and liabilities. In this illustration the inflow and outflow of cash is considered. After the transactions have been analyzed, review exercises provide readers a chance to test your understanding.

TRANSACTION 1

In this transaction, Overdrew City Library receives cash deposits from patrons who check out video equipment and cassettes for home use. These deposits are returned to the patrons when the video equipment and cassettes are brought back into the library (the receipt and repayment of deposits is a continuing process during the year). For illustrative purposes, assume the library collects and repays a $50 deposit. What follows is a transaction analysis of the collection and repayment of this deposit. If, in an actual accounting system, deposits of this type are a fairly common occurrence, they are recorded in total on a daily basis. (It is unlikely that one deposit would be recorded, as shown here. Also, it is important to know the organizational viewpoint from which the transaction is analyzed. In other words, is the viewpoint that of Overdrew City Library or the depositor's accounting system? In this case it is obvious that attention is focused on the library's accounting system, but in other instances the distinction is not as clear.)

The process of transaction analysis begins with a series of questions, the correct answers to which provide the proper debits and credits to a transaction. The procedure is followed with each transaction in the remaining portions of this chapter.

The following step-by-step analysis is useful for anyone who is beginning to classify debits and credits.

Questions	*Answers*
1. What is the library receiving or giving up?	1. The library is receiving Cash.
2. Is Cash an asset, liability, or part of the Fund Balance?	2. Cash is an asset.
3. Is Cash increasing or decreasing?	3. Increasing.
4. What registers an increase in an asset?	4. A debit.
5. Is another asset affected?	5. No.
6. Is a liability affected?	6. Yes. (See following explanation.)
7. Is the Fund Balance affected?	7. No.
8. Is a liability increasing or decreasing?	8. Increasing.
9. What registers an increase in a liability?	9. A credit.

Transaction analysis is a step-by-step procedure that allows the investigator to determine which accounts are affected and how they are affected. Notice that in question 6 it was determined that the amount to be repaid to the depositors was a liability, but in question 7 the effect on the Fund Balance was still investigated. This is an important step because more than one debit or credit may occur in a single transaction. Assets must equal liabilities and the Fund Balance, but this does not mean that only one credit or debit change occurs in every transaction. More than one debit or credit change can occur.

Through transaction analysis it is determined that the Cash account is debited and a liability account (as yet unnamed) is credited.[8] Although it is obvious that the deposit affects the Cash account, the question may arise as to why a liability account is affected. To understand this, it must be remembered that the $50 deposit must be repaid when the patron brings the video equipment and cassettes back to the library, which has a legal obligation to return the deposit. Therefore, the deposit is a liability the library owes the patron upon receipt of the undamaged equipment and cassettes. This type of liability could simply be called "Video Room Deposits" or "Returnable Deposits."

From a learning viewpoint, it is important to understand the effect of debits and credits on the accounting equation. For this purpose, the accounting equation is reviewed after each transaction to ascertain that it remains in balance and to investigate the changes that have occurred in the accounts. (This is not the normal operating procedure in an actual accounting system. Also, most libraries would use a computerized accounting software package in which many of the transactions shown here would be performed automatically and in combination. However, it is important to have an understanding of how transactions are recorded in order to appreciate the financial reports that are eventually prepared.)

Figure 2-4 contains the changes in the accounting equation for the transaction just reviewed. Assume that the library had only one asset, Cash of $10,000, before the $50 deposit was left with the library. In such a case, the accounting equation would appear as shown in figure 2-4, equation 1: Before Deposit.

FIGURE 2-4   Accounting Equation after $50 Deposit Is Recorded

1. Before Deposit:	Assets	−	Liabilities	+	Fund Balance
	$10,000		$0		$10,000
2. After Deposit:	Assets	=	Liabilities	+	Fund Balance
	$10,050		$50		$10,000

After the library receives the deposit, its Cash balance increases by $50, and at the same time the liability balance also increases by $50. This is apparent in figure 2-4, equation 2: After Deposit. The accounting equation is in balance both before and after the transaction. As previously stated, checking the accounting equation after each transaction is not practical, but in all accounting systems the debits and credits must periodically be balanced against one another to determine if they are equal. This is done through use of a "trial balance" (which is explained later).

This analysis also can be shown through T accounts, which illustrate how the balances in the asset and liability accounts change through the entry of debits and credits to those accounts. The first set of T accounts in figure 2-5 represents the situation prior to receipt of the deposit. The second set of T accounts shows the balances after the deposit has been received. When T accounts are used for the analysis, a specific asset and liability account needs to be named in which to record the debit and credit entry. In this case, the asset account Cash and the liability account Returnable Deposits are used.

The $50 deposit appears in the Cash account as a debit of $50, which increases the Cash balance to $10,050. The liability account, Returnable Deposits, also increases as a result of the credit entry to $50. Yet, as the accounting equation showed, the debits and credits are equal.

FIGURE 2-5   T Account Analysis of Receipt of Deposit

Before Receipt of Deposit

Cash	Returnable Deposits	Fund Balance
$10,000		$10,000
Bal. $10,000	$ 0 Bal.	$10,000 Bal.

After Receipt of Deposit

Cash	Returnable Deposits	Fund Balance
$10,000	$50	$10,000
50		
Bal. $10,050	$50 Bal.	$10,000 Bal.

TRANSACTION 2

In this second transaction, assume that the patron returns the undamaged equipment and cassettes to Overdrew City Library within the loan period. At that time, the library must return the deposit to the patron. Another transaction has occurred and will be analyzed through transaction analysis.

Questions	*Answers*
1. What is the library receiving or giving up?	1. The library is giving up Cash.
2. Is Cash an asset, liability, or part of the Fund Balance?	2. Cash is an asset.
3. Is Cash increasing or decreasing?	3. Decreasing.
4. What registers a decrease in an asset?	4. A credit.
5. Is another asset affected?	5. No.
6. Is a liability affected?	6. Yes.
7. Is the Fund Balance affected?	7. No.
8. Is a liability increasing or decreasing?	8. Decreasing.
9. What registers a decrease in a liability?	9. A debit.

Through transaction analysis, we determine that a liability account, in this case Returnable Deposits, is debited and the asset account, Cash, is credited. The next step is to review the changes in the accounting equation.

After transaction 1, the accounting equation appears as shown in equation 2: Before Returning Deposit in figure 2-6. The changes from the debiting and crediting entries in transaction 2 cause Cash to decrease and the repayment of an obligation through decrease in the liability account, Returnable Deposits, to occur. After these changes are reflected in the accounting equation, the equation appears as equation 3 in figure 2-6. Overdrew City Library's accounts have returned to their original balances, prior to receipt of the deposit.

FIGURE 2-6   Accounting Equation Before and After Return of $50 Deposit

2. Before Returning Deposit:	Assets	=	Liabilities	+	Fund Balance	
	$10,050		$50		$10,000	
3. After Returning Deposit:	Assets	=	Liabilities	+	Fund Balance	
	$10,000		$0		$10,000	

The T accounts, with the transactions recorded in them, appear in figure 2-7. These T accounts provide a summary of all transactions from receipt of the deposit to its return.

FIGURE 2-7   T Account Analysis of Return of Deposit

Cash		Returnable Deposits		Fund Balance	
$10,000					$10,000
0	$50 Bal.	$50	$50		
Bal. $10,000			$0 Bal.		$10,000 Bal.

EXERCISE 2-2   Debiting and Crediting Assets and Liabilities

1. Green County Library purchases book shelving for $1,200 in cash. Determine the account classification(s) to debit and credit. What are the names of these accounts?
2. Took City Library has received $2,500 from a patron's estate. The money is to be used specifically for programs for senior citizens. Determine the account classification(s) to debit and credit. What are the names of these accounts?
3. Carter Art Center recently lost a large share of its funding. To continue to operate in the current year, it has received a $17,000 loan from an affiliation of local businesses. It is anticipated that the loan will be repaid when funding is restored. Determine the account classification(s) to debit and credit. What are the names of these accounts?

WHAT ARE REVENUES, EXPENSES, AND EXPENDITURES?

Up to this point, the transactions illustrated have not affected the Fund Balance. As previously stated, the Fund Balance acts as a residual between assets and liabilities. In addition, any increases or decreases in the Fund Balance from one year to the next are attributed to two other account classifications: revenues and expenses. The relationship between the Fund Balance and all these accounts is illustrated in figure 2-8. The Fund Balance is shown as a residual between assets and liabilities. At the same time, the current increase in the Fund Balance occurs because this year's revenues are more than expenses (or expenditures). Therefore, the Fund Balance acts as a connecting point between assets, liabilities, revenues, and expenses. The accounts that create a yearly increase or decrease in the Fund Balance—revenues, expenses or expenditures—will be considered next.

FIGURE 2-8   The Fund Balance

The Fund Balance is equal to the excess of assets over liabilities ($2.5 M). At the same time, current increase in the Fund Balance is due to excess of revenues over expenses ($.5M).

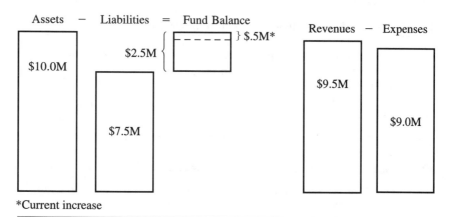

*Current increase

Basically, *revenues* are considered inflows of resources to the organization that will eventually increase the Fund Balance; whereas *expenses* or *expenditures* cause reductions in resources and reduce the Fund Balance. There is a somewhat short-run perspective adopted here as revenues and expenses are tied to the current time period (usually the current year). Expenses also can be seen as causing the expiration of benefits in the current fiscal period. Many expenses are recorded in the accounts at the time a legal obligation for payment is incurred. This may not occur at the same time that the expense is paid for with cash; that is, the legal obligation may be incurred before the cash flows out of the organization.

Before we explore the more detailed characteristics of revenues, a distinction between the terms *expenditures* and *expenses* should be made. A fundamental difference exists between the two terms, and they should not be confused. Expenses are considered to be those reductions of resources that benefit the current reporting period only. Expenditures, on the other hand, can be made for resources that benefit the current and future periods as well as reductions of resources in the current period. Thus, both expenses and expenditures cause a reduction in resources and decreases in the Fund Balance to occur, but expenditures include a broader range of transactions than those included under an expense classification.[9] Therefore, the term "expenditure" includes all expense classifications but goes beyond expenses to include purchases of capital assets such as vehicles, buildings, equipment, and even supplies.

This difference is related to the timing or when expense or expenditure recognition causes a decrease in the Fund Balance. The question of timing between the two methods is most clearly seen in the manner in which the purchase of assets is handled. For example, under the expense concept the purchasing of an automobile increases an asset account called Vehicles and decreases an asset account called Cash. It is assumed that some sort of benefit will be received from the new car as it is used by the organization. As those benefits are received—that is, as the car is used—there are periodic charges called expenses that reduce the Fund Balance over the life of the car. Therefore, the charges against the Fund Balance are made as the car's benefits are provided to and used by the organization. Those readers more familiar with this accounting technique will recognize this charge as depreciation. Depreciation will be discussed in a later chapter.

When the expenditure concept is adopted and an automobile is purchased, an expenditure account is increased for the entire purchase price of the car *at the time it is purchased,* and the Cash account is decreased by an equal amount. The expenditure approach charges the entire purchase cost of the automobile against the Fund Balance during the fiscal year the car is purchased, and it does not allocate expenses against the Fund Balance as the benefits are received from the use of the car. Whether expenses or expenditures are used depend on several new accounting rules that have recently been put into effect.[10] For now, it should be understood that libraries within governmental organizations may use either method depending on their specific circumstances, but it would be more common to find NFOs recording expenditures.

Both expenses and expenditures are usually classified on either a functional or an object basis. Typical examples of expense classifications under these two methods are shown in figure 2-9. The expense accounts used depend on the decision-making needs of the administrators in the entity as well as the needs of outside monitoring agencies. For example, an agency that provides a grant could act as a monitoring agency and require the filing of certain object expense classifications showing how the grant funding was used.

FIGURE 2-9   Object and Functional Classifications

Object Classification	Functional Classification
A. Expenses and Expenditures	A. Libraries
Maintenance	Circulating Library
Supplies	Media Library
Personnel Services	Children's Library
Books and Standing Orders	Regional History Library
Publicity	Community Services
Miscellaneous Expenses	B. Art Center or Museum
Professional Fees	Publicity
Telephone	Exhibits
B. Expenditures	Fellowships
Building	Crafts Education
Equipment	
Vehicles	

As stated, revenues are generally considered an inflow of resources to the NFO. Yet, revenue is not represented by a refund of previous expenses nor by an inflow that creates any form of obligation through a liability. Resources that are refunds or create a liability are not revenues. Revenues are recorded when resources are transferred to the NFO or if it is clear that the organization will receive these funds because they have been earned.[11] In the latter case, revenues are recognized although the inflow has not yet occurred.

Examples of typical revenue accounts vary with organizational activities, but some common types of revenue accounts are presented in figure 2-10.

FIGURE 2-10   Examples of Revenue in Various NFOs

A. Library	C. Botanical Society
User's Fees	Admission Charge
Book Fines	Membership Dues
B. Art Center	D. General Revenue Sources: All NFOs
Admission Fees	Investment Revenue
Tuition Fees	Dividend Income
	Interest Income

EXERCISE 2-3   Revenues and Expenditures

1. Waterford Library received cash from the following sources last month. Determine which sources are revenues.
   a. Borrowed $750 from First National Bank.
   b. Sold an old typewriter for $75 cash.
   c. Charged patrons a $2 user's fee: collected $450.
   d. Received $1,200 in interest from investments owned by the library.
2. Cabell County Library completed the following transactions during the past month. Determine which involve expenditures and expenses.
   a. Paid $100 for repair work on the roof.
   b. Paid $1,200 for new duplicating machine.
   c. Brought $1,500 worth of new books.
   d. Paid $97 for cleaning supplies.

ANALYZING DEBIT AND CREDIT CHANGES IN REVENUE AND EXPENSE ACCOUNTS

To understand the function of revenue and expense accounts, it is necessary to study the effect of debits and credits on them. Transaction analysis will be used to investigate the changes that occur in revenue and expense accounts from recording debits and credits. Later, the study of expenditures will build on this fundamental understanding of expenses.

Previously, equations A, B, and C set forth the relationship between assets, liabilities, and the Fund Balance. When the effect of expenses and revenues is incorporated into the previous forms of the accounting equation, the result is Equation D.

D. Assets = Liabilities + Fund Balance + Revenues − Expenses

An important relationship in Equation D is that the change in the Fund Balance is attributed to the difference between revenues and expenses. This change is determined on a periodic basis, usually yearly, when the financial reports are prepared. Notice that the equation incorporates the term "expenses." If the term "expenditures" were used, the Fund Balance would need to be redefined.

E. Change in the Fund Balance   =   Revenues   −   Expenses

To understand the functions of revenues and expenses in an accounting system, it is necessary to study the effects of debits and credits on them. A method that is useful in remembering the relationship is illustrated in figure 2-11, where expenses are shown as debits and revenues as credits. The Fund

Balance account normally has a credit balance, and the effect of expenses on it is to decrease the "normal" balance, whereas the effect of revenues is to increase the "normal" balance. For this relationship to exist, expenses must normally have a debit balance. Figure 2-12 helps us remember that expenses (on the debit side of the Fund Balance) normally have a debit balance and revenues (on the credit side of the Fund Balance) normally have a credit balance. Although expenses may occasionally be credited and revenues debited, the "normal" entries for these accounts result in a debit to an expense account and a credit to a revenue account.

FIGURE 2-11   Expenses and Revenues

Expenses cause decreases in Fund Balance and are shown as debits, whereas revenues cause increases and are shown as credits.

Fund Balance

Expenses (Dr.) −	Revenues (Cr.) +

These relationships are summarized in figure 2-12, where the effects of debits and credits on expenses and revenues are shown. The Fund Balance is included in the illustration so that the effects of debits and credits on the three account classifications are comparable. A comparison shows that debits and credits affect the Fund Balance account and revenues in the same manner.

FIGURE 2-12   Effects of Debits and Credits on Fund Balance, Revenues, and Expenses

Effect of	Fund Balance	Revenue	Expenses
Debits	−	−	+†
Credits	+*	+*	−

* "Normal" balance is a credit.
† "Normal" balance is a debit.

USING TRANSACTION ANALYSIS WITH REVENUES AND EXPENSES

The following two transactions use the relationships in figure 2-12 in more detail.

TRANSACTION 3

Assume that Howl Creek Library charges an annual user's fee of $2 for each patron. The fees are charged for identification cards, which are required in order to use the library, and the library receives a total of $2,000 in user fees during the year. The technique of transaction analysis is again used to determine the proper accounts to debit and credit.

Questions	Answers
1. What is the library receiving or giving up?	1. Cash is received.
2. Is Cash an asset, liability, part of the Fund Balance, an expense, a revenue item?	2. Cash is an asset.
3. Is Cash increasing or decreasing?	3. Increasing.
4. What registers an increase in an asset?	4. A debit.
5. Is another asset affected?	5. No.
6. Is a liability affected?	6. No.
7. Is the Fund Balance affected?	7. Not immediately.
8. Is an expense recorded?	8. No.
9. Are revenues received?	9. Yes.
10. Are revenues increasing or decreasing?	10. Increasing.
11. What registers an increase in a revenue item?	11. A credit.

Transaction analysis shows that the cash received is a revenue item. The necessary entry is a debit to Cash and a credit to a revenue account, such as User's Fee Revenues. Figure 2-13 shows the effect of receipt of the $2,000 cash on the accounting equation. After transaction 2, the accounting equation appeared as shown in figure 2-13, equation 3: Before Cash Is Received. Once the effect of transaction 3 is recorded, the accounting equation appears as shown in equation 4: After Cash Is Received.

FIGURE 2-13   Accounting Equation Before and After Receipt of $2,000 Revenues from User's Fees

3. Before Cash Is Received:	Assets $10,000	=	Liabilities $0	+	Fund Balance $10,000	
4. After Cash Is Received:	Assets $12,000	=	Liabilities $0	+	Fund Balance $10,000 +$2,000 Rev.	

Although the effect of the revenues is eventually shown as an increase in the Fund Balance account, this change does not immediately occur. This change is transferred to the Fund Balance only at the end of the year—for example, on June 30. The effect of expenses and revenues is not reflected in the Fund Balance immediately as each transaction occurs. As a result, the Fund Balance is not up-to-date until all revenues and expenses are transferred to the Fund Balance. In equation 4, this effect is recorded immediately in the Fund Balance to illustrate the relationship of revenues and expenses on the Fund Balance.

All expense and revenue accounts are considered "temporary" accounts because their balances are cleared to the Fund Balance at the end of each year. The reason for this clearing is that the focus of expenses and revenues is related to a short period. More importantly, it makes no sense to keep accumulating each year's revenues and expenses. Without a clearing of these accounts, an NFO's revenues and expenses are a function of how long the organization has been in existence. To avoid a confusing situation, each financial year's difference between all revenues and expenses is transferred into the Fund Balance. As a result, each year's revenues and expenses are viewed independently of every other year, and yearly comparisons of results can be made.

Assets, liabilities, and the Fund Balance are considered "permanent" because the balances in these accounts are carried on from one year to the next. The procedures for transferring the temporary account balances to the Fund Balance are explained in chapter 5, but equation 4 illustrates the effect.

T accounts summarize the effect of transaction 3 in figure 2-14. The Cash account contains the effects of transactions 1 and 2 as well as transaction 3. In the accounting equation, revenues were recorded in the Fund Balance, but under T account analysis a separate revenue account, User's Fee Revenue, is established. All cash received as user's fees is recorded in this account. At financial year-end, the total balance in the account is transferred into the Fund Balance account as a credit. Prior to the transfer, the accounting equation, as illustrated in equation A or equation 4, will not balance.

FIGURE 2-14   T Account Analysis of Receipt of Revenues

Cash		User's Fee Revenues	Fund Balance
$10,000			$10,000
50	$50	$2,000	
2,000			
Bal. $12,000		$2,000 Bal.	$10,000 Bal.

At this point, it may appear possible to place revenues under the Fund Balance account only and avoid the complications of maintaining a separate revenue account. Although this would be possible, in the sense that debits and credits would balance, such a system makes it difficult to obtain information available about specific revenues. For this reason, it is important to maintain separate revenue accounts.

TRANSACTION 4

The only major account classification remaining to be analyzed is "expense" accounts, and they are the next consideration. In transaction 4, assume the Howl Creek Library is paying $1,500 for roof repairs with a check. Transaction analysis is again used to develop the correct questions and answers about the types of accounts to debit and credit.

Questions	*Answers*
1. What is Howl Creek Library receiving or giving up?	1. Cash.
2. Is Cash an asset, liability, part of the Fund Balance, an expense, a revenue item?	2. Cash is an asset.
3. Is Cash increasing or decreasing?	3. Decreasing.
4. What registers a decrease in an asset?	4. A credit.
5. Is another asset affected?	5. No.
6. Is a liability affected?	6. No.
7. Is the Fund Balance affected?	7. Not immediately.
8. Is an expense recorded?	8. Yes.
9. Are revenues received?	9. No.
10. Are expenses increasing or decreasing?	10. Increasing
11. What registers an increase in an expense?	11. A debit.

The payment for the roof repairs is recorded as an expense. This transaction results in a debit to an expense, such as Repairs Expense, and a credit to the Cash account. The effect on the accounting equation is presented in figure 2-15. Equation 4 illustrates the accounting equation prior to the payment for roof repairs, and equation 5 shows the changes after payment is made. In the equation, assets are reduced by the payment of cash. Furthermore, the expense reduces the Fund Balance account by $1,500. Equation 5 is in balance. The assets and the Fund Balance are both equal to $10,500. Again it should be noted that this summarization of expenses and revenues in the Fund Balance occurs only at year-end. It is presented in this manner to illustrate the effect of expenses and revenues on the Fund Balance.

FIGURE 2-15   Accounting Equation Before and After Payment of $1,500 for Roof Repairs

4. Before Payment:	Assets	=	Liabilities	+	Fund Balance
	$12,000		$0		$10,000
					+2,000 Revenues
5. After Payment:	Assets	=	Liabilities	+	Fund Balance
	$10,050		$0		$10,000
					+2,000 Revenues
					−1,500 Expenses

When this transaction is recorded in the T accounts, it is recorded in specific accounts and not in a general classification, such as "assets" or "expenses." The T account analysis is shown in figure 2-16. It provides the needed accounts; they are Repair Expense and Cash.

FIGURE 2-16   T Account Analysis of Payment for Roof Repairs

	Cash			Repair Expense	
	$10,000			$1,500	
	50	$ 50			
	2,000	1,500			
Bal.	$10,500		Bal.	$1,500	

	User's Fee Revenues			Fund Balance	
				$10,000	
		$2,000			
		$2,000 Bal.		$10,000 Bal.	

Note that the Cash account carries forward all the debits and credits of the previous transactions. This illustrates the summarization process that occurs in a T account. In addition, the User's Fee Revenue account is included as part of figure 2-16 because if this revenue account is excluded, the debit and credit balances in the remaining three accounts do not balance. At present, the debits and credits are equal to $12,000.

As previously stated, when a separate expense or revenue account is established, the accounting equation, as shown in equation 4 or 5, does not balance. It is necessary to transfer the difference in the account balances between all expenses and revenues to the Fund Balance before the accounting equation will balance. This transfer occurs when financial statements are prepared.

EXERCISE 2-4 Debiting and Crediting Revenues and Expenses

1. On the night of July 7, Twin Falls Art Center collects $975 on ticket sales to a production of *Ham and Letty* by Bill Shakepeers. Determine the account classification(s) to debit and credit. What are the names of these accounts?

2. Hanks Public Library received $3,000 in interest and dividends from its investments. Determine the account classification(s) to debit and credit. What are the names of these accounts?

3. Summitville Library recently leased a Xerox machine. The monthly rental of $300 is paid at the beginning of each month. Determine the account classification(s) to debit and credit for May 1. What are the names of these accounts?

4. Five hundred dollars worth of books were purchased on account* by the Maysville-Wallis County Library for the Regional History Collection. Determine the account classification(s) to debit and credit. What are the names of these accounts?

*"On account" means no cash was paid.

ANALYZING TRANSACTIONS, JOURNALIZING, AND POSTING

The accounting equation and the T account analysis illustrate the effect of debits and credits on the various account classifications. These methods are useful for illustrative purposes, but this is not the sequence of accounting procedures in a working accounting system. It is important to understand the proper sequence of accounting procedures used in an actual set of accounts. The fund accounting cycle outlined earlier in this chapter lists the step-by-step procedures actually followed with a set of books. The first three steps in that cycle are of special concern at this point.

The first three steps in the fund accounting cycle are analyzing the transaction, journalizing it, and posting the journal entry to the ledger accounts. Although the accounting equation is a concern when these transactions are recorded, it is not explicitly used in recording any transactions.

The first step in this series of procedures is to use transaction analysis to determine which accounts to debit and credit, as we have done in this chapter. The second step is to record the transaction in a journal called the *general journal,* where the initial entry is made for a transaction that enters the accounting system. All entries are recorded in the general journal in chronological order. When an entry is made in the journal, the debit entry is always placed first; the credit entry, slightly indented, second. The entry is followed by a narrative explanation to indicate the nature of the transaction, and the transaction date is recorded. Figure 2-17 illustrates the format for recording entries in the general journal that will be used in the book. The entry records the recognition of an obligation to repay a patron for a $50 video deposit.

FIGURE 2-17   An Example of a Journal Entry in the General Journal

May 1	Cash	50.00	
	Returnable Deposits		50.00
	Recognition of obligation to repay patron's deposit		

As the entries in a general journal are recorded in the time sequence in which they occur, it is very difficult to summarize total account balances. Therefore, the third step is to transfer the entry from the general journal to a ledger, called the *general ledger,* which contains accounts that are very similar to the T accounts. The general ledger maintains all account balances for the organization in summarized form on an account-by-account basis. The ledger's major purpose is to allow for quick determination of the balance in every account in the accounting system. When an accounting software package is used, these steps are carried out at the same time. See the bibliographical citations for a listing of software packages.

When the entries in the general journal are transferred to the general ledger, it is referred to as "posting to the general ledger." This is a common practice in a set of manually maintained books of accounts, but, as indicated, this process usually occurs at the same time journal entries are entered into an accounting software package. The frequency of posting depends on the number of transactions, but the longest interval between one posting and the next should be one month.

In order to use a set of books properly, cross-referencing is necessary between the general journal and the general ledger. The need for this arises any time it is necessary to trace a transaction through the books from the time it is journalized in the general journal to its entry in a specific account. (Of course, this tracing procedure can be performed in the opposite direction also.) Columns for posting references are usually found in the general ledger and general journal under the abbreviations "PR" or "Post. Ref." The account number of the ledger is used as the citation in the journal, and the page number in the journal is used as the cross citation in the ledger. In a manual system, these cross citations provide for a means of quickly going back and forth in the books. Once this posting process is completed and the correct cross-references are in the journal and the ledger, it is possible to trace an entry from the time it enters the accounting system to its summarization in an account in the general ledger.

The other steps in the accounting cycle are not performed with the same frequency as the first three; these procedures will be described in a later chapter.

SUMMARY

This chapter is an introduction to the debiting and crediting of assets, liabilities, the Fund Balance, expenses, and revenues. Rather than maintain strict adherence to the accounting cycle to illustrate the debiting and crediting procedure, this process has been explained with the use of the accounting equation and T accounts. Although the accounting equation and T accounts are useful for illustrative purposes, the accounting cycle is actually used in a functioning accounting system.

Though reading the material in this chapter will familiarize the reader with the various accounts, one cannot expect to understand all the mechanics of debiting and crediting accounts based on this chapter alone. The bibliography for this chapter includes examples of texts that are helpful for additional review as well as the names of some software packages that take the drudgery out of recording the entries. The basics with which the reader should be familiar before proceeding to the next chapters are in figure 2-18, which shows the effect of debits and credits for the various account classifications, as well as the "normal" balances usually found in these accounts. It is necessary to be familiar with the debiting and crediting of accounts before the material in later chapters can be fully understood.

FIGURE 2-18   Debit and Credit Effects on Accounts

Account	Debit	Credit	Normal Balance
Asset	+	−	Debit
Liability	−	+	Credit
Fund Balance	−	+	Credit
Expenses	+	−	Debit
Revenues	−	+	Credit

EXERCISE 2-5   Review Problems

1. Certain formal accounting documents correspond with specific steps in the fund accounting cycle. Name the internal accounting documents that are associated with (a) journalizing and (b) posting.

(Continued)

EXERCISE 2-5   Review Problems   *(Continued)*

2. Sky Mountain Library has hired a new bookkeeper who recently completed Debit/Credit School at a local career college. The new bookkeeper is uncertain as to which accounts to debit and credit for the following transactions, which occurred during the month of June. Determine for the bookkeeper which accounts should be debited and credited. List the entries in chronological order and use the format illustrated for the June 1 entry.
   Example: On June 1 the library paid $100 for roof repairs. The entry, recorded in "general journal" form:

June 1	Repairs Expense	$100	
	Cash		$100
June 5	Office Supplies for $725 received from previously placed order. (They will be paid for later in the month.)		
June 7	Deposits of $85 received from patrons who checked out videotape equipment.		
June 11	Paid $7 cash for delivery charges to UPS.		
June 16	Check-out deposits of $50 returned to patrons when undamaged video equipment was returned to library.		
June 27	Library collected $75 in fines during month of June.		
June 27	Salaries of $7,500 paid by library. (Ignore any taxes.)		
June 27	Paid invoice on Office Supplies received June 5.		

3. The new bookkeeper (question 2) is even more confused about the posting process. The journal entries below have been taken from page 5 of the library's general journal.
   a. Show the bookkeeper how to post these journal entries into T accounts. Include your posting reference (page number) in the T account.
   b. Determine the "balance" in the Cash account after these entries are posted.

Jan 1	Accounts Payable	250	
	Cash		250
Jan 4	Salaries Payable	750	
	Cash		750
Jan 5	Cash	1,200	
	Interest Revenue		1,200
Jan 6	Miscellaneous Expenses	50	
	Cash		50

4. In question 3, the T accounts were used in place of what document in the formal accounting system?

5. The new bookkeeper assumed that the posting process had been completed in question 3, but when an attempt was made to trace an entry in the general journal to the general ledger, it could not be done. What part of the posting process remains to be completed?

6. Explain to the bookkeeper how it is possible to trace an entry from the general journal to the general ledger and from the general ledger to the general journal.
7. Without referring to figure 2-18, determine the effect of debits and credits on each of the following account classifications:
   a. Assets   d. Expenses
   b. Liabilities   e. Revenues
   c. Fund Balance

FOR MORE INFORMATION

Examples of Accounting Principles Textbooks

Horngren, Charles T., Walter T. Harrison Jr., and Michael A. Robinson. *Accounting.* Englewood Cliffs, N.J.: Prentice Hall, 1999.

Ingram, Robert W., Thomas L. Albright, Bruce A. Baldwin, and John W. Hill. *Accounting: Information for Decisions.* Cincinnati, Ohio: South-Western College Publishing, 1999.

Examples of Fund Accounting Software

Blackbaud, Inc. *Accounting for Nonprofits.* This package includes general ledger, budget management, accounts payable, purchase orders, fixed assets management, miscellaneous cash receipts, payroll, and student billing. (http://www.blackbaud.com)

Cougar Mountain Software. *Fund Accounting.* This software package is a fully integrated accounting and financial management software package for NFOs and government agencies. (http://www.cougarmtn.com)

NOTES

1. Most small to medium NFOs do not have the ability to raise funding by issuing long-term debt as they do not have a revenue base to support the required payments for long-term debt nor do they have, in the form of a guarantee, the backing of an organization that does have a sufficient revenue inflow. Additionally, the NFO may not have legal authority to issue debt obligations. As a result, long-term debt is not commonly found on NFOs' financial reports. Of course, if an asset should be used as collateral for a short-term or long-term loan that needs to be disclosed on the financial reports.

2. In nongovernmental NFOs, this example does not create a liability. Instead, it creates a temporarily restricted portion of the Fund Balance which is called "Net Assets" in nongovernmental NFOs.

3. For the moment, consider the inflow of resources to be revenues.

4. Those readers familiar with fund accounting will recognize that other factors besides the difference between expenses and revenues can cause changes in the

Fund Balance account. For example, differences between the budgetary accounts Estimated Revenues and Appropriations can affect the Fund Balance.

5. It should be noted that there may be restrictions on the amount of the Fund Balance that can be used for current operations. These restrictions are discussed in a later chapter.

6. In a for-profit business, the Fund Balance is called the "equity," and it is considered to be the monies available to the stockholders. Therefore, the owners of the business consider equity increases to be a good sign. In an NFO, no such meaning attaches to the Fund Balance. The different interpretation is due to the differences in the goals of NFOs and for-profit business, i.e., service objectives versus profits. Of course, year-after-year Fund Balance decreases could signify problems. Finally, it should be noted that the residual nature of the Fund Balance is set by the definition of assets and liabilities. If one group of liabilities should not be recognized in an accounting model (and there is more than one NFO model), the residual nature of the Fund Balance is immediately changed.

7. This equation assumes an accrual accounting system (see chapter 3) is in use. Under a cash system, no liabilities are recognized and the equation becomes Assets = Fund Balance, thus creating a very different definition for the Fund Balance. Under the governmental model of accounting, a different definition is used for liabilities. This latter definition will be used in part 2 of the book.

8. The deposits can be kept in an account separate from the Cash accounts as, for example, Cash—Deposits. Of course, each deposit must also be traceable to the patron who left the cash with the library.

9. It should be seen that by simply switching from expenses to expenditures, the amount of profit or net income is changed, and the profit transferred to the Fund Balance is different under the two terms. In essence the accounting meaning of Fund Balance is changed although it remains a residual. For example, expenses reflect a focus on maintaining an NFO's capital, i.e., capital maintenance, whereas expenditures reflect a flow of resources perspective.

10. General Accounting Standards Board, Statement No. 29, *The Use of Not-for-Profit Accounting and Financial Reporting Principles by Governmental Entities* (Norwalk, Conn.: GASB, 1995).

11. The inflow of resources is introduced here as "revenues." In later chapters, a distinction is made between revenues and support. Revenues are earned inflows and support is recognized as those inflows that are given to the NFO without anything given up to receive the support. Examples of support are gifts or grants.

3

Which
Accounting System
Are We Using?

CHAPTER 2 PROVIDED AN INTRODUCTION to debits and credits including an explanation of the various accounts found in a typical NFO. Although the chapter provided an introduction to the basics of an accounting system, a major decision is still necessary prior to recording any debits and credits. The foundation for the accounting system must be selected before any entries can be made in the books. There are significant differences among the accounting systems that can be adopted and the financial statements generated from these systems. In turn, these differences affect the managerial decisions made by those who use this information.

This chapter compares and contrasts the three foundations upon which an NFO's accounting system can be based: cash, accrual, and modified accrual. Each of these methods is defined and explained in the chapter. Many differences between the three methods relate to the time at which a transaction is recorded in the journal and the financial report classifications that result.

CASH BASIS VERSUS ACCRUAL METHOD

The cash basis method of accounting requires the write-up of a journal entry only when cash flows into or out of the organization. This method is very simple to use, compared with the accrual method, and it is the approach we use in recording entries in our personal checkbooks. Although this method appears to be workable, especially in small organizations, there are serious difficulties in its use.

The accrual method of accounting uses other criteria besides the inflow or outflow of cash as the reason to record a transaction in the journal. For example, expenses and revenues are recorded in the time period in which they are incurred or earned, respectively, rather than the period in which cash is paid or received.

To assist in distinguishing these accounting methods from one another, assume that the state government has provided Overdrew City Library with special restricted monies in the form of a grant. The $1,200 grant is for the purchase of minority and ethnic books for the genealogical collection at the library. As this is a special, restricted grant, the monies can only be used for the purchase of minority and ethnic books. The grant has a one-year time limitation: grant monies not used for the purchase of these books within the time period must be returned to the state. The period covered under the grant ends at the end of the current month, June. An invoice (billing statement) for $125 equal to the unexpended portion of the grant is received one day before the end of the month. The invoice does not require payment until a 30-day period has passed.

In a cash-basis system, no record of the purchase is made until the purchase is paid, and that may be up to 30 days after receipt of the invoice. If a grant purchase report is prepared based on the cash accounting records and filed with the state, it will appear that not all the funds were used. In this case, the library has an obligation to repay $125 to the state because the accounting records do not indicate that all the monies have been used for the express purpose for which they had been granted. If off-the-book records are kept to show that $125 was spent, this duplicate system only reduces the efficiency of the NFO by increasing its record-keeping costs.

Under the accrual system, the $125 purchase under the grant is recorded as soon as the obligation for payment is incurred, that is, receipt and acceptance of the invoice. An accrual system shows that grant monies are completely used on the date the invoice is received.

Figure 3-1 shows the general journal entries under the cash basis and the accrual basis for the purchase of the books. In both cases, it is assumed that the library is not going to pay for the books prior to the time that payment is necessary—July 29.

On June 29, when the invoice is received, no entry is made under the cash system, as no cash has flowed out of the organization, but under the accrual system, an obligation for payment is recognized under the liability Accounts Payable. On July 29, both systems record the payment for the book purchase. The cash system records the expenditure, now that cash is flowing out of the library, and the accrual system shows the reduction in the obligation under Accounts Payable. Both systems show a reduction in the Cash account on this date. Note that the terms "expenditures" or "disbursements" may be used under the cash system rather than "expenses." Modified accrual accounting, discussed later, uses the term expenditures rather than disbursements or expenses, but *expenditures* under modified accrual have a slightly different meaning than under cash methods.

FIGURE 3-1 Cash Basis and Accrual Basis for Recording a Liability

Cash			
June 29	No Entry		
July 29	Book Expenditure	125	
	Cash		125
Accrual			
June 29	Book Expense	125	
	Accounts Payable		125
July 29	Accounts Payable	125	
	Cash		125

In reviewing figure 3-1, it can be seen that under the cash system no liability is recognized on June 29. If the end of the financial year, also called the "fiscal year," is June 30, no liability for the purchase is recorded in the year-end financial statements. This results in liabilities and expenditures being understated, and the financial statements not presenting an accurate picture of the organization's activities. Also, it means that the Fund Balance is defined in a way that results in a higher balance than under accrual methods.[1] Expenditures are understated because no expenditure is recognized until July 29. With an end of the fiscal year on June 30, the expenditure will appear in a later year than it was incurred.

The net effect of using the cash basis to account for this particular transaction is to understate both liabilities and expenditures and, in this case, to transfer expenses to a fiscal year in which they were not incurred. None of these problems develop under the accrual system.

ACCRUAL BASIS VERSUS MODIFIED ACCRUAL METHOD

The accrual and the cash systems are on the opposite ends of a continuum from one another. The third method upon which an accounting system can be based is the modified accrual method (MAM). This method uses a combination of accrual- and cash-based methods, and it fits between the cash and accrual methods on the continuum. Even though MAM is the recommended method of accounting for NFOs, it is necessary to be familiar with these other methods of accounting, as they are widely (and often incorrectly) used.[2]

The differences between MAM and the accrual basis can be seen in the way these systems recognize revenues and expenses or expenditures. Under the MAM, revenues that have not been received in cash arc not accrued, that is, journalized, unless (1) they are *material* and there is a delay in the normal time of their receipt or (2) they are recognized as being *available*.[3] An item is considered "material" if the accountant judges it to be of sufficient magnitude as to affect financial or managerial decision making. Revenues that the accountant considers material are recorded even though they have not been received in cash.

"Availability" could be defined in several ways; it could mean revenues will be considered available when the asset related to the revenue has been recognized in the books. For example, when the cash from a revenue item is collected, the revenue is recognized. This is the case in the cash-basis method of accounting. Under MAM, revenues are considered to be available when they are likely to be received in cash within 60 days. Thus, they are assumed to be available if they will be received in time to pay liabilities incurred in the fiscal year just ending. It is not acceptable under accrual methods to hold the books open for a 60-day period after the end of the fiscal year and continue to record revenues. Another consideration under both MAM and accrual is that revenues must be *measurable*. "Measurability" means that it must be possible to reasonably estimate the amount of revenues that will be received at a future date.

As an example of these concepts, assume a state library commission has received a grant for $6,500 which is to be awarded July 15, 20x3, without restrictions, to Overdrew City Library. At June 30, 20x3, the library's year-end, the grant has not been received in cash yet, but it is receivable within two weeks. The criteria of materiality, normal receipt time, and availability are evaluated to determine whether grant revenue is recorded in the accounting records on June 30.

The criterion of measurability is not an issue because the amount of the grant is known. Materiality and delay in this case are not an issue either. The important criterion for deciding to record these revenues in the accounting records is availability. The cash from the grant has not been received, but it is anticipated it will be received in time to pay liabilities of the year just ending.[4] Therefore, it will be recognized as a revenue in the accounts on June 30, 20x3 under both accrual and MAM. The criterion of availability, as defined under MAM, has been met. Furthermore, grants receivable from other governments are usually accrued.[5] Under accrual accounting, the criterion of revenue being earned has been met as there is no requirement for additional performance. So in this case, revenue is recognized under both accrual and MAM.

Book-fine revenues can be used as another example of revenue recognition under MAM. The question of recognition relates to whether such revenues should be recorded before they are collected, and the decision revolves around the measurability of the fines. Fine revenues are defined as not measurable under MAM because they cannot be reasonably estimated before the fines are actually received.[6] Therefore, under MAM, fine revenues are not journalized in the accounting records until they are received in cash, and the question of availability does not arise. Under accrual, revenue recognition occurs when the patron becomes obligated to pay the fine, which is usually before the cash is received.

Figure 3-2 sets forth the decision criteria that are used under the three bases of accounting for determining when revenues are recognized in the accounting records. Notice that the major difference between MAM and the accrual method is that the former is focused around the availability of revenues and the latter on whether they are earned.

In figure 3-2, an important reason for recognizing revenues in MAM is availability. Availability of revenues under MAM has already been explained. This concept slightly contrasts with revenues that are "earned" under accrual as revenues may be available but "unearned." Revenues are earned at the point where the NFO has a right to expect to receive payment for services without the obligation of any further performance. The following are four examples of earned revenues: (1) contracted services have been provided; (2) a sale has been made; (3) a fine has been incurred; and (4) interest revenues are receivable because of the passage of time. Although the two concepts overlap, availability of revenues concentrates on the period of collectibility, whereas earning of revenues focuses on the completion of performance. Under a cash approach, the only criterion is: "has the cash been received?"

With MAM, expenditures are recorded in the same time period as accrual expenses, with several exceptions. One exception is that interest expense on long-term debt is not recognized before the fiscal year in which it is actually paid (which may be after it is owed). A second example is that some accrual assets may be recorded in the books as MAM expenditures.[7] The recording of supplies provides an example of the latter situation. Supplies, a prepaid asset, may be considered an expenditure when they are purchased or when they are used. If they are considered expenditures when they are purchased, they are not recognized as prepaid *assets*. Thus, accrual accounting is likely to recognize more accounting assets, such as supplies, than MAM over the same time period. This is also seen in the accounting recognition of large fixed assets. Under MAM, purchases of fixed assets with long working lives, such as buildings, equipment, and vehicles, are recorded as expenditures in the current accounting period. Purchasing the same fixed assets in an accrual system results in no similar expenses or expenditures on the date of purchase; instead, asset values increase.

FIGURE 3-2   Recognition of Revenues under the Three Models of Accounting

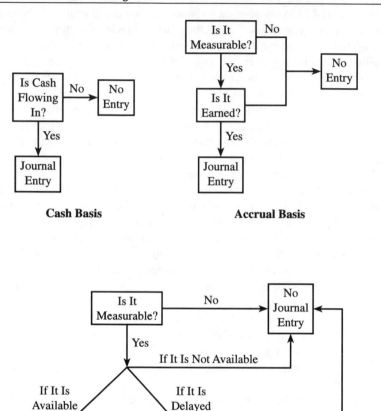

Figure 3-3 illustrates the relationship between expenditures, expenses, and cash disbursements. Cash disbursements have nothing in common with accrual expenses (with the exceptions noted), but cash disbursements overlap some items that are considered expenditures. All expenses are expenditures but not all expenditures are expenses. Thus, some expenses are cash disbursements.

Another difference between the three models of accounting is in the handling of interest on long-term debt. Under MAM, interest on long-term debt is not recorded until the fiscal year in which the interest is actually due be-

FIGURE 3-3   A Comparison of Expenses (accrual), Expenditures (MAM) and
Disbursements (cash)

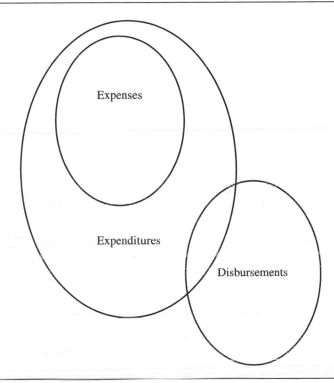

cause of the way monies are allocated by the governing board. For example,
if the interest expenditures are journalized in the year ending December 31,
20x3, but they are not payable until January 15, 20x4, the following year, a
deficit would be created, or at least contributed toward, in the Fund Balance
for December. Recognizing the interest expenditures prior to the time they are
due contributes to such a deficit because no monies are available through appropriations for the interest expenditures in 20x3. Although the new year's appropriations (20x4) are "available" within 60 days, these appropriations can
only legally be spent on 20x4 expenditures and not those arising from the previous year's activities. Creation of a deficit in the 20x3 Fund Balance serves
no useful purpose because monies will be set aside through appropriations by
the governing board in the following year, 20x4, for the 20x4 interest expenditures. For this reason, MAM does not recognize a liability and expenditure
for interest on long-term debt that is owed but not scheduled to be paid until
the following year. The accounting for interest on long-term debt illustrates
another difference between the accrual and MAM expense/expenditure ac-

counting because the accrued-bond interest expense is recognized under the accrual method.

Under accrual accounting, an Interest Expense account and a liability account called Interest Payable would be increased for the amount of interest owed but not yet due on December 31, 20x3. As this interest is owed at the end of the year, it is recognized as both a liability and an expense in the fiscal period ending December 31, 20x3. This difference between accrual and MAM is significant only for those NFOs that might have long-term debt outstanding.

These examples illustrate the differences that can arise in journalizing entries under the three methods of accounting. The examples also indicate the differences that can develop in the financial statements prepared under the different accounting methods. For example, it can be seen that MAM records some revenues before they are recorded under accrual methods. Additionally, many expenditures will be recorded before (possibly years before) they are recognized in accrual-based accounting records. These different accounting practices change the meaning of the Fund Balance as this residual captures the difference between the recorded revenues and expenses, expenditures, or disbursements.

As indicated, another difference between accrual and MAM occurs because the latter method does not have to recognize "prepaid assets"—items that are paid for before they are used and that are recognized as assets with a short life under an accrual system. Under MAM, they are usually recognized as expenditures of the current period. Another common example of this type of item is insurance payments on a car or building. Payment of the insurance applies to a future period; it provides a benefit in the future, a characteristic of an asset. Under the accrual system, it is recognized as an asset, Prepaid Insurance, but under MAM it is recognized as an expenditure, Insurance Expenditures. When the accrual asset account, Prepaid Insurance, is used, it is transferred to an expense classification bit by bit as the period covered by the insurance policy expires. Thus, all things being equal, MAM again shows higher expenditure and cost levels than accrual.

Finally, it should be noted that for control to exist over the use of inventories, the actual physical counts of the inventory should be compared with the amounts shown in the accounts. Under MAM, the inventories may be considered expenditures when they are purchased (cash-based) or when they are consumed (accrual-based). At the end of the fiscal year, the accrual method has an inventory in the books, whereas with MAM there is no "book" inventory. Under the purchases method, without footnotes to the financial statements disclosing the inventory's dollar value there is no means to check the inventory's physical count against its book valuation. As a result, there is a reduced level of control against loss. Under the consumption method, any unused materials or supplies at the year-end are disclosed in an asset account called Material Inventory or Supplies Inventory.

EXERCISE 3-1   Cash, Accrual, and Modified Accrual Systems

Assume fiscal year-end is June 30 in all cases.

1. The City of Tarrinton forwards monies for operational support to the city library each year. These monies are usually received in the first week of July. During the current year, budget revisions have delayed receipt of these monies, and as of the first week in July no monies have been received. Should a journal entry be made at the end of the first week in July for these monies under the following accounting methods?
   a. Cash
   b. Accrual
   c. MAM

2. The Harriet Carry Art Center has pledges receivable of $25,000 from a number of individuals who made pledges of support during a recent fund-raising drive. It is estimated that 10 percent of these pledges will never be collected. After the pledges have been made, which of the following methods of accounting require a journal entry?
   a. Cash
   b. Accrual
   c. MAM

3. An NFO has a long-term debt of $100,000 and the interest rate on this debt is 14 percent. This debt requires a cash interest payment twice each year of $7,000, on July 1 and January 1 ($100,000 × .14 = $14,000/2 = $7,000). Under which method(s) of accounting should the organization recognize a $7,000 expense/expenditure/disbursement on the June 30 financial statement for the interest payment on July 1?
   a. Cash
   b. Accrual
   c. MAM

4. The Stanley-Hanley County Library recently paid $250 for insurance on its bookmobile. How should this payment be recognized under the various methods of accounting?
   a. Cash
   b. Accrual
   c. MAM

5. What is the difference between the "purchases method" and "consumption method" of recording inventory expenditures?

ACCOUNTING UNDER THE CASH, ACCRUAL, AND MODIFIED ACCRUAL SYSTEMS

The three foundations upon which an accounting system can be based have been briefly explained. This section uses a series of transactions to extend those explanations and comparisons.

Whichever method is used in an NFO, it should be deliberately chosen and not used because "it's the one that was used before." Again, it should be noted that the only accounting method that is recommended for NFOs classified as governmental is MAM. If MAM is not used to prepare financial statements and the characteristics of the other methods create significant differences in the amounts shown on the financial statements, extensive misinterpretations of activities can result.

Another reason for using MAM occurs when the NFO's books are audited by an independent accountant. It is important to understand the effect on the audit of using a method other than MAM or choosing MAM and not correctly following its practices. The importance of a successful audit cannot be understated, and it is considered later in the chapter.

A series of transactions is used in this section to highlight the variations between cash, accrual, and MAM. Information about the transactions, in an entity called the Eclectic Organization, is contained in the following paragraphs (numbered 1 through 7). It is assumed that these transactions occurred during the year, and each is analyzed under the three different methods of accounting. It is further assumed that Eclectic's financial or fiscal year ends June 30.

1. On April 15, 20x3, an invoice was received from Acme Supply Company granting 30-day credit terms on a $10,000 purchase of supplies. The goods had been received by June 30. As of June 30, there was $2,000 of supplies inventory on hand, that is, unused. All these supplies had been purchased during the current year.

Figure 3-4 outlines the entries that are necessary on April 15 under the three methods of accounting. No entry is made under the cash basis for the purchase of supplies on April 15 because the supplies are purchased on credit. A cash-based system generates an entry only when cash flows into or out of the entity, and this does not occur when purchases are made on credit.

FIGURE 3-4   Transaction 1: Purchase of Supplies on Credit

Cash

April 15	No Entry		

Accrual

April 15	Supplies Expense	10,000	
	Accounts Payable		10,000

MAM

April 15	Supplies Expenditures	10,000	
	Accounts Payable		10,000

In accrual and MAM, the entries are very similar. The accrual-based entry debits Supplies Expense whereas the account debited under MAM is Supplies Expenditures.[8] In both cases the credit entry is to the liability account, Accounts Payable. It is assumed that MAM records inventories as an expenditure when they are purchased, and at the end of the year the amount of the unused inventory is recognized as a prepaid asset, if it is significant; otherwise, it is not shown as an asset. With MAM, this is known as the "purchases method."

The major difference between the cash basis and MAM or accrual is that the latter two systems recognize a liability for the amount owed to Acme Supply Company. It is obvious that use of the cash basis "hides" the liabilities of the organization.

> 2. The employees are paid every two weeks and the pay schedule is the first and third Friday of every month. The total to be paid for the next pay period is $24,000. The entry for June 30 is considered in this example.[9] (Any taxes, i.e., income taxes or social security taxes, are to be ignored at the present time.)

In a cash-basis system, no entry is made to record the organization's obligation to pay the employees. The employees' last payday was the third Friday in June, which means they have worked for a week without being paid. Salaries for that period are an accrual expense of the current period and not the subsequent fiscal period. The cash system records the expense when it is paid, not when it is actually owed or when the employees perform their tasks for the organization. The cash system transfers the expense to the subsequent fiscal period. As a result, the salary expenditures for the year-end June 30, 20x3, are understated, and the salary expenditures for the fiscal year ending June 30, 20x4, will be overstated.

Accrual and MAM record the amount owed and the expense or expenditure on June 30, 20x3. Expenses/Expenditures for the first week of the two-week pay period are recorded in the fiscal year ending June 30, 20x3, and the second week's payroll is recorded as an expense of the following fiscal period. Figure 3-5 illustrates the debit and credit entries. The accrual entry increases Personnel Expenses by $12,000, which is one-half of the two-week payroll, and Salaries Payable is increased by an equal amount. The only difference between MAM and accrual methods is in the account names, Personnel Expenses and Personnel Expenditures, as shown in figure 3-5. Although both accrual and MAM increase the expenses/expenditures recognized at the end of the year, these methods do it for different reasons. Accrual records the expense and obligation because it is owed at the year end for the services employees provided during the current year. MAM records the entry because budget funding has been provided to pay for these personnel expenditures.

FIGURE 3-5   Transaction 2: Payroll Expenses/Expenditures

Cash

June 30   No Entry

Accrual

June 30	Personnel Expense	12,000	
	Salaries Payable		12,000

MAM

June 30	Personnel Expenditures	12,000	
	Salaries Payable		12,000

3. On July 2, Manual, Hang, Fanner, and Jones, the investment banking firm that handles Eclectic Organization's bond and security investments, notified the organization that it earned $7,500 in interest income for the three-month period ending June 30, 20x3. The interest income will be forwarded to the organization on July 7, 20x3.

The journal entries to record this transaction under the accrual basis are a debit to Interest Income Receivable and a credit to Interest Revenue.[10] There is a credit to the Interest Revenue account, even though the revenues will not be received in cash until July. From an accrual viewpoint, this revenue is earned as of June 30, 20x3, and it requires accounting recognition in that period. The entry under MAM is the same as the accrual entry. The revenue is recognized under MAM because it is considered to be available. These entries are shown in figure 3-6.

FIGURE 3-6   Transaction 3: Recognition of Interest Receivable but Not Received

Cash

June 30   No Entry

Accrual

June 30	Interest Income Receivable	7,500	
	Interest Revenue		7,500

MAM

June 30	Interest Income Receivable	7,500	
	Interest Revenue		7,500

Under the cash system, the revenues are not recognized until the cash is received, which is scheduled for July 7, 20x3. The cash-based procedures cause interest revenues of 20x2–20x3 to appear as revenues of 20x3–20x4, a later period. This is an incorrect classification, as the revenues are earned in the earlier period. This misclassification results in understating current-year revenues and overstating revenues in the subsequent year.

4. Eclectic Organization has received confirmation that as of June 15, 20x3, it had been awarded a special grant from the federal government for a program for the handicapped. The grant is for $75,000, and is expected to be received shortly.

Under the accrual system, the grant needs to be recognized as a receivable in the current period. The grant has been awarded; so as soon as Eclectic Organization is aware of the award, a receivable account, showing the amount owed to the organization by the federal government, is debited for $75,000. The amount owed to Eclectic Organization is its receivable until the monies are collected.

Under accrual accounting methods, which would characteristically be used by an NFO that is classified as "nongovernmental," the credit entry is made to an account called Restricted Contribution Revenue. This is a special type of revenue account, but it is a revenue item.[11]

Under MAM, the credit side of this journal entry is a liability called Deferred Restricted Contribution—Grants. Remember, the monies receivable under this grant can only be used in a program to help the handicapped. If the organization does not use the monies for these purposes, the grant will have to be repaid. In MAM, the monies are considered unearned until they are expended. Grants accepted under such conditions create a contingent liability for Eclectic Organization under which repayment may be necessary, and the contingency rests upon the proper spending of the monies.[12] Due to the contingent nature of the grant, it is established as a liability until the monies are used for the designated purposes. As the monies are expended for helping the handicapped, the liability is reduced, and revenues and expenditures are recognized at the same time. Figure 3-7 illustrates the entries for the three accounting methods.

Accrual and MAM do not recognize the revenue from a grant at the same time. Accrual methods recognize the revenue at the time of notification whereas, under MAM, revenue is not recognized until the obligations under the grant are fulfilled. With the cash method, there is a third choice. As illustrated in figure 3-7, there is no entry under the cash basis as no cash flows into or out of the organization. Compared with the other two methods, the cash method understates assets by not recognizing the receivable from the federal government.

5. Eclectic Organization is required under a lease agreement, signed on May 1, 20x3, to make a six-month rent prepayment of $12,000.

FIGURE 3-7   Transaction 4: The Notification of a Grant Award

Cash

June 30   No Entry

Accrual

| June 30 | Grant Receivable | 75,000 | |
| | Restricted Contributions Revenue | | 75,000 |

MAM

| June 30 | Grants Receivable | 75,000 | |
| | Deferred Restricted Contributions—Grants | | 75,000 |

In this transaction, the same journal entries are used under cash and MAM, and a different entry is used for the accrual method. The initial entry to record the payment of the rent under cash and MAM is shown in figure 3-8 as a debit to Lease Expenditures and a credit to Cash.[13] Although the entry is the same under both methods, the reasons for recording them in this manner are slightly different. Under the cash basis, cash has flowed out of the organization, and this outflow triggers an entry in the accounting system. The prepayment of the lease is a prepaid asset, and with MAM prepaid assets are usually not recognized. Therefore, if an asset is not recognized in the debit portion of this entry, the expended cash for the lease is considered to be an expenditure/disbursement.

Under the accrual method of accounting, the cash payment on the lease is recognized as a prepaid asset, Prepaid Rent. Prepaid assets have a short life and are soon consumed by the organization's operating activities. In this transaction, cash and MAM record the same journal entry. This is an instance in which MAM follows the cash basis.

FIGURE 3-8   Transaction 5: Advance Payment on a Lease

Cash

| May 1 | Lease Expenditures | 12,000 | |
| | Cash | | 12,000 |

Accrual

| May 1 | Prepaid Rent | 12,000 | |
| | Cash | | 12,000 |

MAM

| April 15 | Lease Expenditures | 12,000 | |
| | Cash | | 12,000 |

6. On April 15, 20x3, theatergoers paid a total of $50,000 for season ticket books, entitling them to attend six plays. Three of the plays had been produced as of June 30, 20x3.

Figure 3-9 illustrates the entries made on April 15. (The situation on June 30 will be considered later in the chapter.) The cash-basis system recognizes the inflow of $50,000 in cash on April 15 as a debit to Cash and a credit to Theatrical Revenues. The cash-based system recognizes the entire amount received for the tickets as revenues immediately. At this point the question should be asked, "What happens if the plays are not produced?" The most appropriate action is a refunding of the monies collected. This indicates that once cash is accepted for the tickets, the organization has an obligation either to produce the plays or, if they are canceled, to repay the money. This type of obligation is a liability. These monies are collected in advance of the performance, and as of April 15 they are deferred revenues (a liability). When the monies are collected, the liability account, Unearned Theatrical Revenue, is the account credited for $50,000 under both the accrual and MAM. It would be possible to recognize revenues earned as each of the six plays is completed, but, in practice, revenues for the three completed plays are recorded only on June 30—at the end of the fiscal year.

FIGURE 3-9   Transaction 6: Prepayment for Services

Cash

April 15	Cash	50,000	
	Theatrical Revenue		50,000

Accrual

April 15	Cash	50,000	
	Unearned Theatrical Revenue		50,000

MAM

April 15	Cash	50,000	
	Unearned Theatrical Revenue		50,000

In comparing the cash-based entries with the accrual entries, it is seen that the cash basis understates liabilities in the current period and overstates the revenues. Cash-based accounting systems will continually understate liabilities.

7. On June 28, 20x3, Eclectic Organization made an award to a graduate student working on a master's in library science at a local university. The $1,000 award is for tuition support, and it is to be paid on September 2, 20x3, which is the beginning of the school year.

No entry is made for the award under the cash basis. The reason for not recording an entry is the same as before: no cash flowed into or out of the organization. Under the accrual basis, an expense, Award Expense, is recognized in the current period and a liability for the obligation to pay the award is also recognized in the account Award Payable. These entries appear in figure 3-10.[14]

FIGURE 3-10   Transaction 7: Awarding a Grant

Cash

June 28   No Entry

Accrual

| June 28 | Award Expense | 1,000 | |
| | Award Payable | | 1,000 |

MAM

| June 28 | Award Expenditures | 1,000 | |
| | Award Payable | | 1,000 |

The award is made in the period ending June 30, 20x3, but it will not be paid until the following period. This means that in June Eclectic Organization has an obligation to make a payment to the student in September. This obligation is a liability. It is assumed that the monies for the award come from the current period. Thus, the expenditures should be recognized in the current period under MAM. Then the entry in figure 3-10, under MAM, follows the accrual entry; the only difference relates to use of the terms "expenses" and "expenditures," as is apparent in the name of the account debited.[15]

EXERCISE 3-2   Journalizing Entries under Cash, Accrual, and Modified Accrual Systems

1. Record in general journal form the proper entry for questions 2, 3, and 4 in exercise 3-1 under cash, accrual, and MAM.
2. Assume Battell Library receives and pays for $750 worth of supplies on May 1. The library uses the "purchases method" of recording supplies. What is the correct journal entry on May 1 under cash, accrual, and MAM?
3. Assume the supplies described in question 2 are recorded under the "consumption method." What is the correct journal entry under the three different methods of accounting on May 1?

ADJUSTING ENTRIES

The main objective of this chapter is to illustrate differences between the three accounting methods that can be used for establishing an accounting system. One important difference will be found among the financial statements prepared under cash, accrual, and MAM. Before preparing any financial statements, however, it is necessary to make what are called "adjusting entries." The major emphasis at this point is to highlight differences between the three methods of accounting.

"Adjusting entries" are really "catch-up" journal entries, used to bring account balances up-to-date, made only at the end of the fiscal year, and made prior to preparing financial statements. In the case of Eclectic Organization, they are made on June 30, the year-end. As an example, consider the Prepaid Rent recorded in figure 3-8. The accrual entry for the rent was made May 1. From May 1 to the end of Eclectic's fiscal year, two months have passed, and an adjustment to Prepaid Rent is necessary to bring the account up-to-date. The adjustment is necessary because some of the prepaid rent has been used up. Eclectic's rent is no longer paid ahead for the next six months; that is, the initial prepaid period has been reduced. This means that the asset Prepaid Rent needs to be reduced.

In explaining adjusting entries, we will review each of the previous seven transactions to determine which of them need to be adjusted or updated. This process is not as difficult as it may appear. For one thing, none of the entries made under the cash basis require adjusting entries. Only entries that used the accrual basis or MAM, when the latter follows accrual accounting, need to be considered for adjustment.

Each of the seven transactions is reviewed in figure 3-11 to determine which of them require an adjusting entry. Figure 3-11 shows the transaction number of the item, the type of item, the date it was recorded in the journal, whether it needs an adjusting entry, and the reason it does or does not require an adjusting entry.

The decision for making or not making an adjusting entry begins as a process of elimination. If a journal entry is dated as of June 30, it does not need an adjusting entry, because it is current as of the end of the fiscal year. On this basis, transactions 2 and 3 are eliminated. If the transactions involve a prepaid asset and were recorded before June 30, an adjusting entry is required. On this basis, transactions 1 and 5, both dealing with prepaid assets, require adjusting entries under accrual but not MAM.

The remaining transactions are analyzed individually to determine if they need updating since the time they were recorded in the journal. Transaction 4 records a grant that is to be received. If the monies from the grant have been received, an adjusting entry is necessary. In fact, the entry is made as soon as

**FIGURE 3-11   Guidelines for Adjusting Entries in the Seven Transactions
under Accrual and MAM**

Transaction Number	Transaction Description	Date Recorded in Journal	Does It Need Updating? (Accrual/MAM)	Reason for Update
1	Supplies	June 15	Yes/No	Passage of time
2	Salaries	June 30	No/No	Current as of June 30
3	Interest	June 30	No/No	Current as of June 30
4	Grant	June 15	No/No	Current as of June 30
5	Rent	May 1	Yes/No	Passage of time
6	Revenues	April 15	Yes/Yes	Three plays produced (revenue earned)
7	Award	June 28	No/No	Current as of June 30

the monies are received—which is not necessarily an adjusting entry at the end of the year. The point is academic as the grant monies have not been received as of June 30, and no entries are necessary.

In transaction 6, which deals with Theatrical Revenues, three plays out of six have been produced as of June 30. This means that some of the deferred revenues in the Unearned Theatrical Revenue account are now earned revenues; therefore, the liability needs to be reduced. The last transaction, 7, deals with the tuition award to the graduate student, and it does not require an adjustment, because as of June 30 the award has not been transferred to the student. In other words, nothing has changed since the June 28 transaction.

The transactions that require accrual adjusting entries are 1, 5, and 6. Transaction 6 also requires adjustment under MAM. Each of these adjusting entries is analyzed in more detail in the remaining portion of this section.

As indicated in transaction 1, $2,000 of supplies are in the inventory as of June 30. These supplies need to be shown in the accounts as an asset. The adjusting entry necessary under the accrual method is reflected in figure 3-12.

In the first entry in figure 3-12, the amount of supplies remaining at the end of the year is recorded as a debit to the Inventory of Supplies account. Without this entry, no record would be maintained as to the amount of the remaining supplies. This entry also reduces the Supplies Expense by the amount of the ending inventory. This decrease in Supplies Expense for the total of the unused inventory is necessary; otherwise the Supplies Expense is overstated for the current fiscal year. The accounting for the inventory requires coordination with the employees who are responsible for keeping an inventory count of the supplies. The accounting supervisor must determine if there are discrepancies between the accounting records and the physical count made by the employees. Any significant differences require investigation. Without this type of coordination and recording procedures, there is little control over the supplies at the facility.

FIGURE 3-12   Adjusting Entries for Transaction 1

Cash

June 30   No Adjusting Entry

Accrual

June 30   Inventory of Supplies   2,000
                  Supplies Expense   2,000

MAM

June 30   No Adjusting Entry

The first adjusting entry reduces the Supplies Expense by $2,000. This reduction in expenses automatically causes the revenues to increase. In turn, when the $2,000 increase in revenues is transferred to the Fund Balance, it will make the Fund Balance higher.[16] In the accounting equation, it was shown that when an asset such as Inventory of Supplies increases, either a liability or the Fund Balance must increase for the equation to remain in balance. In this case, the Fund Balance increases. This is an unavailable increase as the only reason the Fund Balance increased was because an Inventory of Supplies account was established as an asset. The reader of accrual financial statements must always recognize that the inventory account does not provide more monies for potential spending in subsequent years.

As previously stated, the cash basis of accounting does not usually journalize any adjusting entries because no cash flows into or out of the NFO at that time. Therefore, an entry would be recorded for inventories under the cash basis only when the invoice is paid. At that time, an Expenditure account is debited and the Cash account is credited.

With MAM, no entry is recorded. This approach is called the purchases method of recording supplies. The purchases method assumes that these supplies are expenditures when they are purchased even if there are supplies remaining in the inventory. It is more common to find this method used in NFOs unless the dollar value of the remaining supplies is significant. If the valuation of supplies is significant, it should be disclosed.

The next transaction requiring an adjusting entry is number 5, which deals with prepaid rent. The entries for this transaction are different under accrual and MAM. In this transaction, the rent was paid for a six-month period, beginning May 1 and ending November 1, 20x3. As of June 30, two months of that rental period have expired. The passage of the two-month period is used to determine the portion of the rent that has changed from a prepaid asset to an expense. In this example, two months of the prepaid asset ($4,000) have changed into an expense for the period ending June 30, 20x3, and the remaining four months' rent ($8,000) is still a prepaid asset. In figure 3-13, an accrual debit is made to Rent Expense and a credit is made to the Prepaid Rent account. The debit and credit are both for $4,000, which is the amount of prepaid rent that has become an expense over the two-month period ending June 30, 20x3. The effect of this entry is to reduce the Prepaid Rent account to an $8,000 balance, after the $4,000 credit is posted to the ledger, and to increase the Rent Expense account by $4,000.

FIGURE 3-13   Adjusting Entries for Transaction 5

Cash

June 30   No Adjusting Entry

Accrual

June 30   Rent Expense   4,000
                   Prepaid Rent   4,000

MAM

June 30   No Adjusting Entry

Under MAM, no adjusting entry is made as the entire amount paid for the lease is recognized as an expenditure at the time of payment. This is the same procedure used in the cash basis. When prepaid assets are involved in a transaction, MAM usually follows cash-basis accounting procedures. Compared with the accrual method, the MAM and the cash basis record higher amounts of lease expenditures in their financial statements for the fiscal year ending June 30, 20x3.

The final transaction requiring an adjusting entry is transaction 6, which deals with the collection of ticket revenues before the production of the plays. As of June 30, three of the plays have been produced, and an adjusting entry is necessary to bring the amount of earned revenue up-to-date. Since half the plays have been produced, only half the cash received still needs to be considered a liability; the rest has been earned, and it is a revenue item. The initial entries for accrual and MAM used the same accounts, and the adjusting entries apply to both of these methods. The adjusting entry, shown in figure 3-14, reduces the balance of the Unearned Theatrical Revenue account by $25,000 and transfers the $25,000 to the Theatrical Revenue account. This $25,000 now represents earned revenues rather than a potential liability. The $25,000 is equal to half of the total advance ticket sales, and it is removed from the liability account, Unearned Theatrical Revenues, because half of the plays have been produced.

FIGURE 3-14 Adjusting Entries for Transaction 6

Cash

| June 30 | No Adjusting Entry | | |

Accrual

| June 30 | Unearned Theatrical Revenue | 25,000 | |
| | Theatrical Revenue | | 25,000 |

MAM

| June 30 | Unearned Theatrical Revenue | 25,000 | |
| | Theatrical Revenue | | 25,000 |

This section demonstrates how adjusting entries differ under the three models of accounting. Under the cash basis, no adjusting entries are necessary; this makes the cash system easy to use although it does not provide for accurate reporting. MAM requires adjusting entries when it records an entry in the same fashion as the accrual method, but when a transaction is recorded in the manner used under the cash basis, no adjusting entry is made.

FINANCIAL STATEMENTS

Obviously, financial statements differ markedly when they are prepared under the three different methods of accounting. Accrual-based financial statements are used by those NFOs that are considered nongovernmental. MAM financial statements are prepared by governmental NFOs and cash-based financial statements are often used by NFOs, but unfortunately such statements do not reflect NFO accounting guidelines except in special circumstances.[17]

To illustrate the differences that arise in the financial statements, we will begin by looking at Eclectic Organization's financial statements for the year ending June 30, 20x2, which appear in figure 3-15. We will then see how the following year's financial statements would be prepared under cash, accrual, and MAM. The emphasis here is not on how the differences between these statements arose but on what they represent, as well as their potential effects on decision making. First we will examine the two financial statements in figure 3-15, the Balance Sheet and the Statement of Receipts and Disbursements. They are formulated on a cash basis.

The Balance Sheet in figure 3-15 represents a listing of all asset accounts, liability accounts, and the Fund Balance. It shows the balance in these accounts at one point in time, which is the date on which the statement is prepared. The complete Balance Sheet for an NFO is usually prepared only at the end of the fiscal year, and it presents a summarization of the year's business activities.

FIGURE 3-15   **Cash-Based Balance Sheet and Statement of Receipts and Disbursements for Eclectic Organization for Fiscal Year Ending June 30, 20x2 (Base Year)**

ECLECTIC ORGANIZATION
Balance Sheet
June 30, 20x2

Assets		Liabilities and Fund Balance	
Cash	$109,000	Liabilities	$ —
		Fund Balance	109,000
		Total Liabilities and	
Total Assets	$109,000	Fund Balance	$109,000

ECLECTIC ORGANIZATION
Statement of Receipts and Disbursements
For the Year Ended June 30, 20x2

Receipts:		
Support	$1,110,000	
Revenues	35,000	
Total Receipts		$1,145,000
Expenditures:		
Personnel	$1,068,000	
Other Expenditures	21,000	
Total Expenditures		1,089,000
Excess of Receipts over Disbursements		$ 56,000

It should be noted that the accounting equation is represented in the Balance Sheet because the total of the asset balances is always equal to the total of the liabilities and the Fund Balance accounts. Under the cash system, no liabilities are recognized, but the total of the assets and the Fund Balance equals $109,000 in the cash-based Balance Sheet for Eclectic Organization.[18]

Under the cash basis, the Statement of Receipts and Disbursements represents receipts of all the cash collected during the current year and disbursements of all the cash actually paid out during the year.[19] The Statement of Receipts and Disbursements in figure 3-15 reflects transactions over the entire year whereas the Balance Sheet is representative of only one point in time. The bottom line in the Statement of Receipts and Disbursements is referred to as Excess of Receipts over Disbursements, and it is transferred to the Balance Sheet at the end of each fiscal year. With Eclectic Organization, the "Excess," in this case $56,000, is transferred to the Fund Balance and added to the existing balance (see chapter 2).[20] For the Balance Sheet to balance (i.e., assets equal liabilities plus the Fund Balance), the transfer of the Excess must have been completed. This makes it important to prepare the Statement of Receipts and Disbursements prior to preparing the Balance Sheet. This transfer may occur only once a year, when the year-end financial statements are prepared, and this means that the Fund Balance is adjusted once every year.

COMPARISONS BETWEEN ACCRUAL- AND CASH-BASED FINANCIAL STATEMENTS

In figures 3-16, 3-17, and 3-18, the financial statements for Eclectic Organization for June 30, 20x3 are presented on an accrual basis. The cash-based statements for Eclectic Organization for the same period, 20x3, are presented in figure 3-19. All of these statements update the financial statements in figure 3-15 by incorporating the seven transactions previously described. In addition, it is assumed that total personnel costs, paid out in cash during the year, amounted to $1,489,000, and Eclectic Organization had received monies for support, in cash, during the year equal to $1,400,000. It should be noted that the use of an accrual-based financial statement assumes Eclectic Organization is not defined as a "governmental" organization. Only organizations that meet the previously described criteria for "nongovernments" should use accrual-based financial statements.

One immediate difference that is apparent in comparing the cash and accrual systems is a change in the names of the financial statements under the accrual system. The Statement of Receipts and Disbursements, under the cash-basis system, is called the Statement of Activities under the accrual system. The Balance Sheet is renamed the Statement of Financial Position, and a third statement, titled the Statement of Cash Flows, is added.

There are other differences, too. The Statement of Activities uses the term "net assets" in place of deficiency or excess. Although the usual revenue and expense items are included on the statement, this financial statement includes restricted assets in determining the total of net assets. The term net assets includes changes in restricted assets; therefore, it has a broader meaning than an "excess" that only represents the difference between revenues and expenditures or disbursements.[21]

These restricted assets include the amount of the grant received by Eclectic Organization to help the handicapped. It is not considered a liability, as under MAM, but rather a revenue item. This restricted asset is only temporarily restricted as its restrictions will be satisfied when expenditures are made under the terms of the grant. Grant earnings that have to be returned to an endowment are an example of a permanently restricted asset that does not become available for general expenditures. As Eclectic has no permanently restricted assets a balance of zero is shown in figure 3-16 for this item. The

**FIGURE 3-16   Accrual-based Statement of Activities for Eclectic
Organization for Fiscal Year Ending June 30, 20x3**

ECLECTIC ORGANIZATION
Statement of Activities
For the Year Ended June 30, 20x3

Changes in Unrestricted Net Assets:
Revenues from Operations:

Contributions	$1,400,000	
Theatrical Revenue	25,000	
Other Revenue:		
Interest Revenue	7,500	
Total Unrestricted Revenues		$1,432,500
Net Assets released from temporary restrictions		0
Total		$1,432,500
Expenses:		
Personnel	$1,501,000	
Supplies	8,000	
Award to others	1,000	
Lease	4,000	
Total Expenses		1,514,000
Increase (Decrease) in unrestricted assets from operations		$ (81,500)
Changes in temporarily restricted assets:		
Restricted Contributions		75,000
Changes in permanently restricted assets		0
Increase (Decrease) in Net Assets		$ (6,500)
Net Assets at Beginning of Year		109,000
Net Assets at End of Year		$ 102,500

Net Decrease in Assets in figure 3-16 is $6,500. This Net Decrease in Assets should be compared with the similar amounts in figures 3-19 (cash) and 3-20 (MAM) to see the variation created by including restricted grants in the Statement of Activities.

When viewing the accrual-based Statement of Financial Position, it can be seen that there is a significant difference between it and cash or MAM statements. One important difference is that the term "fund balance" is no longer used. It is replaced by "net assets." In the Statement of Financial Position, net assets represent the difference between assets and liabilities. This residual is divided into unrestricted, temporarily restricted, and permanently restricted amounts. Those net assets that have a donor-related stipulation restricting the donated resources from being used and only allow the income earned on the resources to be used are permanently restricted net assets. Those net assets that can be used for spending after the expiration of a stipulation or actions of the NFO are classified as temporarily restricted. The remaining net

FIGURE 3-17   Accrual-based Statement of Financial Position for Eclectic Organization for Fiscal Year Ending June 30, 20x3

ECLECTIC ORGANIZATION
Statement of Financial Position
June 30, 20x3

Assets		Liabilities	
Cash	$ 58,000	Accounts Payable	$ 10,000
Grant Receivable	75,000	Salaries Payable	12,000
Interest Income Receivable	7,500	Unearned Theatrical	
Prepaid Rent	8,000	Revenue	25,000
Inventory of Supplies	2,000	Award Payable	1,000
		Total Liabilities	$ 48,000
		Net Assets	
		Unrestricted	$ 27,500
		Temporarily Restricted	75,000
		Permanently Restricted	0
		Total Net Assets	$102,500
		Total Liabilities &	
Total Assets	$150,500	Net Assets	$150,500

FIGURE 3-18   Accrual-based Statement of Cash Flows for Eclectic Organization for Fiscal Year Ending June 30, 20x3

ECLECTIC ORGANIZATION
Statement of Cash Flows
For the Year Ended June 30, 20x3

Cash inflows from operations:	
Cash received from contributions	$1,400,000
Cash received from theatrical revenue	50,000
Cash outflows from operations:	
Cash paid to employees	1,489,000
Cash paid for lease	12,000
Net Cash from operations	$ (51,000)
Cash at beginning of year	109,000
Cash at end of year	$ 58,000

assets are defined as unrestricted. It can be seen that the net assets show a higher ending balance ($102,500) than the cash-based Fund Balance ($58,000) in figure 3-19.

The third and new financial statement for accrual systems is the Statement of Cash Flows. Its purpose is to show how cash flowed into and out of the organization. This statement allows the users of accrual-based financial statements to have information about the NFO's uses and receipts of cash similar to the information on cash-based statements. For example, when the Statement of Cash Flows is compared with the cash-based Statement of Receipts and Disbursements it can be seen that both statements calculate a decrease in cash of $51,000 for the year. Although the Statement of Receipts and Disbursements is supposed to represent a type of income statement under cash methods, it really discloses the cash income for the organization. This is not a recognized income figure, and for that reason, cash-based accounting systems are not considered acceptable under NFO accounting practices. For small organizations the Statement of Receipts and Disbursements provides information comparable with that shown on the accrual-based Statement of Cash Flows.

Another difference relates to the way in which the available cash in the Cash account can be used under the two systems of accounting. Under the cash basis (figure 3-19), it appears that there are no claims on the cash of $58,000 as of June 30, 20x3, which means that the governing board is likely to want to use this cash for operating activities in the subsequent year. Yet it is apparent that there are claims of $48,000 (total liabilities in figure 3-17) against the cash under the accrual-based statement. This is the amount owed to others, i.e., the liability balance.

These liabilities consist of $48,000 worth of claims against the cash, $58,000. When the Cash balance is considered together with the liabilities it will be used to pay, it changes any decision to spend a large portion of the $58,000. The liabilities will have to be paid, within a short period of time, and the balance in the Cash account will be applied against those liabilities.

If the board decides to spend the $58,000, it places the organization in a difficult position regarding the availability of monies to pay the outstanding liabilities when they come due. This situation is not as apparent under the cash basis. The real amount of "free" cash (i.e., with no liability claims against it) amounts to $10,000. In addition, there is a receivable for interest income of $7,500 that appears on the accrual-based Statement of Financial Position. The total amount available for reallocation by the governing board for the subsequent year is $17,500, which is equal to the free cash ($10,000) and the receivable interest income ($7,500).

The accrual amount shown in the unrestricted portion of the Net Assets is $27,500. Although this amount is listed as unrestricted, $10,000 of it is not available for spending in the subsequent year (inventory $2,000 and prepaid rent $8,000). Therefore the board should not assume that the entire balance of $27,500 is available for spending in the next fiscal period. Under accrual, there is only $17,500 of funding available ($27,500 less $2,000 and $8,000) for reallocation in the new budget year.

It should be clear from the two statements that the NFO's governing board needs to understand what is represented on the financial statements in order to determine if any resources from previous years' activities are available for spending in the current period. The different bases for establishing an

FIGURE 3-19 **Cash-based Balance Sheet and Statement of Receipts and Disbursements for Eclectic Organization for Fiscal Year Ending June 30, 20x3**

ECLECTIC ORGANIZATION
Balance Sheet
June 30, 20x3

Assets		Liabilities and Fund Balance	
Cash	$58,000	Liabilities	—
		Fund Balance	$58,000
		Total Liabilities and Fund	
Total Assets	$58,000	Balance	$58,000

ECLECTIC ORGANIZATION
Statement of Receipts and Disbursements
For the Year Ended June 30, 20x3

Receipts:		
Support	$1,400,000	
Theatrical Revenue	50,000	
Total Receipts		$1,450,000
Expenditures:		
Personnel Expenditures	$1,489,000	
Lease Expenditures	12,000	
Total Expenditures		$1,501,000
Deficiency of Receipts over Disbursements		$ (51,000)

accounting system can result in misinterpretations and misinformed decisions affecting the use of monies.

Several other differences are apparent when the two balance sheets are compared. The Statement of Financial Position has a more complete listing of the organization's assets than the cash-based Balance Sheet. A listing of these assets allows for better control over them. For example, under the cash-based system there is no record of supplies. In other words, after the supplies are purchased, there is no accounting for them and little control over them within the organization's accounting system.[22]

Both the Statement of Receipts and Disbursements and the Statement of Activities show higher disbursements or expenses than either receipts or net assets, respectively. Note the change this causes in figure 3-19. The Excess is no longer called the Excess of Receipts over Disbursements, as was in figure 3-15; because disbursements are higher now, it is called the Deficiency of Receipts over Disbursements. A similar change is apparent in figure 3-16 for the Statement of Activities except that it is called a Decrease in Net Assets. The smaller decrease in net assets is due to the effect of the restricted contribution of $75,000. When these decreases are transferred to the residual (either the Fund Balance or the Net Assets), it decreases the corresponding credit or normal balance. In the cash-based statement, there is a decrease of $51,000 to a Fund Balance total of $58,000; whereas in the accrual Statement of Financial Position the Net Assets decrease by $6,500 to $102,500.

Another difference is apparent when the Statement of Receipts and Disbursements is compared with the Statement of Activities. There is a $44,500 difference between the Deficiency and Decrease between the two statements, from $51,000 to $6,500 on the cash- and accrual-based statements, respectively. This is due to the increase in expenses ($30,500) and the restricted contribution being recognized as an increase in net assets ($75,000) under the accrual method. The $44,500 difference between the statements is a significant change from one method of accounting to the other, and it illustrates the point that the accounting method by itself can create widely different interpretations of the NFO's results. Without understanding these differences, it is hard to make comparisons among NFOs, but there is yet a third choice to consider: MAM.

EXERCISE 3-3   Financial Statements

1. Define the Balance Sheet. Compare it with the Statement of Activities.
2. Explain the major differences in balance sheets prepared under the cash method and the accrual method.
3. Explain the differences between "Excess of Receipts over Disbursements" and "Net Assets."
4. What is the major difference between the terms "net assets" and "fund balance"?
5. What is the major problem in using cash-based financial statements to make decisions about allocating monies?

MODIFIED-ACCRUAL STATEMENTS COMPARED WITH CASH AND ACCRUAL STATEMENTS

One major difference between accrual and MAM is that the latter method does not recognize a liability for certain items in the current period for which monies are going to be made available in the subsequent year.[23] For example, interest on long-term debt that is due at the end of the fiscal year is not recognized as being owed, because it is in the subsequent year that the board sets aside monies for the interest payment. Also, MAM does not recognize revenues unless it is clear that they are "available" (or they are material and delays have arisen in collection). The most significant difference between MAM and accrual, as they relate to the seven transactions in this chapter, is in the area of prepaid items. Under MAM, prepaid items do not have to be recognized in the accounts, and they usually are not. This practice is apparent when the Balance Sheet in figure 3-21 is compared with the Statement of Financial Position in figure 3-17. The Prepaid Rent account for $8,000 is "missing" from the MAM Balance Sheet.

Ramifications from the $8,000 difference also are apparent in the totals on the two statements in figures 3-16 and 3-20. There is a $10,000 difference between the "Decrease in Unrestricted Assets from Operations" on the Statement of Activities ($81,500) and the "Deficiency of Support and Revenues over Expenditures" in figure 3-20 ($91,500) that occurs because Lease Expenditures are $8,000 higher under MAM ($12,000 − $4,000); and Supplies Expenditures are $2,000 higher ($10,000 − $8,000). This effect creates a larger decrease for MAM.

FIGURE 3-20 **Modified Accrual–based Statement of Revenues, Expenditures, and Changes in Fund Balance for Eclectic Organization for Fiscal Year Ending June 30, 20x3**

ECLECTIC ORGANIZATION

Statement of Revenues, Expenditures and Changes in Fund Balance

For the Year Ended June 30, 20x3

Support and Revenues:		
Support	$1,400.000	
Theatrical Revenue	25,000	
Interest Revenue	7,500	
Total Support and Revenue		$1,432,500
Expenditures:		
Personnel	$1,501,000	
Supplies	10,000	
Award	1,000	
Lease	12,000	
Total Expenditures		1,524,000
Deficiency of Support and		
Revenues over Expenditures		$ (91,500)
Fund Balance, July 1, 20x2		109,000
Fund Balance, June 30, 20x3		$ 17,500

The $10,000 greater MAM Deficiency over the accrual-based Statement of Activities in figure 3-16 is more than a 10 percent change. Although this is an important change, it is not as significant as the $30,500 difference between the cash and accrual methods ($81,500 − $51,000), which creates a more favorable cash financial picture by reducing the cash disbursements.

Under MAM, the amount of the unrestricted Fund Balance is $17,500, but under accrual Net Asset restrictions, $27,500 are shown as unrestricted. The

**FIGURE 3-21   Modified Accrual-based Balance Sheet for Eclectic
Organization for Fiscal Year Ending June 30, 20x3**

ECLECTIC ORGANIZATION
Balance Sheet
June 30, 20x3

Assets		Liabilities	
Cash	$ 58,000	Accounts Payable	$ 10,000
Grant Receivable	75,000	Salaries Payable	12,000
Interest Income Receivable	7,500	Deferred Restricted	
		Contributions—Grants	75,000
		Unearned Theatrical	
		Revenue	25,000
		Award Payable	1,000
		Total Liabilities	$123,000
		Fund Balance	
		Unrestricted Fund	
		Balance	$ 17,500
		Total Liabilities &	
Total Assets	$140,500	Fund Balance	$140,500

reader of the Statement of Financial Position needs to be aware that not all the
$27,500 can be appropriated in the subsequent year. An over allocation of cash
by the board is not as likely to be made under MAM.

When MAM is compared with the cash-based statements, all distinctions
that were made between the cash and accrual statements still hold true. MAM
provides management with a better financial report than cash-based statements
for making financial decisions.

WHY A FUND BALANCE RATHER THAN NET ASSETS?

At this point, the Reserved accounts in the Fund Balance that impose restrictions on the Fund Balance need to be further explained. In addition, a distinction between these restrictions of the Fund Balance and restrictions such as the
Deferred Restricted Contributions for Grants and Unearned Theatrical Revenue should be made.

The MAM Fund Balance can include a number of reserved accounts. The
purpose of these reserved accounts is to indicate to the reader of the Balance
Sheet that certain portions of the Fund Balance are not available for new
spending.[24] The reason they are not available for spending is that they are represented on the other side of the accounting equation by noncash assets, such
as supplies, or they have been designated for a specific use by the board, such

as the purchase of new equipment or possibly some type of refund. In these cases, the amount available for spending purposes has been reduced. Each time a reserve account is established within the Fund Balance, it reduces the portion of the Fund Balance that can be used for new spending. The establishment of a reserve in the Fund Balance should be considered for representation of any noncash asset, and a reserve should be established for any board restrictions on the Fund Balance.

The major distinction between reserves in the Fund Balance and restricted accounts such as the Deferred Restricted Contributions account is that the latter is a liability account. The restrictions on a liability account are established by parties outside the NFO. In addition, if the obligation is not fulfilled, the monies which have been or will be received may have to be returned to the granting agency or the donor. Under NFO accrual, the term Fund Balance is replaced by Net Assets. From the perspective of accrual accounting, deferred restricted contributions are not considered a liability, but an asset that will undoubtedly be collected after a timed delay. Therefore, these donor-restricted contributions are recognized as revenue at the time of receipt rather than as a liability, and additionally, as we have seen, the arising net assets are divided between permanently and temporarily restricted classifications.

These two differing viewpoints stem from different assumptions about what should be represented in the financial statements. Accrual methods use a for-profit income measurement perspective. As such, it is very important to recognize earnings and expenses in the proper time period. MAM is based on nonprofit budgetary financial flows. From this viewpoint, it is very important to show the amount of funding that is available for spending and identify the purposes for which this funding can be and has been used. As such, determination of profit is deemphasized and availability of funding sources is the first concern.

EXERCISE 3-4   Account Classification

1. Place check marks in reference to the accounts listed below to indicate what type of balance sheet they would likely be found on.

	Balance Sheet Prepared Under:		
	Modified Accrual Basis	Cash Basis	Accrual Basis
Cash			
Interest Income Receivable			
Prepaid Insurance			
Reserve in Fund Balance			
Accounts Payable			
Temporarily Restricted Net Assets			

AUDITS OF NFOS

This chapter highlights some questions that need to be asked regarding the accounting system adopted in a particular NFO. If the organization is small enough, it may be possible to maintain the accounting records on a cash basis. Of course, doing so may lead to another problem, because an independent audit of the NFO's financial records may not find the cash-based accounting system satisfactory. The major purpose of this section is not to describe the procedures in an audit but to illustrate the results of an audit by reviewing the audit opinion.

Before we proceed to the audit opinion, an explanation is needed of the function of an audit and the importance of the opinion rendered by the independent public accountant who performs the audit. An audit is an examination of the NFO's books and records to determine whether generally accepted accounting principles (GAAP) were followed in preparing the financial statements. GAAP, the established body of rules and guidelines that should be followed in the preparation of financial statements, is formulated around the pronouncements of the accounting standard setting bodies described in chapter 1. If the accounting firm that performs the audit discovers, through its investigation of the records, that the organization is not following GAAP, a "qualified opinion" is provided.[25] An opinion that is considered satisfactory is called an "unqualified opinion." The unqualified opinion certifies that the accounting system has been adequately examined and GAAP is being followed. One GAAP recommendation for NFOs is that the financial statements be prepared using MAM rather than a cash or accrual method.

The requirement for MAM relates to the financial statements, but the accounting records themselves can be maintained on a cash basis, with conversion to an accrual basis at the end of the fiscal year. If this conversion is properly handled, the statements should receive an unqualified opinion. Of course, this conversion can be time-consuming and expensive.

Why is an audit required? In many cases it is required by a regulatory agency that has provided a grant to the organization being audited. Some other granting agency could also require this kind of audit. In addition, the NFO may want an audit performed as a further assurance to the public of proper use of the monies for which the NFO has responsibility.

AICPA has issued an audit guide, *Audits of State and Local Governmental Units,* for governmental NFOs and for accountants who perform audits of these organizations.[26] This audit guide provides recommendations to be followed in auditing a governmental organization. Recommendations in the audit guide relate to the specific type of opinion required for NFOs that follow GAAP and those that do not follow it.

The following opinion is an example for the general-purpose financial statements of a component unit of a local government issued by an independent accountant. A component unit is a smaller governmental unit within another larger government unit such as a library, museum, or school district that is part of a city or state government. General-purpose financial statements are the minimum set of financial statements for which an audit opinion is issued, e.g., the Balance Sheet, Statement of Revenues, Expenditures, and Changes in Fund Balance, and disclosure notes to the financial statements. In this example, it is assumed that GAAP is being used.

> We have audited the accompanying general-purpose financial statements of the Eclectic Library, a component unit of Logo County, as of and for the year ended June 30, 20x3. These general-purpose financial statements are the responsibility of Logo County management. Our responsibility is to express an opinion on these general-purpose financial statements based on our audit.
>
> We conducted our audit in accordance with generally accepted auditing standards. Those standards require that we plan and perform the audit to obtain reasonable assurance about whether the general-purpose financial statements are free of material misstatement. An audit includes examining, on a test basis, evidence supporting the amounts and disclosures in the general-purpose financial statements. An audit also includes assessing the accounting principles used and significant estimates made by management, as well as evaluating the overall general-purpose financial statement presentation. We believe that our audit provides a reasonable basis for our opinion.
>
> In our opinion, the general-purpose financial statements referred to above present fairly, in all material respects, the financial position of Eclectic Library, Logo County, as of June 30, 20x3, and the results of its operations for the year then ended in conformity with generally accepted accounting principles.

This three-paragraph opinion is signed and dated by the accountant, and the library makes it available to the public along with its general-purpose financial statements. This opinion is unqualified. The management of the library followed the correct accounting practices, and there is no qualification in the opinion. The next opinion contains a notation that the cash method was followed, but it is not a qualified opinion.

> We have audited the accompanying general-purpose financial statements of the Eclectic Library, a component unit of Logo County, as of and for the year ended June 30, 20x3. These general-purpose financial statements are the responsibility of Logo County management. Our responsibility is to express an opinion on these general-purpose financial statements based on our audit.
>
> We conducted our audit in accordance with generally accepted auditing standards. Those standards require that we plan and perform the audit to obtain reasonable assurance about whether the general-purpose financial statements are free of material misstatement. An audit includes examining, on a test basis, evidence supporting the amounts and disclosures in the general-purpose financial statements. An audit also includes assessing the accounting principles used and significant estimates made by management, as well as evaluating the overall general-

purpose financial statement presentation. We believe that our audit provides a reasonable basis for our opinion.

As discussed in Note 10, Eclectic Library, Logo County, prepares its financial statements on the cash basis, which is a comprehensive basis of accounting other than generally accepted accounting principles.

In our opinion, the financial statements referred to above present fairly, in all material respects, the cash and unencumbered cash balances of Eclectic Library, Logo County, as of June 30, 20x3, and the revenues it received and expenditures it paid for the year then ended on the basis of accounting described in Note 10.

There is notification to the reader in paragraphs three and four that Eclectic Library is not following the correct method of accounting, but the opinion goes on to state that, even so, the financial statements present fairly the results of operations. In some cases, a small public library's accounting system that is audited as part of a city's or county's accounting system does not significantly differ from GAAP, and its small size means it has little effect on the entire organization's audit report. Therefore, it is possible that cash-basis accounting in a public library that is a small part of a larger accounting system could occur without serious audit problems.

In the next opinion a qualification is noted. The qualification, in the third paragraph of the opinion, expresses concern over the omission of an account group showing the cost of the fixed assets owned by the library. This is considered a violation of GAAP as the valuation of buildings, equipment, and other long-lived assets are not recorded.[27]

We have audited the accompanying general-purpose financial statements of the Eclectic Library, a component unit of Logo County, as of and for the year ended June 30, 20x3. These general-purpose financial statements are the responsibility of Logo County management. Our responsibility is to express an opinion on these general-purpose financial statements based on our audit.

We conducted our audit in accordance with generally accepted auditing standards. Those standards require that we plan and perform the audit to obtain reasonable assurance about whether the general-purpose financial statements are free of material misstatement. An audit includes examining, on a test basis, evidence supporting the amounts and disclosures in the general-purpose financial statements. An audit also includes assessing the accounting principles used and significant estimates made by management, as well as evaluating the overall general-purpose financial statement presentation. We believe that our audit provides a reasonable basis for our opinion.

The general-purpose financial statements referred to above do not include the General Fixed Assets Account Group, which should be included in order to conform with generally accepted accounting principles. The amount that should be recorded in the General Fixed Asset Account Group is unknown.

In our opinion, except for the effect on the financial statements of the omission described in the preceding paragraph, the general-purpose financial statements referred to above present fairly, in all material respects, the fi-

nancial position of Eclectic Library, Logo County, as of June 30, 20x3, and the results of its operations for the year then ended in conformity with generally accepted accounting principles.

The possible consequences of using a cash-based system or not following GAAP should be clear to the administrators of an NFO—a qualified opinion. There is another factor which should be mentioned before a library unit or other NFO organization decides to adopt a cash-basis system or not follow GAAP. From a public relations viewpoint, it should be clear that not using GAAP and receiving a qualified opinion may create confusion among some members of the governing board and the general public.

SUMMARY

This chapter has presented the basic differences between cash-basis accounting, accrual-based systems, and systems based on MAM. The differences between these methods can affect managerial decisions. In addition, use of the cash basis can affect the type of audit opinion that is rendered by an independent accountant. Therefore, establishing an accounting system should be a well-considered decision. The decision should not be left to the accounting personnel alone. If improper funding decisions are made because of the decision to use a cash-based accounting system, the responsibility for these inadequacies rests with the director of the organization and possibly with the board. This does not mean that the cash basis should be ruled out entirely. It does mean that the limitations of the cash basis should be understood and accounted for by the director and the board prior to making funding decisions. Figure 3-22 provides a summary of the differences between the three accounting methods.

EXERCISE 3-5 Converting a Balance Sheet

1. The balance shown below is for Outer Banks Pirate Museum. It is a cash-based balance sheet. Convert it to an accrual-based balance sheet by incorporating as necessary the additional three transactions listed below.

OUTER BANKS PIRATE MUSEUM
Balance Sheet
June 30, 20x5

Assets		Liabilities & Fund Balance	
Cash	$75,000	Liabilities	$ —
		Fund Balance	75,000
		Total Liabilities	
Total Assets	$75,000	& Fund Balance	$75,000

(Continued)

FIGURE 3-22 Summary of Major Differences between the Three Accounting Methods

Item	Cash Method	Accrual Method	Modified Accrual Method
Assets	Recognized if cash paid	Assets recognized as they are received and title passes to the organization	Usually no recognition of prepaid assets; capital additions also recognized as expenditures
Liabilities	Not recognized	All liabilities recognized as incurred	Most liabilities recognized as incurred, but not if current funding is not provided (e.g., long-term debt)
Revenues	Represent the amount of cash receipts and not assigned to the correct fiscal period	Correctly assigned to fiscal period where earned. Revenues include changes in donor-restricted contributions. Revenues matched with expenses.	Not always correctly assigned to fiscal period where earned
Disbursements/ Expenses/ Expenditures	Disbursements are not assigned to the correct fiscal period	Correctly assigned to fiscal period where earned. Matched with expenses.	Not always correctly assigned to fiscal period where earned
Fund Balance or Net Assets	Fund Balance: Represents cash available	Net Assets: Represents the accumulated difference between revenues and expenses adjusted for the donor-restricted contributions. Based on income determination methods.	Fund Balance: Represents the amount of funding available for spending in the subsequent fiscal period*
Auditing Effect	Qualified opinion likely	Qualified opinion for governmental NFOs	Unqualified opinion for governmental NFOs
Accounting Equation	Cash = Fund Balance	Assets = Liabilities + Net Assets	Current Assets = Current Liabilities + Fund Balance†
Adjusting Entries	Not required	Required	Required

*Budgetary restrictions on the fund balance will be explained in chapter 4.

†Capital assets with long-term lives (over one year) and long-term liabilities do not appear in MAM's governmental accounts. Prepaid assets (under one year) usually do not appear, either. Therefore, is it more correct to show the accounting equation as Current Assets = Current Liabilities + Fund Balance rather than Assets = Liabilities + Fund Balance.

EXERCISE 3-5   Converting a Balance Sheet   *(Continued)*

The museum is on an island that can only be reached by boat; so it was not an active year for the museum. Assume that the following transactions are the only ones that occurred during the year:

February 15—Purchased $825 worth of supplies. On June 30, 20x5, there are $500 worth of supplies remaining. (Assume no beginning inventory was in existence.)

June 15—The Museum has received notification of the award of a $12,500 grant from the Smithzonen National Museum to be used for the preservation of ship relics. (The grant has not been received as of June 30.)

June 30—As of June 30, 20x5, salaries owed to employees are equal to $3,700.

FOR MORE INFORMATION

American Institute of Certified Public Accountants. *Audits of State and Local Governments.* New York: AICPA, 1996.

American Institute of Certified Public Accountants. *Not-for-Profit Organizations.* New York: AICPA, 1996.

American Institute of Certified Public Accountants. Statement of Position 78-10. *Accounting Principles and Reporting Practices for Certain Nonprofit Organizations.* New York: AICPA, 1979.

Financial Accounting Standards Board, Statement of Financial Accounting Concepts No. 4. *Objectives of Financial Reporting by Nonbusiness Organizations.* Stamford, Conn.: FASB, 1980.

NOTES

1. Under accrual accounting for NFOs defined as "nongovernmental," the Fund Balance is referred to as Net Assets. It still represents the residual between assets and liabilities.

2. General Accounting Standards Board, Statement No. 29, *The Use of Not-for-Profit Accounting and Financial Reporting Principles by Governmental Entities* (Norwalk, Conn.: GASB, 1995).

3. *Codification of Governmental Accounting and Financial Reporting Standards as of June 30, 1995* (Norwalk, Conn.: GASB, 1995). Section 1600.106-116.

4. Liabilities under the grant can usually be incurred prior to the receipt of grant monies.

5. GASB, op. cit., Section 1600.107.

6. Ibid., Section 1600.113. If a fine were clearly collectible from the sale of confiscated assets, it could be recognized as revenues before the fines are collected.

7. This is true with supply inventories which are accrual assets. *Codification of Governmental Accounting and Financial Reporting Standards* (GASB, June 30, 1995). Section 1600.122 dealing with long-term debt, and Section 1600.123, which states "Inventory items . . . may be considered expenditures either when purchased . . . or when used. . . , but significant amounts of inventory should be reported. . . ."

8. Under the accrual method, this debit entry could be made to Supplies Inventory as previously explained, but for consistency in comparing the two methods, a debit is made to Supplies Expense. Either approach is correct.

9. Entries made on June 30 are usually considered to be an adjusting entry. Adjusting entries are more fully explained later in the chapter. In governmental accounting, efforts are made to be certain that the last pay period for the year occurs on June 30. As a result there are no accrued payroll entries made at the end of the year.

10. This journal entry is also an adjusting entry.

11. The $75,000 represents payments for future performance, and it is restricted as to use, but it is regarded as a revenue, not a liability. This revenue is considered a "temporarily restricted net asset." FASB 116, *Accounting for Contributions Received and Contributions Made* (par. 14) and FASB 117, *Financial Statements of Not-for-Profit Organizations* (par. 21).

12. If it is obvious that no repayment would ever occur, it may be possible to recognize a revenue immediately upon receipt of the grant under MAM as is done under accrual.

13. The account debited under the cash method could have been "Lease Disbursements" instead of Lease Expenditures.

14. It is assumed that the monies for the award come from general funds and are not part of the funding in a special award fund.

15. The accrual entries for transaction 1 and 2 recorded a credit to a payable account as did transaction 7, and in these examples MAM followed accrual methods. In these two cases, supplies (transaction 1) and salaries (transaction 2), funding for the expenditures is almost always provided in the period when the entry is made, and MAM followed accrual accounting.

16. Under NFO accrual methods, the term Fund Balance is replaced by Net Assets. Net Assets still represent the residual between assets and liabilities.

17. Those special circumstances occur when there would be no significant differences between cash-based financial statements and the accepted accounting methods for the NFO. This could occur with very small NFOs.

18. In a cash system, there is no standardized system of reporting. As a result, some liabilities may be recognized. For example, notes payable could be a liability recognized in a cash system.

19. In a commercial business, this statement, prepared under different accounting guidelines, is called an income statement, and the phrase "bottom line" developed here.

20. The balance in Eclectic's Fund Balance prior to the $56,000 Excess transfer on June 30 was equal to $53,000, determined as follows: Balance after Excess Transfer ($109,000) − Excess ($56,000) = Balance before Excess Transfer ($53,000).

21. This system of accounting does not strongly support the fund concept whereby assets and related liabilities are grouped into self-balancing funds. This perspective of NFO accounting is to view the entity's assets as a whole using a "net assets view." Fund groups can be used, but they are not considered a necessary part of financial statement reporting.

22. Of course, the organization may maintain off-the-book records on assets, but this defeats the purpose of keeping a centralized set of accounting records.

23. When monies are made available by a board, the monies are referred to as an "appropriation."

24. It should be noted that new spending is made available from the board through budget appropriations, but old appropriations that have not been returned to the board, and thus remain part of the Fund Balance, may still be available for spending purposes in the new budget year. Of course, this depends on the legal status of the unspent appropriations.

25. There can be other reasons for an opinion being qualified (not satisfactory) besides not following GAAP.

26. American Institute of Certified Public Accountants, *Audits of State and Local Governmental Units* (New York: AICPA, 1996).

27. Although fixed assets are recorded as expenditures in one part of the accounting records, their cost also must be recorded separately elsewhere. This practice will be explained in more detail in later chapters.

4

Making Budget Dollars Make Sense

Budgetary accounts help NFO managers track monies that have been provided for the use of the NFO by the governing board. Tracking of these funds is very important as it may be a violation of law if more monies are spent than are provided at the beginning of the fiscal period. Therefore, correct use of budgetary accounts provides a vital service.

Four budgetary accounts (listed in figure 4-1) are used in most governmental fund accounting systems. The effects of debits and credits on these accounts are also shown in figure 4-1. These accounts are used to record the budget handed down by the board of an NFO. The accounts that have been discussed in earlier chapters relate to the measurement of the organization's financial operations, rather than its budgetary activities. Accounts concerned with financial operations are called "proprietary accounts." In governmental fund accounting, both budgetary and proprietary accounts appear on the financial statements.

Using budgetary accounts in conjunction with Expenditure accounting provides the answers to the following questions:

How much money do I have left for my department?

Can monies be transferred from supplies to book purchases?

Do we need additional funds to complete our operating year?

Will we have to curtail our program for disadvantaged readers at the end of the month?

FIGURE 4-1   Budgetary Accounts

Budgetary Accounts	Debit	Credit
Estimated Revenues	+*	−
Appropriations	−	+*
Encumbrances	+*	−
Reserve for Encumbrances	−	+*

* "Normal" balance

All these questions relate to the availability of monies, and the budgetary system provides the answers.

ESTIMATED REVENUES AND APPROPRIATIONS

The budget action of the governing board in approving monies for spending in an NFO is incorporated into the accounting system with a journal entry. This entry actually incorporates the approved budget into the formal accounting system. An entry of this type is shown in figure 4-2, along with its T account effects, as a debit to the Estimated Revenues account and a credit to the Appropriations account for the yearly budget appropriation of $425,000. The Appropriations account simply shows the amounts that have been approved by the board for spending. In this example, the estimated revenues to be collected, in the Estimated Revenues account, are equal to the amount approved for spending, that is, $425,000 in the Appropriations account. The purpose of this entry is to show how much funding is available. If the budget appropriation should be less than the approved spending level, this dollar equality does not occur, as will be explained shortly.

When the budget is approved or passed by the governing board, it means that the organization has been provided with spending authority for the year. This authority can be allocated to the organization as a whole, as shown in the entry in figure 4-2, or the spending authority can be allocated on a departmental level, as is usually the case. In both cases, the spending authority or the budget must be approved by the board. The illustration in figure 4-2 is a simplified example and, as such, does not divide the appropriation of $425,000 among other categories, such as supplies, departments, or programs. Further division of the budget is usually considered necessary for adequate financial control and planning.

In the entry in figure 4-2, the Estimated Revenue account is used as a debit. (This budgetary account is different from the Revenue account.) Estimated revenues are projected amounts that are expected to be received from

FIGURE 4-2   Initial Journal Entry to Record Budget Appropriation of $425,000 and Postings to General Ledger T Accounts

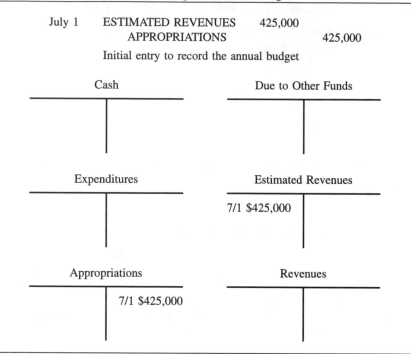

| July 1 | ESTIMATED REVENUES | 425,000 | |
| | APPROPRIATIONS | | 425,000 |

Initial entry to record the annual budget

various funding sources throughout the year, whereas revenues are recognized when the estimated revenues that were projected actually become available to the organization. Although some projections of estimated revenues are very accurate, such as amounts expected to be received from funding agencies, other projected amounts, such as investment income, are not likely to be as accurate. Regardless of accuracy, the total amount of predicted revenue is used as a base for incurring expenditures among the various activities of the organization during the budget year. Once the budget appropriations are approved, each program's spending level in the current year is set. Any difference between the amounts recorded as Estimated Revenue and the actual Revenue collected is recorded in the Fund Balance at the end of the fiscal year. In figure 4-2, for example, if the estimated revenues of $425,000 do not materialize, the difference between $425,000 and the amount collected decreases the balance in the Fund Balance. In such a situation, it would be possible for a debit balance to develop in the Fund Balance.

It may appear that providing a reserve in the Fund Balance account for any possible future decrease is good financial practice. By not appropriating all the estimated revenues projected, it is possible to provide for a reserve. Such a policy assures that some of the estimated revenues are "set aside" for emergencies. But the main objective of an NFO is to provide services to the public, and if the organization withholds services only to ensure that it maintains a credit balance in its Fund Balance or to return monies to its governing board, it is probably not meeting its service objectives. It is not considered acceptable practice to retain resources only for the purpose of maintaining or increasing the Fund Balance account. Accumulating increases in the Fund Balance or continual refunding of appropriations to a governing board by an NFO are justifiable only when the NFO has attempted to provide a full level of services to its public. Therefore, the recommended procedure is to attempt to predict estimated revenues as accurately as possible and to base appropriations for programs on a full-service concept.

After the journal entries to record the budget have been made, it is necessary to post them to the ledger accounts. The general ledger and the posting process were explained in chapter 2, but, as a reminder, the posting process transfers the amounts debited and credited in the journal to ledger accounts. The ledger summarizes all journal entries showing the current balance of that account. The account summarizes all the debits and credits chronologically recorded in the journal relative to that account, and the difference between the debits and credits in the account is called the balance. Figure 4-2 includes ledger accounts for Cash, Due to Other Funds, Appropriations, Revenues, Expenditures, and Estimated Revenues, as well as the initial budget entry. (This ledger is an example of a general ledger.) The journal entry in figure 4-2 has been posted to the proper accounts in the general ledger, and these are the two accounts with balances shown in them.

The transaction in figure 4-2 introduces the concept of appropriations and estimated revenues on a straightforward basis, because there are no additional divisions of appropriations and only one funding source is assumed. Normally, there is more than one funding source, and the appropriations are subdivided among many categories, such as supplies, maintenance, salaries, and employee benefits. When a budget appropriation is separated into detailed appropriation divisions, the accounting system is expanded to incorporate subsidiary ledgers, which are subdivisions of a specific general ledger account. The total of a specific account balance is maintained in the general ledger, but detailed information about the account is kept in the subsidiary ledger. When each subsidiary account is totaled, it should equal the debit or credit balance in the general ledger account to which it is related.

Assume that the authorized budget is journalized to specific appropriation accounts. Under this assumption, specific appropriations for items such as salaries and supplies are posted to the subsidiary-ledger accounts. At the same time, the total of the appropriations is posted to the Appropriations account in the general ledger. With dual posting, the total of the detailed appropriation accounts in the subsidiary ledger should equal the balance of the Appropriations account in the general ledger. The general ledger accounts serve as a check on the subsidiary accounts and, for this reason, they are known as "control accounts."

Without a control account and a subsidiary ledger, detailed information about appropriations would have to be recorded in the general ledger, which would be extremely tedious. Therefore, a subsidiary ledger is a consideration for any general ledger account where extensive detailed account information can be eliminated from the general ledger.

Figures 4-3 and 4-4 expand the initial recording of the budget entry to include the use of subsidiary accounts. The journal entry in figure 4-3 is the same as the one in figure 4-2 except for the listing of three debit subsidiary accounts under Estimated Revenues and nine credit subsidiary accounts under Appropriations. The procedure for entering subsidiary accounts in the journal entry is to place them, slightly indented, under the proper control account. The indentation indicates that they are subsidiary accounts. In figure 4-3, the $200,000 of estimated revenues projected to be received from the City of X is recorded as a debit, slightly indented under the control account Estimated Revenues. In a similar fashion, subsidiary accounts are recorded under the Appropriation control account. All the dollar amounts in these journal entries require posting to the general ledger or the subsidiary ledgers.

FIGURE 4-3   Initial Entry in the General Journal to Record Budget at Beginning of Fiscal Year

July 1 ESTIMATED REVENUES	425,000		
City of X		200,000	
County Commission		125,000	
State Grant		100,000	
APPROPRIATIONS			425,000
Personnel Salaries			250,000
Employee Benefits			39,000
Book Purchases			48,000
Standing Orders			7,950
Supplies			9,350
Maintenance			48,000
Publicity			6,000
Miscellaneous Utilities			10,000
Staff Development			6,700

The three debits to the subsidiary accounts under Estimated Revenues add up to the amount debited to the Estimated Revenues account ($425,000), and the credits to the nine subsidiary accounts are equal to the total credited to the Appropriations account ($425,000). The subsidiary accounts' balances will always sum to the balance in a control account in the General Ledger.

There can be several layers of subsidiary accounts below a designated control account. Subsidiary financial information can be maintained on a departmental level and further subdivided to specific expenditures within a department. As a new subsidiary level is added below the control account, an additional indentation serves to distinguish that subsidiary level in the journal entry. The indentation system in the subsidiary accounts works much like the indentation system in a formal outline. An outline starts with roman numerals representing the major headings or the control accounts in the General Ledger. Lesser topics or departmental financial information are indented below the roman numerals and represented by Arabic numbers. Still lesser topics or specific expenditures in a department are indented and represented by letters in the outline. The decision as to how many layers of subsidiary accounts to use should be based on the information needs of management. As more levels are added more detailed information is available, but if a manual accounting system is used, the addition of more than two levels below the General Ledger control accounts makes the system tedious to maintain. With a computerized system, it makes little difference. At any rate, each subsequent division of subsidiary accounts should total to the control account in the level above it. This upward balancing is apparent in all journal entries in this chapter. The upward control becomes more apparent in figure 4-5 when the department levels are used as a subsidiary level between the General Ledger control accounts and lower subsidiary accounts.

Figure 4-4 illustrates the result of posting the credit journal entry to the Appropriations account in the general ledger. Also, the subsidiary accounts—Personnel Salaries, Employee Benefits, Book Purchases, Standing Orders, Supplies, Maintenance, Publicity, Miscellaneous Utilities, and Staff Development—are posted to the subsidiary ledger. The amounts allocated to each of these subsidiary accounts indicate the manner in which total estimated revenues have been budgeted. It is important to record the approved budget in the books as a means to ensure that spending is limited by the appropriations that have been approved by the governing board. This initial recording of the budget provides control points for limitations on future spending. More information is provided later about these control features, but as an example, consider the $6,700 that has been authorized for the Staff Development account. This account provides monies for attending seminars and professional meetings. Recording this budget appropriation in the subsidiary accounts provides a spending limit for staff development.[1]

**FIGURE 4-4   The General Ledger and Subsidiary Ledgers after Postings
from the General Journal Entry in Figure 4-3**

General Ledger

ESTIMATED REVENUES		APPROPRIATIONS	
$425,000			$425,000

Subsidiary Ledgers

Revenue Ledger | *Appropriation-Expenditure Ledger*

City of X		Personnel Salaries		Maintenance	
$200,000			$250,000		$48,000

County Commission		Employee Benefits		Publicity	
$125,000			$39,000		$6,000

State Grant		Book Purchases		Misc. Utilities	
$100,000			$48,000		$10,000

Standing Order		Staff Development	
	$7,950		$6,700

Supplies	
	$9,350

> ***From the Library Desk:*** If the budget indicates that training funds are not available, and yet a staff member in the Cataloging Department needs training in order to catalog unusual material, I will disregard the accounting information and send that person for training.
>
> Anonymous survey respondent [Note: In some NFOs, it is acceptable to make changes among certain budget lines as long as the total appropriation is not exceeded.]

A subsidiary ledger that is used with an NFO's general ledger is the Appropriation-Expenditure Ledger, and it is illustrated in figure 4-4. One of its purposes is to record detailed information about the allocation of the $425,000 appropriation. The procedure for posting to this ledger is also illustrated in figure 4-4. The Appropriations account in the general ledger is a control account for the Appropriation-Expenditure Ledger. Once the postings have been made to the general ledger and the subsidiary, the balance in the Appropriations account and the total of all the subsidiary accounts are equal to $425,000. If postings to both ledgers are up-to-date, the balance in the control account should always equal the total of the balances in the subsidiary ledger. This relationship between a control account and its related subsidiary ledger allows for easier detection and isolation of mistakes in the account balances.

In addition to the introduction of subsidiary accounts under the Appropriations credit entry, the journal entry in figure 4-3 introduces subsidiary accounts for estimated revenues. The three subsidiary accounts are the City of X, the County Commission, and the State—the sources of funding for the NFO. All three funding sources are posted to a subsidiary ledger called the Revenue Ledger, which is illustrated in figure 4-4. The $425,000 debit entry in the journal for estimated revenues is posted to the Estimated Revenues account in the general ledger, and this account acts as the control account over the Revenue Ledger. The balances in the three subsidiary accounts in the Revenue Ledger are equal to the Estimated Revenue account's balance in the general ledger. Again, this illustrates the relationship between a control account and its subsidiary ledger.

The journal entry illustrated in Figure 4-3 is adequate for an NFO that does not require any departmental or program budget information or control. If an organization requires more detailed information about departments and programs, the entries require the introduction of another subsidiary account, based on a departmental or program classification. For example, an account such as Circulating Library is a program classification.

Before we proceed to the next entry, which incorporates additional accounting information about programs and departments, an assumption must be made about the relationship between a program and a department. When a program, such as an audiovisual program, is established, it is assigned, as nearly as possible, to one department. The reason for this one-on-one relationship is to ensure that control and responsibilities are clearly established for the program. When program activities are spread over a number of departments, the primary responsibility for the program becomes less clear. In addition, any allocation of central administration's salary costs to programs that are partially run by two or more departments can lead to difficulties. Finally, assignment of a program to a single department should result in less duplication of effort. Although this problem would not be expected in a small NFO, assignment of one program's activities to several departments tends to contribute to its development. Therefore, for our purposes, the assumption is made that programs are assigned within departments. For example, programs related to children are considered to be part of the Children's Library, a separate department in the main library.

In the next series of journal entries, illustrated in figure 4-5, departmental divisions have been introduced as new accounts in the subsidiary ledgers. The departments are listed as Audiovisual, Regional History, and Children's Library. The specific appropriations are separately entered in the journal under each departmental account. The detailed appropriation accounts under each departmental account are equal to the total departmental appropriation. For example, in the Audiovisual Department the total appropriation is $25,000, and this amount is equal to the total appropriations for personnel, books, and supplies. All these amounts are posted to the proper accounts in figure 4-6. The number of specific appropriations under each department has been limited for illustrative purposes.

The entries to the Estimated Revenue control account and its subsidiary accounts in figure 4-5 are the same as in figure 4-3, except the dollar amounts have changed. As there is no other difference, the posting process for the Estimated Revenue account and its subsidiary accounts is not illustrated in figure 4-6, where only the General Ledger and the Appropriation-Expenditure Ledger are presented.

The manner in which the subsidiary accounts are coded in the Appropriation-Expenditure Ledger should be noted. Each account is classified to a department by the first two digits in the account code, and the decimal digits indicate whether the credit is for supplies, books, or a personnel item. For example, account number 14.02 indicates the account is part of the Regional History Department (14), and the specific item is a book purchase (.02). With a computerized system, it would be common to have account numbers with nine or more digits. Each group of subsidiary accounts and fund types would be depicted within the account's numerical coding. Such systems allow data to be easily classified and analyzed across various groupings.

Figures 4-5 and 4-6 disclose budget information according to departments. As is apparent in the journal entry in figure 4-5, the departmental bud-

FIGURE 4-5 Initial Entry to Record Budget Includes Departmental Accounts

		Debits	Credits
July 1	ESTIMATED REVENUES	55,500	
	City of X	28,500	
	County Commission	15,000	
	State Grant	12,000	
	APPROPRIATIONS		55,500
	Audiovisual		25,000
	Personnel		12,000
	Books		10,500
	Supplies		2,500
	Regional History		12,500
	Personnel		6,700
	Books		4,800
	Supplies		1,000
	Children's Library		18,000
	Personnel		12,500
	Books		3,700
	Supplies		1,800

get information is subcategorized between the Appropriations credit entry and specific appropriation accounts, such as Supplies and Books. Supplies and books are called "object" classifications of appropriations or expenditures. The departmental account is maintained in the subsidiary ledger, along with the specific appropriation accounts for supplies, etc. The department accounts act as a control account over the expenditures of each department, and the total of all departments equals the total in the Appropriations account in the general ledger.

This method of categorizing departmental budget information utilizes another layer of accounts in the subsidiary ledger. These additional accounts are useful if this information is needed or frequently requested (on a total departmental basis) by the director or the board. If the information is needed only by the separate appropriations in each department, such as Supplies and Books, it is possible to eliminate the departmental accounts. Using these account classifications, a computerized accounting system will quickly report appropriations or expenditures for all supplies or personnel salaries. Of course, in a manually maintained set of books it is more important to be judicious in the number of accounts and layers of subsidiary ledgers that are maintained in order to reduce the work of maintaining the accounting records.

It is always possible to separate the specific appropriation accounts with the use of account numbers. For example, the Supplies account for Administration could be designated as account number 16.03, and the Supplies account

FIGURE 4-6   Postings to the Appropriation-Expenditure Ledger and General Ledger, with Departmental Accounts

General Ledger

ESTIMATED REVENUES	APPROPRIATIONS
$55,500	$55,500

Appropriation-Expenditure Ledger

Audiovisual 13.00	Regional History 14.00	Children's Library 15.00
$25,000	$12,500	$18,000

Personnel 13.01	Personnel 14.01	Personnel 15.01
$12,000	$6,700	$12,500

Books 13.02	Books 14.02	Books 15.02
$10,500	$4,800	$3,700

Supplies 13.03	Supplies 14.03	Supplies 15.03
$2,500	$1,000	$1,800

for the Regional History Collection as account number 14.03. It would be obvious to which department the supplies appropriation belongs without having a separate *departmental* control account. The major difference in an accounting system without departmental control accounts is that departmental information, in total, can be generated only by adding all the department's specific object appropriations. This information is already available in a system that uses departmental accounts.

EXERCISE 4-1 Journalizing Initial Budget Entry

1. In the current budget year the Montclair Heritage Art Center has received or will be receiving monies from the following sources: (1) investment income, $75,000, (2) federal awards for general operations, $25,000, and (3) anticipated collections in a fund-raising campaign, $10,000. In its June meeting, these monies received final approval for spending as follows:

Personnel	$75,000
Administrative Supplies	4,500
Craft Supplies	5,200
Utilities	10,100
Staff Development	1,100
Publicity	1,200
Repairs and Maintenance	4,000

   a. Journalize in general-journal form the entry necessary to record the budget, assuming departmental account classifications and subsidiary expenditure ledgers are not used.
   b. Journalize in general-journal form the entry necessary to record the budget, assuming departmental account classifications are not used but subsidiary revenue and expenditure ledgers are used.
   c. If the accounts are maintained without some sort of departmental information on expenditures, what type of problems can arise?
   d. Assume that the Art Center is reorganized into a Craft Education Department and an Exhibit Department and that all the expenditures are divided equally between them. How would this change the journal entry necessary to record the budget?

ESTIMATED REVENUES, REVENUES, AND THE REVENUE LEDGER

We have seen that estimated revenues are projections of funding that will become available to the organization. When these funds actually become available, they are recognized as revenues. The journal entry for recording estimated revenues has been illustrated; at some point after the estimated revenues are recorded in the accounts, the monies from various funding sources begin to be received. Prior to this time, a receivable is recognized in the accounts. When the funds are actually received, Cash is debited in the journal and the receivable is canceled. All revenues in this subsidiary ledger will sum to the balance in the Revenue control account in the general ledger.

In figure 4-7, a debit and credit entry is made to the account Due from the City of X and Revenues, respectively, to recognize an increase in revenues. This type of entry can be made for any of the funding sources. The journal entry for the City of X should be made shortly after the estimated revenues from the city have been recognized, on July 1, in figure 4-5. The receivable Due from the City of X will appear in that account in the general ledger. The credit entry will be posted to the Revenue account in the general ledger. Also recorded in the journal entry is a credit to the subsidiary account City of X. The amount credited to this account will be posted to the City of X in the Revenue Ledger.

FIGURE 4-7   Recognition of Revenues for Subsidiary Account, City of X

July 2	DUE FROM CITY OF X	28,500		
	REVENUES		28,500	
	City of X			28,500
July 5	CASH	7,125		
	DUE FROM CITY OF X		7,125	

Although this journal entry used the receivable account Due from City of X, a receivable is not always used in recording revenues. In many cases the funds are received in cash. If no previous receivable had been recognized in the accounts, a receipt of cash is recognized as a debit to Cash and a credit to Revenues and the City of X account.

In the July 5 journal entry in figure 4-7, the cash from the City of X is received in the form of a quarterly payment. The receipt of this payment increases the cash available and decreases the amount receivable from the City of X. Both of these accounts are posted to the general ledger, and no subsidiary ledger accounts are affected by this transaction.

In using a revenue ledger, as for example with the City of X, it is necessary to consider the actual format of the accounts incorporated in the ledger. Although T accounts can be used to illustrate the debit and credit process in any account, figure 4-8 illustrates a more useful format for the revenue account, City of X, in the revenue ledger. Figure 4-8 records the estimated revenues and revenues in the same account. The initial entry in this account is the estimated revenues projected for this funding source at the beginning of the fiscal year. For the City of X, this amount is $28,500. As the actual revenues are received in cash, or recognized as a receivable, they are recorded in the account and the balance in the account is reduced.

This is seen when the July 2 entry for $28,500 is posted into the revenue ledger, causing the balance in the Balance of Estimated Revenues column to decrease to zero.[2] At the end of each fiscal year, a schedule

FIGURE 4-8   Format and Entries in the Revenue Ledger Account, City of X

REVENUE LEDGER
Account No.: 27   Year: 20x3–20x4
Account Title: City of X

Date	Description	PR	Estimated Revenues	Actual Revenues	Balance of Estimated Revenues
7/1	Initial budget entry	GJ 1	$28,500.00		$28,500.00
7/2	Recognition of receivable	GJ 1		$28,500.00	0

should be prepared to show the differences between estimated revenues projected at the beginning of the year and the actual revenues received. The purpose of this comparison is to show the accuracy of the revenue projections and to indicate where adjustments may be necessary in subsequent year projections. An example of a comparison of estimated and actual revenues is shown in figure 4-9 for the library in the City of X. This report is prepared at the year-end, June 30, and as the organization increases in size, the number of revenue accounts would expand. In figure 4-9, a significant mistake was made in estimating Contribution Revenues. A mistake of this magnitude would likely result in a deficit in the fund balance assuming annual expenditure levels were based on budgetary estimates that did not materialize.

FIGURE 4-9   Comparison of Budget and Actual Revenues

CITY OF X LIBRARY
June 30, 20x4
Revenue Analysis—Budget and Actual

Revenue	Budget	Actual	Variance Favorable (Unfavorable)
Federal	$ 12,000	$ 12,000	$ 0
Local Government	120,000	120,000	0
Fines	5,700	5,500	(200)
Contributions	140,000	80,000	(60,000)
Other Revenues	25,000	26,500	1,500
Totals	$302,700	$244,000	$(58,700)

As the Revenue account and the Estimated Revenues account in the general ledger are temporary accounts, they must be "closed" at the end of the year. (The process used to close temporary accounts is described in chapter 5.) Basically, the process results in any temporary accounts with a debit or credit balance being reduced to a zero balance by transferring the current balance to the Fund Balance account. This procedure is said to "zero balance" an account.

Two closing procedures can be followed with the revenue ledger in figure 4-8. It, too, can be zero balanced at the end of the fiscal year, or it can simply be filed away and a new ledger opened for the current year. The method selected is a matter of choice. In either case, the revenue ledger is relatively easy to maintain.

ENCUMBRANCES, RESERVE FOR ENCUMBRANCES, AND EXPENDITURES

We will now examine the interrelationship of the three accounts, Encumbrances, Reserve for Encumbrances, and Expenditures. Only Encumbrances and Reserve for Encumbrances accounts are part of the budgetary system, but Expenditures accounts are also a necessary part of the budgetary procedures needed to determine the amount of uncommitted monies. Therefore, this type of account is included with the explanation of the two budgetary accounts.

In an NFO, the question continually arises as to the amount of monies still available for spending by the organization. The introduction of an encumbrance system into a fund accounting system allows this question to be answered readily. In some NFOs, expending more funds than have been appropriated can lead to possible legal action against the official responsible. Fortunately, overexpending appropriations is not likely to result when an encumbrance system is in use.

An "encumbrance" discloses a commitment of monies for an anticipated purchase at the time the purchase order is issued by the NFO. If a monetary commitment is made without using a purchase order, an encumbrance is still created (with certain specific exceptions noted later). A journal entry for an encumbrance is made prior to the time the ordered items have become a liability or have been paid. The ordered items create a liability only when the billing statement or invoice is received and accepted. However, an encumbrance entry shows the commitment of budgetary funding. At the time a purchase order is issued, an entry is made in the journal, debiting the Encumbrances account and crediting a Reserve for Encumbrances account. At this time, the funds have been "encumbered" by the debit to the Encumbrances account. The Encumbrances account in the general ledger acts as another control account over the appropriation-expenditure accounts in the subsidiary ledger. It should be noted that in addition to the Encumbrances account's acting as a control account over the Appropriation-Expenditure ledger, the Appropriations and Expenditure accounts in the general ledger are also control accounts over this subsidiary ledger.

At the time the Encumbrances account is debited, the effect is to reduce the amount that has been appropriated for a specific account. Assume that a purchase order is issued for supplies in the amount of $300 and recorded in the journal as a debit to Encumbrances and a credit to Reserve for Encumbrances. As soon as these journal entries are posted to the ledgers, they reduce the appropriation for supplies. This procedure provides accurate information to the department head as to the amount of monies available for future spending in this supplies account.

In the year-end Balance Sheet, the Reserve for Encumbrances account acts as a restriction on the Fund Balance, indicating that not all funds are available for use by the entity. The role of the Reserve for Encumbrances in the Fund Balance is the same as the other reserve accounts that show the limitations on the amount available for appropriation.

The typical journal entries that are used in an encumbrance system are illustrated in figure 4-10, where issuance of a purchase order on July 15 results in a journal entry debiting the Encumbrance account and the Audiovisual Supplies account (the latter being slightly indented to indicate it will be posted to a subsidiary ledger), as well as crediting the Reserve for Encumbrance account. The debit to Encumbrances and the credit to Reserve for Encumbrances will be posted to the general ledger. The appropriations for supplies in the Audiovisual Department has been reduced by $37. This change is apparent in the subsidiary ledger.

After the vendor receives the purchase order and accepts the order, the goods are shipped and a sales invoice (or billing statement) is sent to the purchasing organization. When the purchasing organization receives the sales invoice and the goods, it is necessary to approve the invoice and make payment on it. At the time of payment, two situations can develop. The amount of the invoice is assumed to be equal to the amount of monies which had previously been encumbered, in which case the original encumbrance entry is simply reversed and the invoice is paid. The journal entry to record the payment of the invoice is a debit to the Expenditure account and a credit to the Cash account. The second type of situation occurs when the invoice is not equal to the amount that had previously been encumbered. Under these conditions, the same accounts are debited and credited, but although the dollar amount for the reversal of the encumbrance is the same as the amount originally encumbered (see $37 entry on August 10), the amount on the invoice is different. This difference is reflected in figure 4-10 for the entry on August 10, where it can be

FIGURE 4-10   Typical Sequence of Entries for Encumbrance System

July 15	ENCUMBRANCES	37		
	Audiovisual Supplies		37	
	RESERVE FOR ENCUMBRANCES			37
	Recording initial obligation on appropriation for Purchase Order #11			
Aug. 10	RESERVE FOR ENCUMBRANCES		37	
	ENCUMBRANCES			37
	Audiovisual Supplies			37
	Recording reversal of encumbrances			
Aug. 10	EXPENDITURES	40		
	Audiovisual Supplies		40	
	CASH			40
	Recording payment of cash for supplies received			

seen how the $3 difference between the amount originally encumbered and the actual amount paid is handled in the journal entries. This is an increase in expenditures, and it will be reflected in the postings to the subsidiary ledger. There must be an adjustment for the difference to the subsidiary account balance in the Appropriation-Expenditure Ledger so that it will properly reflect that the amount available for future spending is further reduced by an additional $3.

Before these transactions are posted to the ledgers, a new format for the subsidiary accounts needs to be illustrated. This format is used to save recording time and effort. Encumbrances, expenditures, and appropriations are all recorded in the Appropriation-Expenditure Ledger.[3] If the standard form of account is used in the ledger, as represented by the T accounts in figures 4-4 and 4-6, the recording process is difficult because an account has to be established for the appropriations in (for example) supplies, another account for the expenditures in supplies, and a third account for the encumbrances in supplies. To determine the amount of funds available, all three accounts have to be consolidated and compared. To avoid this cumbersome process, encumbrances, appropriations, and expenditures are not separated into three different accounts; instead, they are combined into one account. The balance in that account is the amount of appropriated monies still available. In other words, the account balance provides the answer to the question, How much money do we have available to *spend?*

> **From the Author's Desk:**   The typical paper-based, in-triplicate purchase order and invoice forms that are mailed back and forth between seller to purchaser of goods are about to undergo significant changes in the new world of electronic commerce. The Internet is expected to become the medium for this change. The customer will make purchases directly from an electronic catalog. An immediate check of inventory is made to ensure the merchandise is available. The goods are shipped almost immediately from the warehouse. The merchant's accounting department bills the purchaser electronically, and money is sent directly to the merchant's bank. Electronic orders will eliminate the need for countless forms and the duplication of data entry into accounting systems with savings in the cost of system maintenance for both the seller and the buyer.

The type of format for this account is illustrated in figure 4-11, one of several formats that can be used to combine appropriations, expenditures, and encumbrances into one account. The first columns of the account contain information about the date, type of transaction, posting reference, and purchase-order number. The first column under Encumbrances, called "Issued," records the journal entry debiting the encumbrance, and the second column, "Liquidated," records the credit entry which reverses the initial encumbrance entry. The third column, "Outstanding Balance," maintains the total amount of the appropriation that is encumbered or committed. (Different headings may be used for these columns than the ones chosen here.)

Following the three encumbrance columns is a column that records the amount of the actual expenditures. The expenditure is recorded at the same time the encumbrance is reversed, which usually occurs when the invoice has been approved for payment. The last column in the account contains the information which answers the question of the department head or director: How much of the appropriation remains for future spending? The portion of the appropriation that has not been spent or obligated is called the *unencumbered balance.*

The first entry on July 1 in the account in figure 4-11 relates to the initial appropriation which was allocated for supplies in the Audiovisual Department by the governing board. The appropriated amount is equal to $2,500, and it is the same amount that was shown in the T account for Audiovisual Supplies in figure 4-6. The present figure illustrates the way the account would appear in an Appropriation-Expenditure Ledger. In the initial entry, the appropriation is equal to the unencumbered balance, but as encumbrances and expenditures are made, the appropriation is reduced.

FIGURE 4-11 Example of Account Format for an Appropriation-Expenditure Ledger Containing Information about Appropriations, Encumbrances, and Expenditures

APPROPRIATION-EXPENDITURE LEDGER
Account No.: 13.03
Account Title: Audiovisual Supplies
Appropriation: $2,500

Year: 20x3–20x4
Fund: General Fund

| Date | Description | PR | Purchase Order No. | Encumbrances | | | Expenditures | Unencumbered Balance |
				Issued	Liquidated	Outstanding Balance		
7/1	Appropriation							$2,500
7/5	Cleaning Supplies		7	$225		$225		$2,275
7/15	Catalog Cards		11	$ 37		$262		$2,238
7/25	Cleaning Supplies		7		$225	$ 37	$220	$2,243
8/10	Catalog Cards		11		$ 37	0	$ 40	$2,240

The July 5 entry in the account has been posted from a journal entry that is not shown, but the entry records Purchase Order 7, for cleaning supplies. It is recorded under the "Encumbrances–Issued" column, and it reduces the amount of unencumbered funds to $2,275. This indicates to anyone who uses the account that the appropriation has been reduced by the amount of the purchase order, and that the purchase order is considered a commitment of these funds. (It is not a liability.)

The July 15 entry in the account corresponds with the journal entry on July 15 in figure 4-10, in response to issuance of another purchase order, and it is recorded in the same manner as the previous entry. It, too, reduces the unencumbered balance, indicating a further commitment of funds.

On July 25, the invoice for the July 7 purchase of cleaning supplies is approved for payment and paid. This transaction (which has not been illustrated as a journal entry) liquidates the $225 outstanding encumbrance, and it is entered under the "Encumbrances–Liquidated" column. After this liquidation, a balance of $37 remains encumbered. At the same time that the $225 encumbrance is liquidated, the expenditure is recorded for the actual amount of the invoice.

The actual amount that was paid for the purchase was $220, rather than the $225 that was encumbered. It is not uncommon to find that the amount of the original encumbrance is different from the invoice that is forwarded by the vendor. These differences can arise from price changes. To ascertain that any differences between encumbered amounts and invoices are recognized, a comparison should always be made between the two dollar amounts. Any difference can be easily accounted for by subtracting or adding it to the unencumbered balance. In this case, the encumbrance was for more than the invoiced amount; therefore, $5 is added to the unencumbered balance. At this point, the amount of funds available for additional purchases of supplies is equal to $2,243.

On August 10 the invoice for the catalog cards ordered under Purchase Order 11 is approved for payment and paid. The journal entries for this transaction are recorded in figure 4-10, where it can be seen that the first entry on August 10 is a reversal of the entry on July 15. The reversal occurs because the invoice is being paid and the unencumbered funds are no longer obligated under an encumbrance; instead, these funds become an actual expenditure. In figure 4-10, under the control account, Encumbrances, the journal entry to the Audiovisual Supplies account is recorded. The $37 encumbrance reversal is entered in the subsidiary ledger account in figure 4-11 under the "Encumbrances–Liquidated" columns. The date, description, and purchase-order number are also entered under the proper columns. This entry in the "Liquidated" column of the Audiovisual Supplies account removes the remaining $37 encumbrance and results in a zero balance in the "Encumbrances–Outstanding Balance" column.

The journal entry to record the payment of the invoice is shown in figure 4-10. In that final journal entry, a debit is made to the control account, Expenditures, and a credit to Cash in the general ledger. Beneath the debit to the Expenditures account, another debit is made to the Audiovisual Supplies account. This entry is recorded in the Appropriation-Expenditure Ledger in figure 4-11, under the "Expenditure" column, as the $40 entry. It should be noted that the $3 difference between the amount that was encumbered and the actual expenditure is deducted from the unencumbered balance. When the expended amount is more than the encumbered amount, the difference must be deducted from the unencumbered balance; when the encumbrance is higher, the difference is added to the unencumbered balance.

Figure 4-11 illustrates detailed information for one account, Audiovisual Supplies. In many cases, budgetary reporting does not provide the detail shown in this account. Figure 4-12 is an example of a computer-generated report, with fewer details, provided for a department manager on departmental appropriations. This information does show, in the last columns, important information about the unencumbered balance on each appropriation in the department and the percentage of the appropriation currently remaining.[4] The report may also be arranged to present comparative information over a two-year period. The information reported in figure 4-12 comes from the detailed account information in figure 4-11, but detailed account information may not be important to the department manager except in special circumstances.

The introduction of the subsidiary ledger in this chapter changes the relationship between the accounts illustrated in chapter 2, where no subsidiary accounts were used and all expenditures were maintained in the general ledger. With introduction of the subsidiary ledger, specific expenditure account classifications are transferred to the subsidiary ledger accounts and a control summarization account for each subsidiary ledger is maintained in the general ledger. A budgetary system and subsidiary accounts are required parts of a fund accounting system if control is to be maintained over the spending of appropriations, to ensure that appropriations are not over expended.

From the Library Desk: Our library receives the following monthly accounting reports: Detail listing of Obligations vs. Budget with Percents; Trial Balance by Accounting Distribution. These reports tell me how much money we have encumbered, and all expenditures are listed. They also tell me how much is unobligated and the budgeted percent remaining.

Eva Poole, Denton Public Library, Denton, Texas

FIGURE 4-12 Example of a Year-to-Date Operating Report for City of X Library

City of X Library
Fund: 0100100
For Month Ending November 30

Year: 20x3

Description	Object Code	Month-to-Date Expenditures	Year-to-Date Expenditures	Year-to-Date Encumbrance	Unencumbered Balance	Percent Available
Personnel	0300	$12,500.00	$ 78,000.00	0	$95,000.00	54.9%
Equipment	0500	0	$225,000.00	$125,000.00	$17,500.00	4.8%
Contract Services	0700	$ 6,000.00	$ 30,000.00	0	$42,000.00	58.3%
Supplies	0800	$ 1,000.00	$ 15,700.00	$ 7,500.00	$ 8,000.00	25.6%

SUMMARY

This chapter has explained the function of budgetary accounting in a fund accounting system. A fund accounting system can be established without budgetary accounts, but budgetary accounts, used in conjunction with expenditures, allow for quick determination of the amount of monies left in each appropriation classification.[5] They allow the director and the head of a department to easily determine how much money is available for spending. This is particularly important at the end of the fiscal year, when overspending of the year's appropriation can have serious consequences.

As part of the budgetary accounts, the use of two subsidiary ledgers—the Revenue Ledger and the Appropriation-Expenditure Ledger—was explained. In addition, this chapter introduced a more extended type of account format to use with budgetary subsidiary ledgers. These techniques make it possible to determine the amount of monies still available without an extensive search through the records.

EXERCISE 4-2   Using the Appropriation-Expenditure Ledger

1. The Hennin County Library has recently introduced a budgetary system in its fund accounting system. The bookkeeper was not happy about the change and has resigned. However, the bookkeeper used the new account format for awhile, and the director is afraid mistakes were made in the accounts.

   You have been asked to review a typical account—Craft Supplies—to determine if the accounts were properly handled. Craft Supplies records expenditures for supplies that are used to decorate the library. The transactions in this account for the last several months are described below; the Craft Supplies account (#72-734) is also shown. As you review the transactions and the account, correct the bookkeeper's mistakes. Also, make a recommendation to the director as to whether you think there are other mistakes in the budgetary accounting system.

   July 1   Budget approved at $975 for Craft Supplies.
   July 15   Issued Purchase Order #15 for Craft Supplies for $185.
   July 25   Received and approved payment invoice on Purchase Order #15. Invoice was for $200.
   Aug. 1   It was discovered that some of the craft supplies received under Purchase Order #15 were damaged, and adjustment was requested (and granted) from vendor for $25.
   Aug. 15   Issued Purchase Order #18 for $240 for Office Supplies.
   Sept. 5   Money was transferred from Craft Supplies account to Regional History account. Amount was $300.
   Sept. 9   Issued Purchase Order #25 for $225 for purchase of craft supplies.

APPROPRIATION-EXPENDITURE LEDGER
Account No.: 72-734
Account Title: Craft Supplies
Appropriation: $975

Year: 20x2–20x3
Fund: General Fund

Date	Description	✓	Purchase Order No.	Encumbrances			Expenditures	Unencumbered Balance
				Issued	Liquidated	Outstanding Balance		
July 1	Appropriation							$975
July 15	Craft Supplies		15	$185		$185		$790
July 25	Invoice Received		15		$185	—		$790
Aug 1	Returned Damaged Goods/ Reduced Appropriation		15					$765
Aug 15	Supplies		18	$240		$240		$525
Sept 5	$300 Transferred to Regional History Fund		25				$(300)	$825
Sept 9	Supplies		25	$225				$600
Oct 3	Invoice Received		7			$225		$600

(Continued)

EXERCISE 4-2 **Using the Appropriation-Expenditure Ledger** *(Continued)*

Oct. 3   Received and approved for payment invoice on Purchase Order #25. Invoice was for $250.

2. The Muskegon Art Center is represented by the organization chart shown below; the dollar amounts appropriated by the board are shown under each organizational unit. The monies to operate the Art Center are received from one major source, investment income. In addition, earned monies are received from play ticket sales, craft education tuition, and receipts from trip ticket sales. These revenues amount to $25,000, $57,000, and $12,200, respectively.

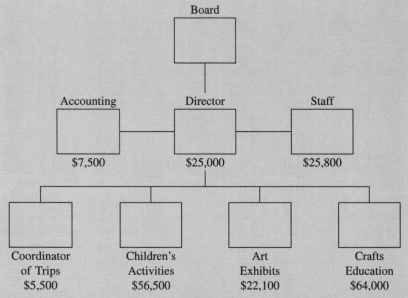

Board

Accounting	Director	Staff
$7,500	$25,000	$25,800

Coordinator of Trips $5,500	Children's Activities $56,500	Art Exhibits $22,100	Crafts Education $64,000

Journalize the initial budget entry, which should be divided down to a divisional level on the Art Center; that is, departmental accounts should be used in the entry. The following description of each organization unit provides an indication of the type of activities taking place in each department. Assume the initial budget entry contains a credit entry to the Fund Balance for $6,600. You will have to estimate the amount of other appropriations in each department (other than those for personnel salaries).

Accounting. This function is staffed by a part-time bookkeeper who maintains the ledgers and handles mailing of purchase orders, as well as receipt of invoices. He works with the auditor, who comes in once a year to audit the records. The bookkeeper's salary is $6,700, and the remainder of the budget is used for supplies.

Director and Staff. This position is held by an individual with an art center management background who makes $25,000 a year. She has a

staff of two secretaries; one is full time and the other is part time. Together, they earn a total of $16,000. The director and staff are responsible for publicity, telephone charges, the entire organization's training program, and the payment of professional fees to the auditor.
Coordinator of Trips. The Art Center sponsors bus trips to see major theatrical productions in New York City. This position is staffed by one part-time person who earns $4,000. This person also has responsibilities under the Crafts Education Department. The trip scheduling requires reservation deposits for bus transportation.
Children's Activities. This department is staffed by a full-time production director and an assistant. Their salaries are $17,800 and $14,700, respectively. Their activities involve the production of plays, including the construction of sets for plays.
Art Exhibits. This department opens selected art works to the public for viewing. It includes paintings and crafts of local artists as well as occasional traveling art exhibits. It is staffed by one full-time employee who earns $15,100 per year.
Crafts Education. A series of classes and workshops is continually conducted in the Art Center. These classes range from stained glass making to calligraphy. Local artists are hired as faculty for the classes and some supplies are provided by the Art Center. Eventually, each of these classes must be self-supporting through the tuition that is collected. The part-time coordinator of trips works half-time in scheduling classes for Crafts Education and earns $6,500.

NOTES

1. Some budget appropriations may allow for the switching of monies among budget lines. When this is possible, these budget lines are not considered to be true budgetary control points. When control points are established by the board, switching monies is not allowed.

2. Although this balance is reduced to zero, this reduction does not always immediately occur. In the case of some revenues (such as fines), it takes longer to collect the estimated revenues for the year as they are recognized only when the cash is received; that is, they are not recognized as a receivable.

3. This example provides a very detailed format. Various accounting software packages allow the amount of detail to be determined by those who use the reports.

4. The "percent remaining" is calculated by adding expenditures to date, encumbrances to date, and the unencumbered balance, then dividing this total into the unencumbered balance.

5. NFO accounting without separating the accounts for fund budgetary accounting is more accepted in NFOs that are classified as nongovernmental. See chapters 1 and 2.

5

End of a Year:
Closing Entries

ALL ACCOUNTING SYSTEMS DIVIDE the financial history of organizations into equal time periods such as quarters and annual periods. It is necessary to subdivide the life of an organization into equal time periods to measure its financial progress from one period to another and to evaluate organizational revenue and expenditure pattern between similar time periods.

Annual periods are either calendar years or fiscal years. The calendar period follows the January-December calendar year whereas the fiscal year is a twelve-month period that more closely corresponds with the activities of the organization. For example, in an agriculture-related business the most active period is during the summer months and the least active time is the winter. A fiscal year for this type of business might be the twelve months from the beginning of March to the end of the following February. A common business practice is to schedule the end of the financial year with the end of a business cycle, so that inventories are low and it will be easier to count the "ending" inventories.

In an NFO, the fiscal year usually begins July 1 and ends on the following June 30, because this period is likely to correspond with sessions of state legislatures and approval of the budget. Although a July-June fiscal year is common in NFOs, the example in the chapter adopts a January-December calendar year.

At the end of a fiscal or calendar year, certain accounting procedures occur. Usually this is the time when financial statements, as described in chapter 3, are prepared. The end of the year is also the time when "closing entries" are prepared, and this chapter explains the process of making those entries.

We have already seen that a number of accounts are considered temporary accounts; that is, they are closed at the end of the fiscal year. Temporary accounts are established only to reflect financial events during the current fiscal year; therefore, their balances should not be carried into the next year. For example, if a governing board approves the budget appropriations for the current fiscal year and they are recorded in the ledgers for the current year, there is no reason to continue to carry these balances or add to them in subsequent years. To eliminate these balances from the accounts, they are closed or "zero balanced" at the end of the year.

Expenditures and revenues accounts and budgetary accounts are considered temporary accounts, and all are closed at the end of the fiscal year. This closing process results in transfers to the Fund Balance. Any unexpended appropriations are added to the Fund Balance, and if there are any excess of expenditures over appropriations, they contribute to a deficit in the Fund Balance. A difference between estimated revenues and actual revenues also affects the Fund Balance account. The remaining portions of this chapter deal with the entries that must be made to close the temporary accounts.

CLOSING TEMPORARY ACCOUNTS

In a commercial enterprise, the closing process results in credits to all expense accounts and debits to the revenue accounts. Any difference between the debits and credits is transferred to the retained earnings section. In an NFO, the difference is also transferred, but in this case to the Fund Balance account. The determination and final handling of the difference are more complicated in an NFO than in a commercial enterprise because of the conditions under which initial budgetary appropriations are approved.

An appropriation is considered to be either a lapsing or nonlapsing appropriation. A lapsing appropriation is one that has not been encumbered by the NFO during the fiscal year and is therefore returnable to the granting agency that provided the original appropriation. With a *completely* nonlapsing appropriation, the NFO is allowed to keep whatever monies remain from the unexpended appropriation at the end of the fiscal year. Many motivational implications are associated with lapsing and nonlapsing appropriations, but only the difference in accounting for these appropriations is presented here.

In this chapter, it is assumed that with a lapsing appropriation any unexpended appropriations are returned even if they are encumbered. Although this is generally the case, there may be variations from this assumption in some NFOs. Under nonlapsing appropriation authority, it is assumed that any unencumbered monies are returned, but monies encumbered at the end of the fiscal year are not returned to the agency that granted the NFO its spending authority. The policy could be changed so that *no* monies are returned to the agency that granted the spending authority. If the monies do not have to be returned, they automatically create an increase in the Fund Balance in the year-end closing entries. Thus nonreturnable appropriations are the easiest to handle.

The closing entries for the two types of appropriations are illustrated in figures 5-1 and 5-3. In those examples, the entries are presented for the entire fiscal year in a consolidated form. The initial entry is recorded on January 1, 20x5, to record the budget. On November 30 the encumbrances are recorded for the entire year, and on December 15 all expenses are paid. The entire year's transactions are consolidated into these few entries to illustrate the closing process. The closing process is illustrated with the December 31 entries.

"Closing" an account refers to the process of putting a zero balance in the account and carrying the balance that was in the account to the Fund Balance. For example, the entry on January 1 put a $320,000 credit balance in the Appropriations account in the general ledger. At year-end, the Appropriations account is debited for $320,000, which eliminates any balance in this account (December 31 entry). In figures 5-2 and 5-4, the entries shown in figures 5-1 and 5-3 are posted to T accounts to illustrate more fully the closing process. Review of these accounts quickly reveals accounts that have zero balances—that is, those accounts that have been closed.

The closing entries, shown in figure 5-1, are for lapsing appropriations. Under the assumptions of the lapsing appropriation, all funds that are not expended must be returned to the agency that granted the spending authority. The granting agency can use the previous year's unexpended funds by reallocating them in the subsequent year in any manner.

In reviewing the entries in figure 5-1, it is apparent that $320,000 was appropriated under the current year's budget and the remaining estimated revenues of $5,000, anticipated to be collected during the year, were credited to the Fund Balance. On November 30, $320,000 was encumbered, but only $305,000 was paid on the invoices by December 15, as is apparent by the debit to the Expense account. On the same date, a reversal of the encumbrance occurs.

If we assume that no additional payments were made from December 15 to December 31, this leaves encumbered, but unexpended, funds equal to $15,000. The closing entries on December 31 indicate how this $15,000 is handled with a lapsing appropriation. It can be seen in the first entry on December 31 that the $15,000 is transferred into the Fund Balance, and the Encumbrances and Reserve for Encumbrances accounts, which had balances of $15,000, are closed.[1] This is also apparent in the T accounts in figure 5-2. At this point, the $15,000 can be returned to the granting agency. Return of the cash to the granting agency is shown as a journal entry by debiting the Fund Balance and crediting Cash for $15,000 on December 31. The granting agency would then determine where these monies are to be used in the subsequent year. If this last entry were not made, the balance in the Fund Balance would be $15,000 too high.[2]

The December 31 entries contain the closing entries for a lapsing appropriation. The first entry, on December 31, closes the Appropriations, Reserve

FIGURE 5-1   Sequence of Accounting Entries for Lapsing Appropriations

20x3			
Jan. 1	ESTIMATED REVENUES	325,000	
	APPROPRIATIONS		320,000
	FUND BALANCE		5,000
	Recording the budget		
Nov. 30	ENCUMBRANCES	320,000	
	RESERVE FOR ENCUMBRANCES		320,000
	Recording total encumbrances during the year in one entry		
Dec. 15	RESERVE FOR ENCUMBRANCES	305,000	
	ENCUMBRANCES		305,000
	Reversal of encumbrances at time invoice is approved and paid		
Dec. 15	EXPENSES	305,000	
	CASH		305,000
	Recording payment of invoices		
Dec. 20	CASH	331,000	
	REVENUES		331,000
	Recognition of receipt of estimated revenues previously projected		
Dec. 31	APPROPRIATIONS	320,000	
	RESERVE FOR ENCUMBRANCES	15,000	
	EXPENSES		305,000
	ENCUMBRANCES		15,000
	FUND BALANCE		15,000
	Closing entries		
Dec. 31	REVENUES	331,000	
	ESTIMATED REVENUES		325,000
	FUND BALANCE		6,000
	Closing entries		
Dec. 31	FUND BALANCE	15,000	
	CASH		15,000
	Return of the cash to granting agency		

for Encumbrances, Expenses, and Encumbrances accounts. The effect of all these closings is apparent in figure 5-2. It should be noted, as was illustrated by the fund accounting cycle, that closing entries are journalized after the financial statements are prepared. This is the necessary sequence of accounting events because it would be impossible to prepare a Statement of Revenues, Expenditures and Changes in Fund Balance after the closing entries had been jour-

FIGURE 5-2   Posting Closing Entries to the General Ledger Accounts

Estimated Revenues			Encumbrances		
1/1	$325,000	12/31 $325,000	11/30 $320,000	12/15 $305,000	
				12/31 15,000	
Bal.	$0			Bal. $0	

Appropriations			Reserve for Encumbrances		
12/31 $305,000		1/1 $320,000	12/15 $305,000	11/30 $320,000	
			12/31 15,000		
		Bal. $0		Bal. $0	

Expenditures			Revenues		
12/15 $305,000		12/31 $305,000	12/31 $331,000	12/20 $331,000	
Bal. $0			Bal. $0		

Cash			Fund Balance		
12/20 $331,000		12/15 $305,000	12/31 $15,000	1/1 $ 5,000	
		12/31 15,000		12/31 15,000	
				12/31 6,000	
Bal.	$ 11,000			Bal. $11,000	

nalized and posted to the ledger, as all the temporary accounts would have zero balances. Remember, Revenues and Expenditures are temporary accounts.

The second entry on December 31 relates to closing the Revenues and Estimated Revenue accounts, which are also temporary accounts. The Estimated Revenue account was debited on January 1 for the amount of revenues projected to be collected during the year, $325,000. During the year, $331,000 was collected in actual revenue. The entry recorded on December 20 is a cumulative entry of the entire year's revenue collections. As of December 31, these accounts need to be closed. The accounts are closed by "reversing out" the amounts previously placed in them. This is done on December 31 by debiting Revenues for $331,000 and crediting Estimated Revenues for $325,000. The difference, $6,000, which is the increase in actual revenues collected over those estimated, is entered as a credit to the Fund Balance account.

> **From the Library Desk:**   Some materials can be purchased at lower cost if paid for in advance (or for 2- or 3-year subscriptions). Yet restrictions on expenditures for only one fiscal year prohibit the library from taking advantage of such "deals." We can only spend *this* fiscal year's appropriation in the current fiscal year.
>
> Anonymous survey respondent's concern about lapsing appropriations

Up to now, these journal entries have described lapsing appropriations. The next example illustrates nonlapsing appropriations.

Figure 5-3 illustrates a situation slightly different from figure 5-1 because the assumption is made that if the funds are encumbered, they do not have to be returned to the agency that granted the spending authority. The entries and dollar amounts are the same in figures 5-3 and 5-1 until the first closing entry is made on December 31. In figure 5-3, the debit and credit entries in that closing entry are equal to the appropriations that have been expended. The amount of the expended appropriations is equal to the expenses, which total $305,000 for 20x3. The remainder of the appropriations are kept

FIGURE 5-3   Sequence of Accounting Entries for Nonlapsing Appropriations

20x3			
Jan. 1	ESTIMATED REVENUES	325,000	
	APPROPRIATIONS		320,000
	FUND BALANCE		5,000
Nov. 30	ENCUMBRANCES	320,000	
	RESERVE FOR ENCUMBRANCES		320,000
Dec. 15	RESERVE FOR ENCUMBRANCES	305,000	
	ENCUMBRANCES		305,000
Dec. 15	EXPENSES	305,000	
	CASH		305,000
Dec. 20	CASH	331,000	
	REVENUES		331,000
Dec. 31	APPROPRIATIONS	305,000	
	EXPENSES		305,000
	Closing those amounts that are encumbered or expended		
Dec. 31	REVENUES	331,000	
	ESTIMATED REVENUES		325,000
	FUND BALANCE		6,000
	Closing entries		

open in the Appropriations-Expense Ledger's subsidiary accounts and the Appropriations control account in the general ledger until the encumbered amounts are either paid or canceled.

These open accounts are apparent when the T accounts in figure 5-4, which represent the postings from the journal entries in figure 5-3, are reviewed. It can be seen that the Encumbrances, Reserve for Encumbrances, and Appropriations accounts all have $15,000 balances. These balances represent the amount of outstanding encumbrances at the end of the year. If the appropriation were a lapsing appropriation, all these accounts would have zero balances. This difference is clear when these accounts are compared with one another in figures 5-2 and 5-4.

The three temporary accounts with balances can be labeled with the year in which the encumbrance originated, or as "Prior Year" accounts. If this alternative is not satisfactory, the account can be closed—and reopened as a new account with a new name. There is room for choice in this matter; see the appendix to this chapter.

FIGURE 5-4   Posting Closing Entries to the General Ledger

Estimated Revenues

1/1	$325,000	12/31 $325,000
Bal.	$0	

Encumbrances

11/30	$320,000	12/15 $305,000
Bal.	$ 15,000	

Appropriations

12/31 $305,000	1/1	$320,000
	Bal.	$ 15,000

Reserve for Encumbrances

12/15 $305,000	11/30 $320,000
	Bal. $ 15,000

Expenses

12/15 $305,000	12/31 $305,000
Bal. $0	

Revenues

12/31 $331,000	12/20 $331,000
	Bal. $0

Cash

12/20 $331,000	12/15 $305,000
Bal. $ 26,000	

Fund Balance

	1/1	$ 5,000
	12/31	6,000
	Bal.	$11,000

Depending on the size of the accounting system, the closing procedures may transfer the outstanding balances into new accounts specifically established for these prior-year amounts. This change is made at the beginning of the new year. It is an easy process that involves closing out the balances in the accounts from the previous year and recording these same balances in new accounts, with such names as Appropriations–Prior Year, Encumbrances–Prior Year, and Reserve for Encumbrances–Prior Year. If this process seems unnecessary, it may be possible to keep the old accounts open and relabel them. If the accounting system is a large one, new accounts should be established, but in a small accounting system it can be a matter of choice.

EXERCISE 5-1 Lapsing and Nonlapsing Appropriations

1. The Herchal Public Library completed its fiscal year as of June 30, 20x3. Its accounts and the balances in those accounts as of June 30, 20x3, are listed below.

Debits		Credits	
Cash	$ 15,000	Accounts Payable	$ 25,700
Grants Receivable	18,000	Revenues	118,000
Inventory	2,200	Appropriations	120,000
Investments	125,000	Reserve for:	
Estimated Revenues	120,000	Encumbrances	5,000
Encumbrances	5,000	Inventory	2,200
Expenses	122,500	Fund Balance	136,800
	$407,700		$407,700

a. Journalize in general-journal form the closing entries, assuming a lapsing appropriation.

b. Journalize in general-journal form the closing entries, assuming a nonlapsing appropriation.

c. In the case of a nonlapsing appropriation, should accounts payable be equal to encumbrances?

d. Prepare a balance sheet for Herchal Public Library after the closing entries have been made under both a lapsing and nonlapsing appropriation assumption.

e. What are the differences and similarities between these two balance sheets?

f. How much is the difference between projected revenues at the beginning of the year and the actual revenues collected? If there is a difference, is it a serious difference?

OUTSTANDING ENCUMBRANCES IN SUBSEQUENT YEAR

With a nonlapsing appropriation, the 20x3 encumbered monies will be used to pay invoices received on outstanding encumbrances in the subsequent year,

20x4. This is not a concern with lapsing appropriations as all unexpended monies are returned. Figure 5-5 contains the 20x4 entries for the payment of invoices with the 20x3 encumbered funds from figure 5-3 ($15,000). When the payment is made from the previous year's encumbered amounts, three types of situation could develop between expenses and encumbrances. Although expenses could be exactly equal to encumbered monies, the journal entries illustrate those other two cases where the expenses are not equal to the amount encumbered.

In figure 5-5, case 1 represents expenses that are less than the amount encumbered, and case 2 represents expenses for more than the encumbered amounts. It is apparent that they are journalized in the year following the one in which they were encumbered. In 20x3, the Encumbrances and Reserve for Encumbrances accounts had been left open at the end of the year for the $15,000 that was encumbered. When these amounts are paid, in the early part of 20x4, the encumbrance entries are reversed (as always) and the expense is recorded. If the actual amount of the expense is not equal to the amount of the funds that were encumbered, the difference affects the Fund Balance. In case 1, the February 1 entry reverses the encumbrances and recognizes the expense. These expenses should be clearly separated from the 20x4 expenses by having the date, "20x3," appended to the account's name or noted in the account's numeral code.

The posting of the February 1 journal entry for Encumbrances and Reserve for Encumbrances is made in the previous year's general-ledger control accounts as the balances in these accounts are assumed to have remained open. (The chapter appendix illustrates a process for closing these accounts.) The new account, Expense, 20x3, is maintained in the current year's General Ledger. In all cases, where journal entries are made that relate to these previous-year transactions, the year should be appended to the account name so that these expenses are not confused with current-year expenses, making it appear that appropriations for the current year are being overexpended. Any 20x3 expenses should clearly be shown as expending the portion of that year's appropriations which remained open on the books at the end of the previous year. This separation should be reflected in the preparation of financial statements.

On December 31, 20x4, the closing entry is made. This entry closes the account Appropriations, 20x3, which was left open from the previous year; it also closes out the account Expenses, 20x3, which contains the expenses paid in 20x4 for 20x3 encumbrances. Any differences between the two accounts are transferred to the Fund Balance account.

In case 2, journal entries for the accounts are the same as case 1, except that the expense is for more than the amount encumbered in the previous year. The $2,000 increase is apparent in the entries for the February 1 journal entry. When the expense for the purchase is more than the encumbrance, payment of this additional amount may require approval from the governing board be-

FIGURE 5-5 Closing Entries for Nonlapsing Appropriations in Subsequent Year

Case 1

If expenses are less than encumbered amounts, the Fund Balance will increase.

20x4

Feb. 1	RESERVE FOR ENCUMBRANCES, 20x3	15,000	
	ENCUMBRANCES, 20x3		15,000

Reversal of encumbrances from previous year occurs when invoice is paid in 20x4

Feb. 1	EXPENSES, 20x3	12,000	
	CASH		12,000

Recording payment of invoice

Dec. 31	APPROPRIATIONS, 20x3	15,000	
	EXPENSES, 20x3		12,000
	FUND BALANCE		3,000

Closing entry for appropriations left open from previous year

Case 2

If expenses are more than encumbered amounts, the difference will contribute toward a deficit in Fund Balance.

20x4

Feb. 1	RESERVE FOR ENCUMBRANCES, 20x3	15,000	
	ENCUMBRANCES, 20x3		15,000

Feb. 1	EXPENSES, 20x3	17,000	
	CASH		17,000

Dec. 31	FUND BALANCE	2,000	
	APPROPRIATIONS, 20x3	15,000	
	EXPENSES, 20x3		17,000

cause there are insufficient prior-year appropriations available to pay for the more costly purchase.

In case 2, the remaining 20x3 appropriations were $15,000, but the invoice was for $17,000. The $2,000 increase in purchase cost has an effect on the Fund Balance, as can be observed in the December 31 entry. In this entry, the Fund Balance is decreased with a $2,000 debit entry when the Expenses, 20x3, and Appropriations, 20x3, accounts are closed. Again from the governing board approval may be necessary. (This requirement for board action varies among organizations.)

When outstanding encumbrances from the previous year are considered, the interests of the organization are best served if a policy (with guidelines) is instituted as to when all prior-year purchase orders, those issued in 20x3, are to be canceled if the orders have not been received. Without such a policy, monies that can be used elsewhere are committed to encumbrances and appropriations. A policy might require that all purchase orders from the previous year be canceled after a two-month period if the materials have not been received. When a purchase order is canceled, the encumbrance is reversed and the remaining appropriations that applied to the canceled orders are closed with a debit entry to Appropriations. The corresponding credit entry is made to the Fund Balance.[3]

The closing entries for an NFO have been illustrated in this chapter, and these entries will be used again in chapters 6 through 10. Before we begin chapter 6, a brief review of the procedures introduced in the first five chapters is in order.

REVIEW OF THE FUND ACCOUNTING CYCLE

The fund accounting cycle, described in chapter 2, outlines the steps that are followed and the order in which they are followed in a typical accounting system. Step 1, analysis of transactions, was explained in chapter 2. Step 2, the journalizing of transactions, was covered in chapters 2 through 5. The posting process, step 3, was explained in chapter 2. The adjusting entries, described in step 4, were covered in chapter 3. Financial statements were described in chapter 3, and chapter 5 illustrated the closing entries for an NFO.

The only part of the fund accounting cycle that has not yet been illustrated is preparation of a trial balance, which is simply a totaling of the debit and credit balances in the accounts in the general ledger to ensure that they are equal. As noted in the fund accounting cycle, trial balances are prepared after the adjusting entries have been posted to the accounts and again later, after the closing entries have been posted. Preparing a trial balance after the adjusting entries are posted ensures that the accounts are in balance prior to preparing the financial statements. If all the debits and credits in the general ledger are not equal, there is probably an error in the accounts, and if it is not corrected, it will be carried into the financial statements.

A trial balance is also prepared after the closing entries have been posted. This ensures that all the debits and credits are equal prior to beginning the journalizing process in the new fiscal year. If an error is carried forward into the new year, it is very difficult to find it without reopening the prior year's records.

A trial balance should also be prepared at the end of each month during the fiscal year to ensure that debit and credit errors are caught as early as possible. Preparing a trial balance at the end of each month is a good procedure

FIGURE 5-6   Trial Balance for Ronald Library on June 30, 20x2

RONALD LIBRARY
Trial Balance
June 30, 20x2

Cash	$ 25,000	
Marketable Securities	20,000	
Due from Other Governments	35,000	
Inventory	12,000	
Prepaid Items	18,000	
Encumbrances, 20x2	17,000	
Appropriations, 20x2		$ 17,000
Reserve for Encumbrances, 20x2		17,000
Reserve for Inventory		12,000
Fund Balance		81,000
	$127,000	$127,000

to follow to detect debit and credit errors at reasonable intervals during the fiscal year. A computerized accounting system allows for the preparation of a trial balance at any point in time. In fact, it is so easily done that one could be prepared after each debit and credit transaction.

The trial balance can be a formal statement, with all accounts and their balances listed and totaled (as in figure 5-6), or it can be an informal document. With a manual accounting system, if a formal document is not considered necessary it is possible to use an adding-machine tape to provide a simple running total of debit and credit balances in the general ledger accounts. The tape should be dated, initialed by the preparer, and kept in the records for future reference. In any case, it is not always necessary to prepare a formal statement.

Figure 5-6 represents the trial balance for Ronald Library on June 30, 20x2, after the closing entries have been posted. The library receives a nonlapsing appropriation each year, and the trial balance shows the balances in the budgetary accounts that have not been closed at the end of the fiscal year because of outstanding encumbrances. The debit and credit balances in the accounts are equal to a total of $127,000, and this equality indicates that the journalizing process can begin in the new year with the accounts in balance.

SUMMARY

This chapter explains the concept of closing temporary accounts. It is necessary to close accounts that are used only to reflect the current year's financial activities. The budgetary accounts are related to the current year's budget;

therefore, these accounts are considered temporary. The revenue and expenditure accounts are related to the current year's financial activities in the sense that the balances in these accounts do not accumulate from year to year. Therefore, they are temporary accounts too.

The accounting procedure for closing these accounts was presented and adapted to situations in which the appropriations are either lapsing or nonlapsing. The procedures outlined in this chapter assist in allocating funding sources to the correct fiscal year. The closing entries are not really the end of anything, as the accounting cycle immediately begins again, once the closing entries have been posted and a trial balance has been prepared.

EXERCISE 5-2   Nonlapsing Appropriations in a Subsequent Year

1. The Andes Public Library has a nonlapsing appropriation. Its balance sheet for the fiscal year ending June 30, 20x1, is reproduced below.

ANDES PUBLIC LIBRARY
Balance Sheet
June 30, 20x1

Assets

Cash		$ 7,500
Prepaid Assets		8,000
Inventory		6,700
Investments		69,700
Total Assets		$91,900

Liabilities, Appropriations, and Fund Balance

Liabilities		
Accounts Payable		$15,000
Appropriations	$12,700	
Less: Encumbrances	12,700	
Fund Balance		—
Unreserved		49,500
Reserved for:		
Encumbrances		12,700
Inventory of Supplies		6,700
Prepaid Assets		8,000
Total Liabilities, Appropriations,		
and Fund Balance		$91,900

a. On July 1, 20x1, open new accounts for outstanding encumbrances as of June 30, 20x1.

b. An invoice for $13,200 is received and paid on July 15 for outstanding encumbrances on June 30, 20x1. Journalize the proper general-journal entry on July 15.

c. Journalize the closing entries on June 30, 20x2.

2. The John Able Free Library has a nonlapsing appropriation. The balance sheet for the June 30, 20x1, fiscal year is reproduced below. The library has a policy of canceling all outstanding encumbrances from the previous year on August 31 of the current year.

JOHN ABLE FREE LIBRARY
Balance Sheet
June 30, 20x1

Assets

Cash		$ 9,300
Prepaid Assets		4,100
Inventory		5,500
Investments		23,100
Total Assets		$42,000

Liabilities, Appropriations, and Fund Balance

Liabilities		
Accounts Payable		$ 4,000
Appropriations	$7,500	
Less: Encumbrances	7,500	—
Fund Balance		
Unreserved		$20,900
Reserved for:		
Encumbrances		7,500
Inventory of Supplies		5,500
Prepaid Assets		4,100
Total Liabilities, Appropriations,		
and Fund Balance		$42,000

a. On July 21, 20x1, an invoice for $7,100 is received and paid for $7,100 of encumbrances outstanding as of June 30, 20x1. This is for the actual amount that was encumbered under the purchase order. Journalize the proper general-journal entry for July 21.

b. Journalize the proper general-journal entry on August 31, the cutoff date (assuming no additional invoices were received since July 21).

c. Journalize any necessary closing entries on June 30, 20x2.

3. The Burgburg City Library has outstanding encumbrances at the end of the June 30, 20x2, fiscal year as follows:

Encumbrances	$7,300
Reserve for Encumbrances	7,300

An amount equal to $7,300 has been left in the Appropriations account. The library has a policy of canceling all outstanding encumbrances from the previous year on August 31 of the current year.

(Continued)

EXERCISE 5-2 Nonlapsing Appropriations in a Subsequent Year *(Continued)*

During the first two months of the new year, the following transactions affecting encumbrances occurred:

July 16   A $1,200 invoice is received and paid on a purchase order encumbered for $1,250.

July 31   A purchase order for $525 is canceled.

Aug. 10   A $5,500 invoice is received and paid on a purchase order encumbered for $5,175.

Aug. 31   The remainder of purchase orders encumbered and unfilled from the June 30, 20x2, fiscal year are canceled.

a. Open new accounts for the old encumbrances and appropriations on July 1, 20x2.

b. Journalize the transactions for July and August in general journal form.

c. Make any necessary closing entries on June 30, 20x3.

APPENDIX: CLOSING ACCOUNTS WITH OUTSTANDING ENCUMBRANCES

If the Appropriations and Encumbrances accounts in the current year are to be closed when there are outstanding encumbrances, the following entries are made on December 31, 20x3. These entries are for a nonlapsing appropriation.

APPROPRIATIONS	320,000	
EXPENSES		305,000
FUND BALANCE		15,000

Closing the Appropriations account to zero balance

FUND BALANCE	15,000	
ENCUMBRANCES		15,000

Closing Encumbrance out to Fund Balance

The only account that contains outstanding encumbrances at the end of 20x3 is the Reserve for Encumbrances account. This account is closed to a new account, which indicates that these encumbrances are from the previous year. This entry is also made on December 31, 20x3.

RESERVE FOR ENCUMBRANCES	15,000	
RESERVE FOR ENCUMBRANCES, 20x3		15,000

Opening new, dated Reserve for Encumbrances account

When the invoice is received in the following year, assume it is for $15,000, and the expense is recognized as a 20x3 expense. At the end of the fiscal year the Expense, 20x3 account is closed to the Reserve account.

EXPENSE, 20x3	15,000	
CASH		15,000

Recognizing Expense for prior-year encumbrances

RESERVE FOR ENCUMBRANCES, 20x3	15,000	
EXPENSE, 20x3		15,000

The closing entry

NOTES

1. An NFO with lapsing appropriations does not cancel all its outstanding purchase orders as it canceled its outstanding encumbrances at year-end. Outstanding purchase orders are honored in the following year even though the corresponding encumbrances are canceled.

2. It is assumed that the $11,000 remaining in the general ledger accounts (Cash and Fund Balance) is not part of the appropriation from the granting agency.

3. We will see in a later chapter that for purchases that require a long construction or installation period, a special fund is used. Those purchase orders are not canceled at the end of fiscal periods.

PART 2

Accounting for the Major Fund Groups

The five chapters in part 2 go beyond the foundation concepts explained in part 1. Part 2 introduces the General, Special Revenue, Capital Projects, Endowment, Agency Funds, and the General Fixed Asset Account Group. In addition, this section provides an example of individual fund statements and the combined financial statements used by NFOs. Each dated transaction in the next five chapters will be used in the formulation of the combined financial statements for the H. K. Fines Library in chapter 10.

At this point, it is interesting to note the responses of a random sample of librarians who were asked about the usefulness of financial information in their decision making. Survey data from a sample of 150 library directors and other librarians were collected during the writing of this book. The random sample was based on the names listed in the *American Library Directory.* The response rate was 26 percent with only one mailing. Some of this group's open-ended comments are included in the book as part of "From the Library Desk."

In another part of the questionnaire, the respondents were asked to rate a list of financial terms and reports as to their usefulness for managerial decision-making purposes. The choices were "very important," "not very important," and "not used." The percentage of respondents describing each item as "very important" to managerial decision making is shown below.

- Annual budget allocation   97%
- Revenues   71%
- Expenses/Expenditures   100%
- Year-end budget account balances   89%
- Encumbrances   47%
- Balance sheet   63%
- Income/Revenue statement   51%

The annual budget allocation is considered very important by most of the respondents, but encumbrances that are used to control the budget allocation/appropriations were not rated as being "very important" by about half the respondents. A similar split in responses occurred between expenses/expenditures and the income statement. The latter report is used to report expenses and expenditures. These differences may occur because expenses and expenditures are reported on some other document than the income statement for these librarians. Also, the income statement may only be prepared once a year.

The balance sheet also received a low score, but without using balance sheet information, there is little control over the NFO's assets. Some of these responses may arise from the different understandings attached to these terms.

In part 2, the accounting definition and recommended terminology is explained. In chapters 6 through 10, numerous examples show why an understanding of all these accounting terms can provide a decision-making advantage to library and other not-for-profit managers.

6

Introduction to the Twin Funds: The General and Special Revenue Funds

An NFO's FUND ACCOUNTING system is composed of a set of self-balancing accounts called *funds*. These self-balancing accounts are composed of assets, liabilities, the Fund Balance, expenses, and revenues. As a result, each fund in the fund accounting system has its own set of financial statements or reports. The two funds introduced in this chapter are the General Fund and Special Revenue Fund.

The previous five chapters, concerned with the basics of fund accounting, explained the account types: assets, liabilities, etc., as well as debits and credits, the different foundations upon which an accounting system can be established, budgetary accounts, and how to make closing entries. These are preliminary topics of fund accounting. This chapter introduces the General Fund and the Special Revenue Fund.[1] These are two of the "governmental" funds used in governmental NFOs.

The General Fund and Special Revenue Fund can be thought of as twin funds because the entries for both are recorded in essentially the same manner. For that reason, only the General Fund will be explained in detail in this chapter. The General Fund is the most widely used fund and the transactions recorded in it are the daily, routine activities of the NFO. The funding available in the General Fund can be used to support the general operations of the entity, and the NFO uses only one General Fund. On the other hand, several special revenue funds can be used within the same NFO. A Special Revenue

Fund is used when designated revenues are to be used only to finance a specific operation within the NFO. These continuing revenues, such as a special tax, can be expended only on the specific activities being accounted for in the Special Revenue Fund.

The financial statements prepared for these funds are the Balance Sheet (Statement of Financial Position), Statement of Revenues, Expenditures, and Changes in Fund Balance, and usually, Statement of Revenues, Expenditures, and Changes in Fund Balance—Budget and Actual. A set of notes accompanies these financial statements to explain in detail many of the accounting positions taken in the financial statements. It should be noted that these financial statements can be prepared for each separate special revenue fund and later combined into one financial statement. For example, all separate special revenue funds in an NFO would eventually appear on one Special Revenue Balance Sheet. This report is known as a "combining" balance sheet. Once all similar funds have been aggregated, they can be combined into a financial statement that contains only one column for each type of fund (one aggregate Special Revenue Fund). Such a statement is called a "combined" financial statement, and it is the most aggregated NFO financial statement. In the following chapters, it will be assumed that there is only one fund of a specific type, such as one special revenue fund, and combining financial statements of similar funds will not be shown.

Some of the transactions that would appear in the General and Special Revenue Funds, as well as the periodical accounting procedures, were introduced in part 1. Even so, there are unique aspects to these funds. Therefore, chapters 6 and 7 explain the functioning of these funds in more detail. Chapter 6 illustrates and discusses the financial statements used by the General and Special Revenue Funds, and chapter 7 uses a series of transactions to illustrate the workings of the two funds. Throughout the two chapters major emphasis is placed on the General Fund.

THE FINANCIAL STATEMENTS

Three financial statements are used in the General Fund. Two of these statements, the Balance Sheet and the Statement of Revenues, Expenditures, and Changes in Fund Balance (SREF), were introduced in an earlier chapter. The third, the Statement of Revenues, Expenditures, and Changes in Fund Balance—Budget and Actual (SREF2), has not yet been explained. It provides a comparison between actual and budgeted revenues and expenditures. This comparison is important in determining the accuracy of annual forecasts and discovering if spending levels were exceeded. Each of these statements will be reviewed in this chapter.

It should be noted that these financial statements are not usually prepared as comparative statements. Although the SREF2 does compare budget and actual dollars in the current year, this is still not considered a comparative financial statement. Comparative financial statements show the reader current year and previous year data on the same financial statement. Corporate financial statements are usually prepared in this manner. Therefore, governmental financial statements do not allow for the financial comparisons to be easily made between years. As a result, it is difficult to determine whether support or expenditures in various classifications have increased or decreased from last year, and in order to make such a comparison, additional reports need to be prepared.

Another characteristic of these financial statements should be noted. NFO reporting emphasizes combined statements over consolidated statements. Consolidated statements require that reciprocal accounts between various parts of an entity (accounts payable and receivable between two subparts of the same organization) be eliminated when financial statements for the whole entity are prepared. In corporate financial statements, this procedure is used to avoid double counting. Consolidated statements are not used in NFOs. Instead NFO accounts are combined or added across.[2] For this reason, the total columns on the financial statements shown in chapter 6 are labeled "memorandum only." This notation emphasizes the concept of cross-added totals.

The financial statements in figures 6-1, 6-2, 6-3, and 6-4 have been prepared for a hypothetical library, called the "Harold Know Fines Library." The SREF is illustrated in figures 6-1 and 6-2, the Balance Sheet in figure 6-3, and the SREF2 in figure 6-4. All statements are typical of an actual library's financial reports prepared under GAAP.

COMBINED STATEMENT OF REVENUES, EXPENDITURES, AND CHANGES IN FUND BALANCES

In figure 6-1, revenues and expenditures are separated from each other on the SREF. Often, nonoperating revenues from government grants, intergovernmental revenues are reported separately from operating revenues such as charges for services, fines, and miscellaneous revenues. Here only one classification is used for revenues. The H. K. Fines Library earned revenues from book sales, charges for photocopying, and user's card fees as well as from various grants and contributions.

In figure 6-1, the term "expenditures" includes all expenses, as previously defined, and capital outlays. The expenditures in the SREF are reported on a program basis with programs defined along a departmental basis. As we saw in chapter 2, this is sometimes called a functional classification. Care needs to be taken when program expenditures overlap more than one department. If program expenditures do not follow departmental lines, it may be difficult to clearly assign responsibility for making expenditures to one individual.

FIGURE 6-1   Statement of Revenues, Expenditures, and Changes in Fund Balance for the General Fund at the H. K. Fines Library

H. K. FINES LIBRARY
General Fund
Statement of Revenues, Expenditures, and Changes in Fund Balance
For the Year Ended June 30, 20x0

Revenues:		
Government grants	$90,000	
Other grants	3,500	
Contributions and bequests	24,000	
Book fines and sales	2,100	
Photocopying	3,785	
Library ID charges	3,000	
Total Revenues		$126,385
Expenditures:		
Program Services:		
Reference	$33,000	
Children's Library	17,300	
Circulation	32,000	
Regional Library	13,700	
Administration	24,000	
Total Expenditures		120,000
Excess of Revenues over (under) Expenditures		$ 6,385
Fund Equity, July 1		45,190
Residual Equity Transfer		0
Fund Equity, June 30		$ 51,575

For decision-making purposes, it is also advantageous to provide expenditure reports using an "object" basis. (Object expenditures are classified according to such uses as maintenance, supplies, or personnel services.) Object, department, or program reporting are all necessary to maintain control over an NFO's costs and detect cost increases. For financial reporting purposes, it is more common to find expenditures reported on a departmental basis. Therefore, it may be necessary for the library director to request that additional expenditure reports be prepared using an object or program classification. In any case, good review procedures require that expenditures be analyzed using more than one of these classification methods.

In figure 6-1, there is no reporting of comparative financial information for the previous fiscal period. As a result, the financial report provides no means to analyze this year's spending levels with those of the previous year or earlier. This short-term perspective is a characteristic of governmental financial reporting. Financial activities tend to focus on the current period and the annual budget. This one-year financial focus leads to managerial decisions being made with a short-term view even though the best decisions would be based on long-term objectives.

The final balance in figure 6-1, $51,575, also appears as the June 30 total of the Fund Balance on the Balance Sheet in figure 6-3. The subdivisions of the Fund Balance shown on the Balance Sheet will be discussed shortly. In these examples, a residual equity transfer account is shown for illustrative purposes in the Fund Balance. There are two types of interfund transfers that can occur in NFOs. One is the residual equity transfer and the other is an operating transfer. A residual equity transfer occurs if there is a nonrecurring and nonroutine transfer made between funds. A transfer that is considered routine, and usually made on a periodic basis, is called an operating transfer.[3] Operating transfers, either in or out, are reported under a section of the SREF called Other Financing Sources that often appears after the Excess but before the Fund Balance on the SREF.

The SREF is considered a "combined" statement when at least two different funds are shown on it. Figure 6-2 illustrates such a statement for the Fines Library. In this statement, the General Revenue and Special Revenue Funds are shown together. The Special Revenue Fund accounts for those monies that are to be used for a specific activity or purpose. The combined totals for the two funds are shown as memorandum totals in the column on the right.[4] This column is identified as a "memorandum only" to highlight the fact that these totals are not consolidated. As we work with *combined* statements through the remaining chapters additional funds such as the capital projects fund will be added to this report. In figure 6-2, the Special Revenue Fund has no Fund Balance at the beginning or end of the year because all revenues were expended. Usually, this fund will have a year-end balance in its Fund Balance, but it is not shown in this introductory statement.

THE BALANCE SHEET

The Balance Sheet records balances in the NFO's assets, liabilities, and the Fund Balance accounts. Although the Balance Sheet in figure 6-3 for the Fines Library is similar to those prepared earlier under MAM, there are several differences here that need to be considered.

First, the divisions in the Fund Balance section of the Balance Sheet provide information for the Board regarding the money that is available for use (i.e., the amount that can be appropriated) in the subsequent year, or, if the budget has to be revised in the current year, the current amount available for reallocation. In figure 6-3, it can be seen that only $11,180 of the Fund Balance is classified as "Undesignated" and therefore available for appropriation.

FIGURE 6-2   **Combined Statement of Revenues, Expenditures, and Changes in Fund Balance for the General Revenue and Special Revenue Funds at the H. K. Fines Library**

H. K. FINES LIBRARY
Combined Statement of Revenues, Expenditures, and Changes in Fund Balance
For the Year Ended June 30, 20x0

	General Fund	Special Revenue	Memo Totals
Revenues:			
Government grants	$ 90,000	—	$ 90,000
Other grants	3,500	—	3,500
Contributions and bequests	9,000	$15,000	24,000
Book fines and sales	2,100	—	2,100
Photocopying	3,785	—	3,785
Library ID charges	3,000	—	3,000
Total Revenues	$111,385	$15,000	$126,385
Expenditures:			
Program Services:			
Reference	$ 25,000	$ 8,000	$ 33,000
Children's Library	13,000	4,300	17,300
Circulation	32,000	—	32,000
Regional Library	11,000	2,700	13,700
Administration	24,000	—	24,000
Total Expenditures	$105,000	$15,000	$120,000
Excess of Revenues over (under) Expenditures	$ 6,385	—	$ 6,385
Fund Equity, July 1	45,190	—	45,190
Residual Equity Transfer	0	—	0
Fund Equity, June 30	$ 51,575	—	$ 51,575

The undesignated fund balance represents one section of the *"Unreserved Fund Balance."* The other section, $17,000, is classified as "Designated for subsequent year expenditures." The board has put a hold on this portion of the Fund Balance for use in a subsequent year. It may be a commitment that has been approved for future spending. Its use could be designated for specific asset purchases, for example, and the board has the discretionary authority to decrease or increase this amount. For that reason, both board-designated and undesignated amounts are considered to be "unreserved" and not reserves of the Fund Balance. Thus, the amount available for appropriations is $28,180.

The reserved portion of the Fund Balance is completely unavailable to the Board. The reserves are for outstanding encumbrances, inventories, and re-

FIGURE 6-3   Combined Balance Sheet for the General and Special Revenue Funds at the H. K. Fines Library

H. K. FINES LIBRARY
Combined Balance Sheet—General Fund and Special Revenue Fund
June 30, 20x0

	General Fund	Special Revenue	Memo Totals
Assets:			
Cash, including interest bearing savings	$17,000	$14,700	$31,700
State grant receivable	16,000	—	16,000
Pledges receivable, at net realizable value	7,200	—	7,200
Investments, at cost or amortized cost	23,750	—	23,750
Total Assets	$63,950	$14,700	$78,650
Liabilities and Fund Balance:			
Liabilities:			
Vouchers Payable	$12,375	—	$12,375
Deferred Revenues	—	$14,700	14,700
Total Liabilities	$12,375	$14,700	$27,075
Fund Balance:			
Reserved for:			
Encumbrances	$11,700	—	$11,700
Inventory	6,750	—	6,750
Employee retirement	4,945	—	4,945
Unreserved:			
Designated for subsequent year expenditures	17,000	—	17,000
Undesignated	11,180	—	11,180
Total Fund Balance	$51,575	—	$51,575
Total Liabilities and Fund Balance	$63,950	$14,700	$78,650

tirement monies of $11,700, $6,750, and $4,950, respectively. Reserves for Encumbrances are a commitment of future budget monies on purchase orders outstanding at the end of the year. Under assets, no amount is shown for inventories, but there are inventories of supplies within the Fines Library. To indicate to Board members that inventories decrease the amount of the Fund Balance that is available for new appropriations (inventories cannot be spent) a reserve of $6,750 is established. Therefore, although there are inventories in the library, they are not recorded in an asset account. The reason for this will be fully explained in another chapter, but for now, it should be remembered that MAM is concerned with the flow of resources. As a result, inventory purchases are shown as expenditures and not recorded under assets.[5] Another reserve is for employee retirement. This reserve is an actuarial determined commitment that is legally required to be paid by the General Fund for employees' pensions. As the Special Revenue Fund is similar to the General Fund, all the subdivisions shown for the General Fund could also have appeared as part of the Special Revenue's Fund Balance, but for simplicity, those subsections are not illustrated.

Under the Liabilities, two accounts are listed. They are Vouchers Payable and Deferred Revenues. Vouchers Payable is a liability similar to accounts payable. The term "voucher" is more commonly used in MAM, and it indicates that liabilities for goods and services are vouchered—approved for payment—but not yet paid. Deferred revenues can represent cash revenues that have been received but not earned. Thus, there is an obligation or liability for revenues received in advance of services being provided. Deferred revenues have an obligation attached to them, and a possibility exists that if the obligation is not fulfilled, the monies could be returnable. As the Fines Library performs activities to earn these revenues, deferred revenues become actual revenues. Deferred revenues are recorded in the Special Revenue Fund in figure 6-3. Usually, the Special Revenue Fund includes more accounts, but for illustrative purposes here, only this liability account and the Cash account appear in the Special Revenue Fund. It should be noted that the Cash balance is equal to the Deferred Revenue liability. The cash represents the advance monies received and also recognized as a liability.

The asset section includes four different accounts. Cash is common to both funds. The General Fund's assets include a State Grant Receivable. A grant recorded in the General Revenue Fund means that grant monies can be used in paying for the general operations of the Fines Library. If the grant were recognized in the Special Revenue Fund, it could be used only for the special purpose for which the Special Revenue Fund had been established. Another asset included as part of the General Fund is Pledges Receivable. The balance in this account is recorded at its net realizable value. Here, net realizable value is determined by deducting the amount of pledges expected to be uncollectible (based on past experience) from the total amount of pledges made to the library.

The last asset listed is Investments. Investments represent the purchases of bonds and other short-term investments that pay interest to the library.[6] These investments are made to receive the highest return on idle cash. The investments are recorded at cost or amortized cost. Cost is simply the price paid for the bond. Amortized cost is a more complex issue.

A debt security can be valued at *amortized* cost. It should be noted that bond investments purchased by the library are issued for a specific period, and when the end of that time period arrives, the holder of the bond is paid back the face value of the bond. This amount is also called the "maturity" value of the bond. The purchaser of the debt has received interest payments for holding the debt, and at the bond's maturity date, the face value is repaid to the investor. Amortized cost arises when a debt security is purchased at more or less than its face value.

For example, a $10,000 bond (the "face" value) may be purchased for $9,700, in which case it is purchased at a "discount." If the same bond were purchased for $10,300, it would have been purchased at a "premium." At the maturity date of the bond, the purchaser receives its face value, $10,000. The purchaser who paid $10,300 loses $300 over the period the bond was held (to maturity) whereas the purchaser who paid $9,700 gains $300. Premiums and discounts are usually related to the differences between the current (market) rate of interest for this type of bond and the rate the bond is paying. For example, if the bond is paying a rate of 4 percent and the current rate of interest for this type of bond is 12 percent, no one would be willing to buy the bond at its face value of $10,000, and the only way the bond could be sold is for less than $10,000.

The amortized cost of a bond can be computed and recorded under Investments on the Balance Sheet at any time during the period the bond is held. If a $10,000 bond is purchased for $9,700, it is sold at a $300 discount, and the holder of the bond, when it matures, will receive $10,000. Thus, there is a $300 "gain" to the purchaser of the bond. The gain should not be recognized at the maturity date, and in fact, it is *not* considered a gain. Instead, it is considered an adjustment to the interest earned on the bond over the life of the bond. If the bond were purchased on June 30, 2000, and it will mature in five years, or on June 30, 2005, the $300 discount is written off to revenues over each of the five years on an equal basis of $60 per year. The amortized cost of this bond shown on the Balance Sheet is 2001, $9,760; 2002, $9,820; 2003, $9,880; 2004, $9,940; and in the last year, 2005, it will reach its maturity value of $10,000. Therefore, the amortized value of a bond is determined by writing off any discount or premium associated with the bond. If a $300 premium had been paid on the bond, the amortized cost of the bond would have been above $10,000 for four years and in its fifth year it would have been $10,000 also.

Bond valuations on the Balance Sheet recognize a "write-down" on an investment only when a permanent and significant decline in the investment's value has occurred. Under such circumstances, the Investment account is written off by an amount equal to the reduction in value, and the loss is recognized on the SREF.

STATEMENT OF REVENUES, EXPENDITURES, AND CHANGES IN FUND BALANCE—BUDGET AND ACTUAL

The next financial report is important in evaluating the spending performance of the Fines Library during the fiscal year. In figure 6-4, the Statement of Revenues, Expenditures, and Changes in Fund Balance—Budget and Actual (SREF2) shows the manager the variances between expenditures and budgeted amounts appropriated for the current year as well as the variances between estimated (budget) revenues and actual revenues. This statement should be prepared for every fund that enacts a budget, and it should include only purchases made with current-year appropriations. The purpose of the statement is to show dollar-for-dollar accountability between appropriations and spending levels.[7]

The SREF2 validates the accuracy of beginning budget estimates. If the actual revenues are more than the estimated revenues a favorable variance is recorded, otherwise it is unfavorable. In figure 6-4, it can be seen that beginning of the year projections anticipated the receipt of $85,000 from government grants during the year but instead, $90,000 was received—a favorable variance of $5,000. When expenditures are reviewed, it can be seen that all are favorable except in Administration where there is a $6,000 unfavorable variance. When these expenditures are more closely analyzed, it can be seen that the unfavorable expenditure variances in Administration are compensated for by reducing expenditures in each of the other departments. As a result, *total* expenditures of $116,700 are not over budgeted amounts. In many budgets, the only budgetary control point is total amount expended. Consequently, managers are allowed to change appropriations among internal spending points (in this case, the various departments). It should be noted that the variance of $5,485 of revenues over (under) expenditures is favorable because the actual deficit ($5,315) is *less* than the projected budget deficit ($10,800).

From the Library Desk: An example is today's decision—how to make a $35,000 collections purchase, when only $7,500 remains in the acquisitions budget? We must decide what other funds can be transferred to cover the shortfall.

Anonymous survey respondent's response to how budgetary information aids decision making

---

In figure 6-4, the Fund Balance on June 30 is calculated only under the actual column. SREF2s may show the Fund Balance calculation under both the budget and actual column for comparative purposes, but as neither represents GAAP showing the calculation under the actual column is adequate.

FIGURE 6-4 **The Statement of Revenues, Expenditures, and Changes in Fund Balance—Budget and Actual (Non-GAAP) for the H. K. Fines Library**

H. K. FINES LIBRARY
Statement of Revenues, Expenditures, and Changes in Fund Balance—
Budget and Actual (Non-GAAP)
For the Year Ended June 30, 20x0

	Budget	Actual	Variance, Favorable (Unfavorable)
Revenues:			
Government grants	$ 85,000	$ 90,000	$5,000
Other grants	—	3,500	3,500
Contributions & bequests	11,000	9,000	(2,000)
Book fines and sales	2,000	2,100	100
Photocopying	3,900	3,785	(115)
Library ID charges	4,000	3,000	(1,000)
Total Revenues	$105,900	$111,385	$5,485
Expenditures:			
Reference	$ 27,000	$ 26,000	$1,000
Children's Library	16,000	15,000	1,000
Circulation	35,700	34,700	1,000
Regional Library	18,000	15,000	3,000
Administration	20,000	26,000	(6,000)
Total Expenditures	$116,700	$116,700	—
Revenues over (under) Expenditures	$(10,800)	$ (5,315)	$5,485
Fund Balance, July 1		235,190	
Residual Equity Transfer to Capital Projects Fund		(190,000)	
Fund Balance, June 30		$ 39,875	

The SREF2 initially appears to report the same information as the SREF in figure 6-1, but it does not. For example, the SREF shows a June 30 Fund Balance total of $51,575 while in SREF2 it is $39,875. The reason for this difference is that SREF2 uses the NFO's legal basis rather than GAAP (as is done in SREF) for reporting. In some NFOs, the budget is legally required to be prepared on a cash disbursement basis, and its year-end, outstanding encumbrances are combined with its disbursements all under the heading of "expenditures." How is it possible to determine whether a non-GAAP method is being followed? First, the title of the statement, as in figure 6-4, should state that the financial report is a "non-GAAP" statement. Second, a reconciliation to

GAAP should be provided in the financial statement itself or in the notes to the statement. Finally, the notes to the financial statements should provide complete information as to the method followed. Figure 6-4 is a non-GAAP report, as noted in the statement's heading.

In figure 6-4, the encumbrances outstanding at the year-end in each department have been added to the expenditures shown in the SREF in figure 6-2, General Fund. The total outstanding year-end encumbrances are $11,700. If budgetary control is to exist, it is important for senior managers to compare the total of expenditures *and encumbrances* with budget appropriations. Without combining budget expenditures and encumbrances, it would be possible for the budget appropriations to be exceeded by managers who overencumbered current appropriations at the end of the fiscal year. Thus, while expenditures themselves would be within budgetary guidelines, the NFO could still be committed to future spending above budget amounts from large and undisclosed encumbrance commitments. In the Fines Library, there are $11,700 of encumbrances that are added to its expenditures in the SREF2.

The expenditure of $116,700 shown under the Actual column in figure 6-4 includes $11,700 of outstanding encumbrances as well as the $105,000 of expenditures shown in figure 6-2 under the General Fund column. The reconciliation between the Actual column and the General Fund columns follows. The General Fund follows GAAP accounting methods, in which expenditures do not include encumbrances. The difference between actual and GAAP columns represents the outstanding encumbrances of $11,700 that were added to each department's expenditures and are now separately recorded. This reconciliation needs to be shown on the SREF2 or in the notes to the statement. It should be restated that expenditures listed on the SREF2 are not GAAP expenditures.

Reconciliation between Budgetary and GAAP Expenditures:

	Budgetary (Fig. 6–4)	−	GAAP (Fig. 6–2)	=	Difference (Outstanding Encumbrances)
Reference	$26,000	−	$25,000	=	$1,000
Children's Library	15,000	−	13,000	=	2,000
Circulation	34,700	−	32,000	=	2,700
Regional Library	15,000	−	11,000	=	4,000
Administration	26,000	−	24,000	=	2,000
					$11,700

NOTES TO THE FINANCIAL STATEMENTS

An integral part of the previously described financial statements is the notes to these statements. (The notes for the H. K. Fines Library are presented in figure

6-5). These notes provide additional disclosures about the financial activities of the NFO that cannot be conveniently placed in the financial statements themselves. In this example, the notes are shorter than usual because only the General Fund and Special Revenue Fund have been introduced at this point.

FIGURE 6-5   Notes to Accompany the June 30, 20x0 Financial Statements of H. K. Fines Library

H. K. FINES LIBRARY
Notes to the Financial Statements
June 30, 20x0

NOTE 1. Summary of Significant Accounting Policies

The H. K. Fines Library is part of the City of Fines. The Library operates under a Director and an appointed Board of Directors. The Library provides general library, reference, community resources, and administrative services. The accounting policies of the H. K. Fines Library conform to generally accepted accounting principles (GAAP) as applicable to local governments. The following is a summary of the more significant policies.

A. Financial Reporting Entity

The Library's financial statements include all funds and account groups over which the Board exercises oversight responsibility. Oversight responsibility includes such aspects as the appointment of governing body members, designation of management, the ability to significantly influence operations and accountability for fiscal matters.

The branch libraries at Cabin Creek and Moore Head are included within the Library's reporting entity since the Library's Board is the governing body for each branch library.

The Library is includable as a component unit with the City of Fines.

B. Basis of Presentation

The accounts of the Library are organized on the basis of funds or account groups; each is considered a separate accounting entity. The operation of each fund is accounted for within a set of self-balancing accounts composed of the Library's assets, liabilities, fund balances, revenues, and expenditures. The various funds are grouped by type in the financial statements. Account groups are used to record transactions that do not directly change expendable financial resources.

Total columns on the combined statements are "memorandum only" totals to indicate that this data is not comparable to consolidated information and that the data in these columns do not conform to generally accepted accounting principles. Interfund eliminations have not been made in aggregating the data in this column.

The following fund types and account groups are used by the Library: [For the present illustration, only the General and Special Revenue Funds are listed.]

(Continued)

FIGURE 6-5   Notes to Accompany the June 30, 20x0 Financial Statements of H. K. Fines Library   *(Continued)*

Governmental Funds

The General Fund: To account for all financial resources except those required to be accounted for in other funds. This fund is the general operating fund of the Library and it is used to account for administration, library services, supplies, and maintenance of library building and collections.

The Special Revenue Fund: To account for the proceeds of specific revenue sources (other than expendable trusts, debt service, or major capital construction projects) that may be restricted by donors, administrative actions, or legal statutes.

C. Basis of Accounting

The accounting and financial reporting treatment applied to a fund is determined by its measurement focus. All governmental funds are accounted for using a current financial resources measurement focus. With this measurement focus, only current assets and current liabilities generally are included on the balance sheet. Operating statements of these funds present increases (i.e., revenues and other financing sources) and decreases (i.e., expenditures and other financing uses) in net current assets.

The modified accrual basis of accounting is used for all governmental and agency funds. Under this method, revenues are recognized when received, except for those accruable, which are recorded as receivable when measurable and available to pay current-period liabilities. The Library considers revenues available if they are collectible within 60 days of the year-end.

Expenditures are generally recognized under the modified accrual basis of accounting when the related fund liability is incurred.

The Library recognizes deferred revenues. Deferred revenues arise when resources are received by the Library before it can legally claim them, as when grant revenues are received before the qualifying expenditures are made. When the qualifying conditions of the grant are met, the deferred revenue is removed from the balance sheet liabilities and recognized as a revenue.

Encumbrance accounting, under which purchase orders, contracts, and other commitments for the expenditure of monies are recorded in order to reserve a portion of the appropriation, are used by the Library. Encumbrances outstanding at year-end are carried forward to the new fiscal year. These encumbrances are the equivalent of expenditures for budgetary purposes. Outstanding encumbrances are reported as reservations of fund balances on the balance sheet and represent commitments that will be honored in the subsequent fiscal year. All unencumbered appropriations lapse at the end of the fiscal year.

D. Budget

The Library is required under City Ordinance 45(a)(7) to adopt an annual balanced budget by July 1 each year. The Board usually approves a preliminary budget in

March or April for the fiscal year beginning July 1. The Board uses a legally adopted budget with actual data on a basis that includes encumbrances and is inconsistent with generally accepted accounting principles. A reconciliation between budgetary and generally accepted accounting principles is provided at the end of this paragraph. The budget is approved during a public board meeting and published in the paper as required by city ordinance. The Director is authorized to transfer budget amounts within line items, but supplemental appropriations that amend total appropriations of any fund require a Board passed resolution.

Reconciliation between Budgetary and GAAP Expenditures:

	Actual	−	GAAP	=	Difference (Outstanding Encumbrances)
Reference	$26,000	−	$25,000	=	$ 1,000
Children's Library	15,000	−	13,000	=	2,000
Circulation	34,700	−	32,000	=	2,700
Regional Library	15,000	−	11,000	=	4,000
Administration	26,000	−	24,000	=	2,000
					$11,700

E. Inventories

The costs of supplies are charged to expenditures as purchasesd in the year in which the expenditure is budgeted. Inventories of these items are immaterial at year-end.

F. Fixed Assets

Fixed assets used in governmental funds are accounted for in the general fixed assets account group rather than in the governmental fund, and no depreciation is recorded on general fixed assets. Donated fixed assets are valued at their estimated fair market value on the date of their donation. Library books are recorded as expenditures when they are purchased.

G. Retirement Plan

Pension costs are funded as they accrue. All funds that have employees transfer their share of such benefits to the employee benefits fund from which the costs are paid.

H. Comparative Data

Complete comparative data, with the presentation of prior year totals by fund type have not been presented in each of the statements since their inclusion would make the statements unduly complex and difficult to read.

NOTE 2. Pooled Cash and Investments

Investments in certificates of deposit, U.S. Government obligations, repurchase agreements, and other investments are recorded at cost or amortized cost except for donated investments and those in the City's pooled investment fund which are recorded at market value.

(Continued)

FIGURE 6-5   Notes to Accompany the June 30, 20x0 Financial Statements of H. K. Fines Library   *(Continued)*

NOTE 3. Fund Equity

The reserved accounts indicate the portion of the fund balance which has been legally segregated for specific purposes and is not appropriable. The unreserved designated accounts indicate the portion of the fund equity set aside for future projects. The unreserved undesignated account indicates the fund balance available for future appropriations.

In the current year, there was an excess of budgetary expenditures over revenues of $10,800 and actual expenditures over revenues of $5,315 in the General Fund. Although this was a planned level of spending, continued spending leading to an excess of expenditures over revenues could eventually lead to a deficit in the Fund Balance.

Note 1 relates to the significant accounting policies followed by the library. The basis on which the financial statements are prepared must be clearly described. In this case, MAM is used. If a library does not use MAM, that fact should be disclosed in two places. First, if the financial statements are audited, the use of an accounting method other than MAM is likely to be disclosed as a qualification in the audit opinion rendered by the independent public accountant. Second, it should be disclosed in the first note to the financial statements.

The first part of note 1 describes the significant accounting policies used by the NFO and also presents an overview of the NFO itself including governance responsibilities, entity scope, and component unit status. In this case, the library is a component part of the city's financial reporting system.

Section B of note 1 discusses the library's funds and account groups. Funds have already been described as self-balancing account groupings. Account groups, yet to be described in a later chapter, are used to account for those transactions of a governmental fund that are related to fixed assets and debt. The account groups largely provide a listing of the NFO's fixed assets and long-term debt.

The second paragraph of section B describes characteristics of the financial statements that readers should understand. Many readers of the NFO's financial statements have some familiarity with the financial reports of corporations. This paragraph sets forth some of the differences between corporate and NFO financial statements. These differences were described earlier in the chapter. Interfund eliminations are made in a corporation's books, but in an NFO's, they are not recorded. This difference means that the amounts owed between subsidiaries in the same corporation are eliminated in a consolidated set of financial reports. Exactly the opposite happens in an NFO. The interfund transactions are not eliminated unless they are between funds of a similar type, e.g., two Special Revenue Funds.

Section C of note 1 uses the phrase "current financial resources measurement focus." This measurement focus uses expenditures rather than expenses and as a result, only current assets and liabilities are recorded on the balance sheet of governmental funds such as the General Fund and Special Revenue Fund. Even in these cases, many times current assets (prepaid assets) are not recorded on the Balance Sheet. These methods are typical of MAM. Under MAM, a 60-day criterion is used for the recognition of revenues, and although this is a common practice, another NFO may choose to use a shorter period such as 45 days. Whatever time period is chosen, it should be disclosed in the notes to the financial statements and it should not exceed 60 days.

In the third and fourth paragraphs of section C, the manner used to record expenditures and deferred revenues is noted. The final paragraph in this section deals with encumbrances. This paragraph is used to explain the NFO's policies toward outstanding encumbrances at the year-end. For the H. K. Fines Library, the outstanding encumbrances are carried over to the new budget year. Any unencumbered appropriations are returned to the Board or other budget granting authority at the end of the year. For organizations facing a return of unencumbered appropriations, there is always a year end rush to encumber these appropriations. Although only unencumbered appropriations are returned by the H. K. Fines Library at the end of the fiscal year, in many organizations all unexpended appropriations are returned. In other words, "if you don't expend it, you lose it."

Section D, Budget, describes the budget policies followed in the NFO. The accounting method used in developing the budget should be described in this paragraph. The H. K. Fines Library incorporates encumbrances and expenditures together in developing its budget, as was explained earlier. Additionally, the reconciliation that was explained in the chapter follows this paragraph. There are other legally designated ways in which to adopt a budget besides the one illustrated here. In each case, a reconciliation to GAAP should be made in the notes to the financial statements. An example of the disclosures that could be used if a cash budget is legally required follows:

> Budgets for the general and special revenue funds are adopted on a cash basis, which is inconsistent with GAAP which requires modified accrual accounting. All budgeting comparisons presented in this report are on a non-GAAP budgetary basis and are compared with actual cash receipts and disbursements.

It is important in this section to clearly disclose the method of budgetary accounting used. Even if an MAM budget is used by the NFO, it should be disclosed with statements such as the following:

> All budgets are prepared on a modified accrual basis of accounting.

> A final operating budget is adopted for all governmental funds on a modified accrual basis used to reflect actual revenues and expenditures.

In this first paragraph under section D, it is also disclosed that the director has the authority to transfer budget appropriations within internal line items in the library as long as the total appropriation is not overexpended. This is the situation that occurred in the current year when budgetary dollars were added to reduce overexpenditures in Administration, and at the same time, appropriations in the other library departments were reduced.

In section E, the method used to value inventories is described. It is also noted there that the dollar value of the supply inventories is insignificant, and not listed on the Balance Sheet. Fixed assets are described in section F. Capital outlays are recorded as expenditures when purchased, and only listed in the account group for fixed assets. Accounting for fixed assets in this account group will be explained later. For the present, it should be noted that no depreciation is recorded on fixed assets. This is a significant difference from the accounting for fixed assets under accrual accounting.[8] For that reason, we will briefly examine the concept of depreciation.

The concept of depreciation is based on the inherent difference between types of assets. For example, when fixed assets, such as equipment and buildings, are compared with inventories of supplies, it is clear the supplies are used up much more quickly than most buildings. The service benefits received from the inventory of supplies cannot last as long as the service benefits received from a building. The value of a building or equipment is reduced over a lengthy time through wear and tear, as well as by obsolescence. When the processes that cause reductions in the value of a fixed assets are recognized in the accounts, it is called "depreciation."

Depreciation provides a means of assigning the value or benefits of a long-lived asset to the periods over which that asset provides a service to the organization. To recognize this value in the accounts, the cost of a fixed asset (i.e., its value) is assigned to yearly time periods over the asset's estimated life. This is not a cash allocation method for the replacement or renewal of assets, but simply a method to allocate the benefits received from the use of the asset over the asset's life. No cash inflows or outflows occur when this entry is recorded. Under MAM, accounting concerns are directed at expendable financial resources. As depreciation creates no expenditures, and it is not appropriated, even though it is considered an expense, it has little application in MAM.[9] Yet, there are accounting methods used by some NFOs that do record depreciation (see chapter appendix). Finally, it should be noted that some types of assets are never depreciated. Land is one such asset. The characteristic of land that makes it different from other long-lived assets is that it is inexhaustible. Inexhaustible assets such as landmarks and rare books are not depreciated either.

In Section G, retirement plans are mentioned. The accounting for pension plans is very complex and it will not be discussed in this book. Section H explains why comparative data for the previous year are not shown.

Two additional note disclosures appear in figure 6-5. Note 2 lists the investments made by the H. K. Fines Library. Repurchase agreements will be discussed in a later chapter. Amortized cost has already been described in the chapter as a way to value investments. Market value is another method of valuation. Securities that are purchased on a national exchange are bought for the market price when they are initially acquired, but changes occur in that market value on a daily basis, so that a difference occurs between the original price paid for the securities (their cost) and the current market price of those same securities. The market value of a security is its current market price, and when the market-value method is used for valuing securities, this current market price is recorded in the accounting records. This is the value at which the H. K. Fines Library should have its investments valued in an investment pool (to be described later) so that if withdrawals are made, the market value (current value) is received.

Note 3 in figure 6-5 describes the Fund Balance. If there is a potential for a deficit in the Fund Balance, it should be disclosed here. When revenues are less than expenditures, that fact should also be disclosed in this note. The H. K. Fines Library is facing the latter situation, and adequate disclosures are provided in the note to outline the situation.

SUMMARY

This chapter provides an overview of the financial statements that are prepared for the General Fund and Special Revenue Fund. The General Fund is the most important fund in an NFO because so many transactions are recorded there.

Although the Balance Sheet and the Statement of Revenues, Expenditures, and Changes in Fund Balance were introduced in an earlier chapter, more information about them is provided in this chapter. Additionally, a budget and actual version of the SREF is introduced. Chapter 7 continues the explanation of the General Fund and the Special Revenue Fund through the recording of the typical journal entries in these funds. These transactions will culminate in a second set of updated financial statements for the H. K. Fines Library.

As previously stated, governmental NFOs have two choices to follow in preparing their financial statements: MAM or accrual for NFOs. The method that has been illustrated in this chapter is MAM. It is believed that this is the accounting method that will prevail in this area, but the appendix to this chapter presents a set of financial statements that are prepared under accrual for NFOs. The directors of some libraries may find that their financial statements are prepared using the method found in the appendix.

EXERCISE 6-1   The General Fund and Special Revenue Fund

1. Name the three financial statements that are needed to describe the financial activities of the General Fund.

2. Explain the function of the General Fund for an NFO.

3. What is the difference between cash received in the General Fund and the Special Revenue Fund?

4. What are discretionary board restrictions in the Fund Balance?

5. Prepare the proper footnote disclosures and any necessary journal entries for the following two events:
    a. During the 20x0 fiscal year, the Pole Town Library transferred $75,000 to the Pole Town City Commission. These monies had been donated to the library for the remodeling of the library. The City Commission used the money to buy snow removal equipment. At the present time, the library is being sued by the donor's estate for the return of the monies. The library's attorney has indicated that the library has a high probability of losing its case.
    b. During the 20x1 fiscal year, the Mason-Dixon Library has been party to a lawsuit brought against the Library by a patron who fell and broke his arm in the library. The suit is for damages of $125,000. The library's attorney has indicated that the library is not likely to have to pay these damages, and when the case is settled the amounts likely to be paid are in the range of $1,000 to $3,000.

6. Distinguish between earned revenue and contributions received by the NFO.

7. In the Oxford County Library, the budget line dollar appropriation at the beginning of the year for the Children's Library was $100,000. During the year this amount was reduced by $10,000. At the end of the year, the Children's Library has $15,000 of encumbrance outstanding. On checking the amount of expenditures made by the Children's Library, the Director sees that $80,000 was spent. Should the Director reward Mr. Thomas, the head of the Children's Library?

8. Define depreciation.

APPENDIX: USING THE ACCRUAL METHOD

The appendix illustrates the Balance Sheet and Statement of Support, Revenues, Expenses, and Changes in Fund Balance based on NFO accrual. The third statement, required in an accrual framework, is the Statement of Changes in Cash Flow. This statement is not used under MAM for governmental funds. Likewise, the Statement of Revenues, Expenditures, and Changes in Fund Balance—Budget and Actual is not used in NFO accrual financial reports.

In the Statement of Support, Revenues, Expenses, and Changes in Fund Balance, figure 6A-1, there is no General Fund or Special Revenue Fund. The General Fund is replaced by the Operating Fund, and instead of using a Special Revenue Fund, the restricted monies are in the Operating Fund under a "restricted" heading. Financial statements in accrual NFO are usually prepared on a comparative basis, and here the comparative data for 20x0, the previous year, are shown. Additionally, expenditures are replaced by expenses. The amount in the investment account includes net gains and thus, it becomes a more complex calculation to determine the balance in this account. In this financial statement, depreciation would be recorded as one of the expenses on the SREF. Although the bottom line of $51,575 is the same as in figure 6-1, this similarity would not continue through an entire year's transactions because of the differences in the accounting model upon which these financial statements are based.

The Balance Sheet in figure 6A-2 is a comparative statement with an unrestricted and restricted account division. The division is established to make it clear that restricted monies are being used only for those purposes designated by the donor. Further, it should be noted that the restricted accounts are very abbreviated. In this case, only Cash and Deferred Restricted Contributions are used. These two accounts are equal because the liability account, Deferred Restricted Contributions, is reduced only when cash is expended on a qualified expense specified by the donor.

The Statement of Cash Flows is not used with governmental funds under MAM. The financial reports prepared under MAM more closely reflect cash results than NFO accrual reports; therefore, under NFO accrual, it is considered important to provide information reflective of cash results. The Statement of Cash Flows, shown in figure 6A-3, provides information about the Library's cash flows during the year. Except for the beginning and ending cash balances on the Balance Sheet ($212,190 and $31,700), this information is not available through reviewing the Balance Sheet or the SREF. The basic purpose of the Statement of Cash Flows is to provide a summary of how cash was used during the year. Using the Statement of Cash Flows, the reader can quickly determine where cash was obtained or used during the year. In the Statement, a distinction is made between cash sources from operations, financing, and investing activities. These divisions help the reader determine whether normal operations are supporting the cash needs of the NFO. In this case, they are not. In fact, the H. K. Fines Library used its large cash reserves at the beginning of the year to fund its operations during the current year. This is not a viable method of operating in the long run.

FIGURE 6A-1   Statement of Support, Revenues, Expenses, and Changes in Fund Balance for H. K. Fines Library

H. K. FINES LIBRARY
Operating Fund
Statement of Support, Revenues, Expenses, and Changes in Fund Balance
For the Year Ended June 30, 20x1
(with Comparative Totals for 20x0)

	Unrestricted	Restricted	Total	June 30, 20x0 Totals
Support and Revenue				
Support:				
Grants (Note 1)*				
Governments	$ 90,000	—	$ 90,000	$ 85,000
Other	3,500	—	3,500	11,000
Contributions and				
Bequests	9,000	$15,000	24,000	3,000
Total Support	$102,500	$15,000	$117,500	$ 99,000
Revenue:				
Book Fines and Sales	$ 2,100	—	$ 2,100	$ 3,000
Photocopying	3,785	—	3,785	4,000
Investment Income,				
incl. net gains	3,000	—	3,000	2,700
Total Revenue	$ 8,885	—	$ 8,885	$ 9,700
Total Support and Revenue	$111,385	$15,000	$126,385	$108,700
Expenses (Note 4)*				
Program Services:				
Reference	$ 25,000	$ 8,000	$ 33,000	$ 34,000
Children's Library	13,000	4,300	17,300	15,000
Circulation	32,000	—	32,000	28,000
Regional History	11,000	2,700	13,700	12,000
Total Program Services	$ 81,000	$15,000	$ 96,000	$ 89,000
Supporting Services				
Administration	$ 24,000	—	$ 24,000	$ 40,000
Total Expenses	$105,000	$15,000	$120,000	$129,000
Excess (Deficiency) of				
Support and Revenue over				
Expenses	$ 6,385	—	$ 6,385	$(20,300)
Fund Balance at Beginning				
of Year	235,190	—	235,190	270,490
Transfers	(190,000)	—	(190,000)	(15,000)
Fund Balance at End of				
Year	$ 51,575	—	$ 51,575	$235,190

*Notes are included in figure 6A–4.

FIGURE 6A-2   Balance Sheet for H. K. Fines Library

H. K. FINES LIBRARY
Operating Fund
Balance Sheet
June 30, 20x1
(with Comparative Totals for 20x0)

	Unrestricted	Restricted	Total	June 30, 20x0 Totals
Current Assets:				
Cash, including interest bearing savings accounts	$17,000	$14,700	$31,700	$212,190
State grant receivable	16,000	—	16,000	7,100
Pledges receivable, at estimated net realizable value (Note 1)*	7,200	—	7,200	—
Prepaid Assets and Other Current Assets	6,750	—	6,750	900
Total Current Assets	$46,950	$14,700	$61,650	$220,190
Investments (Note 2)*	$17,000	—	$17,000	$ 40,000
Total Assets	$63,950	$14,700	$78,650	$260,190
Liabilities and Fund Balance:				
Current Liabilities:				
Accounts Payable	$12,375	—	$12,375	$ 15,000
Deferred Restricted Contributions (Note 3)*	—	$14,700	$14,700	$ 10,000
Total Current Liabilities	$12,375	$14,700	$27,075	$ 25,000
Fund Balances:				
Unrestricted				
Designated by Board for:				
Office Equipment	$ 4,945	—	$ 4,945	—
Investments	17,000	—	17,000	$ 40,000
Undesignated	11,180	—	11,180	193,290
Restricted:				
Encumbrances (Note 1)*	11,700	—	11,700	1,000
Inventory	6,750	—	6,750	900
Total Fund Balance	$51,575	—	$51,575	$235,190
Total Liabilities and Fund Balance	$63,950	$14,700	$78,650	$260,190

*Notes are included in figure 6A–4.

FIGURE 6A-3   The Statement of Cash Flows for the H. K. Fines Library

H. K. FINES LIBRARY
Operating Fund
Statement of Cash Flows
For the Year Ended June 30, 20x1

Cash flows from operating activities:		
Cash received from grants	$ 87,385	
Cash paid to employees	(81,000)	
Cash paid for current assets	(5,850)	
Cash paid to suppliers	(2,625)	
Net cash used by operating activities		$ (2,090)
Cash flows from financing activities:		
Cash received from unrestricted contributions	$(16,100)	
Cash received from restricted contributions	4,700	
Cash transferred out	(190,000)	
Net cash used by financing activities		(201,400)
Cash flows from investing activities:		
Proceeds from sale of investments		23,000
Net decrease in cash		$(180,490)
Cash at the beginning of the year		212,190
Cash at the end of the year		$ 31,700

The Statement of Cash Flows is not shown on a comparative basis. Without comparative data, as is available in figures 6A-1 and 6A-2, it can be seen that the usefulness of the statement is reduced. In concluding, it can be stated that the accounting techniques used in preparing NFO accrual statements are more complex than MAM. Further, the accrual-based statements do not provide the budget variance information that many library directors are interested in reviewing.

The notes to the financial statements shown in figure 6A-4 provide similar information to that found in figure 6-5, but it should be clear to the reader of these notes that a different accounting model is being used to prepare these financial statements than the one used in the main part of chapter.

FIGURE 6A-4   Notes to 20x1 Financial Statements of H. K. Fines Library

H. K. FINES LIBRARY
Notes to the Financial Statements
June 30, 20x1

NOTE 1. Summary of Significant Accounting Policies

The financial statements of H. K. Fines Library have been prepared on the accrual basis. The significant accounting policies followed are described below to enhance the usefulness of the financial statements to the reader.

Fund Accounting

To ensure observance of limitations and restrictions placed on the use of resources available to the library, the accounts of the library are maintained in accordance with the principles of fund accounting. This is the procedure by which resources for various purposes are classified for accounting and reporting purposes into funds established according to their nature and purposes. Separate accounts are maintained for each fund.

The operating funds, which include unrestricted and restricted resources, represent the portion of expendable funds that is available for support of library operations.

Expendable Restricted Resources

Operating funds restricted by the donor, grantor, or other outside party for particular operating purposes are deemed to be earned, and reported as revenues of operating funds when the library has incurred expenditures in compliance with the specific restrictions. Such amounts received but not yet earned are reported as restricted deferred amounts.

Grants

The library records income from unrestricted grants in the period designated by the donor.

Other Matters

All gains and losses arising from the sale, collection, or other disposition of investments and other noncash assets are accounted for in the fund that owned the assets. Ordinary income from investments, receivables, and the like is accounted for in the fund owning the assets.

Legally enforceable pledges less an allowance for uncollectible amounts are recorded as receivables in the year made. Pledges for support of current operations are recorded as operating fund support. Pledges for support of future operations and plant acquisitions are recorded as deferred amounts in the respective funds to which they apply. Encumbrances represent obligations in the form of purchase orders, contracts, or other commitments which have been appropriated, but for which no liability has yet been incurred.

(Continued)

**FIGURE 6A-4   Notes to 20x1 Financial Statements of H. K. Fines
Library**   *(Continued)*

NOTE 2. Investments

Investments are presented in the financial statements in the aggregate at the lower of cost (amortized cost, in the case of bonds) or fair market value.

	Cost	Market
Operating Fund	$17,000	$21,000

Investments are composed of the following:

	Cost	Market
Corporate Stocks	$ 7,000	$11,000
U.S. Government Obligations	10,000	10,000
	$17,000	$21,000

Fair market value is determined by aggregating all current marketable securities. At June 30, 20x1, there was an unrealized gain of $4,000 pertaining to the current portfolio. This portfolio had a cost on June 30, 20x0, of $30,000, and a market value of $32,300.

A net realized gain of $2,690 on the sale of marketable equity securities was included in the determination of Excess (Deficiency) of Support and Revenue over Expenses for 20x1. The cost of the securities sold was based on a first-in, first-out method in both years.

NOTE 3. Changes in Deferred Restricted Amounts

Balances at beginning of year	$10,000
Additions:	
Contributions and Bequests	8,000
Investment Income	1,700
	$19,700
Deductions—Funds expended during year	5,000
Balance at end of year	$14,700

NOTE 4. Functional Allocation of Expenses

The costs of providing the various programs and other activities have been summarized on a functional basis in the Statement of Support, Revenues, Expenses, and Changes in Fund Balance. Accordingly, certain costs have been allocated among the programs and supporting services benefited.

NOTE 5. Commitments and Contingencies

The library receives a substantial amount of its support from federal, state, and local governments. A significant reduction in the level of this support, if this were to occur, could have an effect on the library's programs and activities.

NOTES

1. In some organizations, the General Fund is known as the Operating Fund.

2. The only time cross-accounts are eliminated is when funds of the same type are combined, such as the combining of two special revenue funds, prior to moving the data to another financial report.

3. An example of a residual equity transfer would be a one-time monetary transfer made to the Capital Projects Fund to help pay for the construction of a new annex to the library. An example of a operating transfer is a yearly transfer of money made to the Endowment Fund from the General Fund.

4. To prepare figure 6-2, the amounts shown in figure 6-1 were divided between the General Fund and Special Revenue Fund and recorded in figure 6-2. For this reason only, the total columns are equal to the amounts in the General Fund in figure 6-1.

5. Inventory amounts are not shown if they are considered not "significant." If the inventory amounts are significant, an Inventory account will appear in the Asset section of the Balance Sheet and expenditures will be reduced by an equal amount. It should be repeated that there is a tendency under MAM not to show prepaid assets such as Inventories on the Balance Sheet.

6. Other types of investments, such as repurchase agreements and reverse repurchase agreements, will be discussed later.

7. The definition of "spending levels" can vary from NFO to NFO. Therefore, spending that is actually the same may be reported differently under different accounting methods.

8. Library accounting can use three distinctly different methods. Even "governmental" libraries can use two different methods of accounting. One of those governmental methods recognizes depreciation. This system is an accrual-based method for NFOs. A brief description and an example of the financial statements using this method are found in the appendix to this chapter.

9. Under MAM, the recording of depreciation is considered an option. As a result, it is rarely recorded. If it were recorded, it would be recorded in the General Fixed Asset account group, and this account group has no effect on the NFO's expendable financial resources.

7

The General Fund and Special Revenue Fund with Journal Entries

Accounting transactions in the General Fund and Special Revenue Fund are important enough that they deserve additional consideration. These transactions are considered in this chapter, and a number of illustrative journal entries for the H. K. Fines Library are presented. Special attention should be paid to these transactions, as they will be used to revise the financial statements in chapter 6 into a set of new financial statements for the H. K. Fines Library for the period ending June 30, 20x1 (in the appendix to this chapter).

ALLOTMENTS

An allotment is a restriction on appropriations imposed by higher management or the board. If an allotment system is used, the appropriation dollars are designated for use in specific time periods. For example, the appropriation for the Reference Department may be divided into four quarterly allotment periods. If the total appropriation is for $70,000, each quarter's allotment is $17,500. The spending plans developed by the head of the Reference Department cannot exceed $17,500 for any quarter. Thus the allotment system gives management greater control over departmental spending patterns.

Use of an allotment procedure introduces another account into the general ledger—the Allotment account, which acts as a temporary holding account from which the appropriation is allocated to each period. If we assume that a $125,000 budget appropriation is made to Flavor Library and it is divided into four equal quarterly allotments ($31,250), the following entries record the accounting for allotments.

ESTIMATED REVENUES	125,000	
ALLOTMENTS		125,000
Reference		48,000
Children's Library		35,000
Circulation		27,000
Regional History		15,000

Recording initial budget entry as allotment

ALLOTMENTS	31,250		
Reference		12,000	
APPROPRIATIONS			31,250
Reference			12,000
Personnel			8,000
Travel			250
Supplies			1,700
Maintenance			800
Book Purchase			1,250

Recording first-quarter allotment to Reference Department [This is a partial entry as other departments are not shown.]

These entries are based on the journalizing format used in chapter 4, with subsidiary accounts slightly indented under the General-Ledger Control accounts (Allotments and Appropriations, in this case). The subsidiary accounts provide detailed information about the allotments to each department, as well as the specifics of the quarterly appropriations.

The first entry journalizes the initial budget approved. The debit to the Estimated Revenues account and the credit to the Allotments account are recorded in the general ledger. The various department accounts act as subsidiary accounts under the general-ledger control account, Allotments. In the second entry, the first quarterly allotment is credited to the departments and to the object expenditures of that department (in the illustration, only the Reference Department's appropriations are shown). The amounts credited to subsidiary departmental accounts are recorded in the Appropriation-Expenditures ledger, as previously explained. The illustration shows the yearly allotment evenly divided into quarterly amounts.

The equality of these allotments depends on the cycle of activity in the organization. If there are peaks of activity, it is not a good idea to divide the appropriation into equal allotments, as more monies are expended during peak activity periods during the year. For example, the summer session is a slower period for a private elementary school, and the appropriations should be divided so that the largest allotments occur during the school term.

The second entry also contains a debit to the Allotment account and a reduction in the Reference Department's allotment in the subsidiary account. This debit entry records the amount by which the allotments have been reduced in the first quarter or the partial amount of the appropriation made available for spending.

The entries for the H. K. Fines Library will not use an allotment system. The major reason for using this type of system is for more detailed control over the organization's use of appropriations.[1]

THE GENERAL FUND

As indicated, the unrestricted assets in the General Fund are available for use in the routine daily activities of an NFO. They have not been restricted for specific uses. Transactions of this nature are the first consideration in the chapter, followed by an explanation of transactions in the Special Revenue Fund.

RECORDING THE BUDGET

The H. K. Fines Library has had its 20x1 budget approved by the governing board of the library, and on July 1 the budget is recorded in the general journal with the following entry.

July 1				
ESTIMATED REVENUES	183,500		
City of Fines		78,000	
Backlog County		66,000	
State Grant		26,000	
Book Fines		2,500	
Book Sales		3,000	
Photocopying		8,000	
APPROPRIATIONS			171,000
Administration			45,000
Reference Department			35,000
Children's Library			37,000
Circulation			40,000
Regional History			14,000
FUND BALANCE—			
Undesignated			12,500
Recording the 20x1 budget			

In this entry, the appropriations are made to the departments in the library and are not further subdivided into object expenditures accounts, such as supplies or maintenance. (This simplification makes the example a more workable illustration.) The departmental accounts in the July 1 entry are maintained in the Appropriation-Expenditures ledger, a subsidiary ledger.

REVISING THE BUDGET

Shortly after the budget was recorded in the accounts, it was learned that the City of Fines would be able to contribute only $68,000 to the library. In response to this $10,000 appropriation reduction, the director called a meeting of department heads and the budget was revised. The revised budget reduces the amount that had been appropriated to the Reference and Circulation departments by $1,500 each, the Fund Balance is reduced by $7,000, and Estimated Revenues is reduced, along with the estimated revenues to be available from the City of Fines. Although there was a $10,000 reduction in estimated revenues from the city, the appropriations were reduced by only $3,000 because amounts in the Fund Balance were used to make up the shortfall.[2]

July 7	FUND BALANCE—Undesignated	7,000	
	APPROPRIATIONS	3,000	
	Reference		1,500
	Circulation		1,500
	ESTIMATED REVENUES		10,000
	City of Fines		10,000
	Recording revision of original budget		

Budget revisions, due to reductions in anticipated support from various governments or from changes in the way the budget was originally appropriated among departments and programs, are not unusual. Budget reductions and revisions require good communications between the professional finance staff and library management to avoid potential misunderstandings

---

From the Library Desk: Sometime near the beginning of our fiscal year, I am given a budget, $10,000, for example. I have no input into that amount. Near the end of our fiscal year I hear by way of a staff meeting, for instance, that there is not much money left and no large orders should be made until the new budget. The fact that I still have money available for Children's Room books according to my records is of no importance. There has never been a budget meeting to which I have been invited, nor any of the rest of the staff to the best of my knowledge. There is no discussion of the budget, whether we are spending a lot or a little, too much, too soon, not enough, etc.

Anonymous survey respondent

RECEIPT OF CASH FROM GOVERNMENTS

On July 14, 20x0, the monies from all three government authorities are received in cash and recorded in the general journal.

July 14	CASH	160,000	
	REVENUES—Intergovernmental		160,000
	City of Fines		68,000
	Backlog County		66,000
	State Grant		26,000

Recording receipt of revenues from governments that support the library

As indicated in chapter 4, portions of the estimated revenues available from a government may not be immediately received in the form of Cash. The amounts that are not quickly available should be recognized as a receivable by debiting a "Due from" account in such a case. As the estimated revenues are received in the form of cash, the receivable is reduced. In the case of the H. K. Fines Library, the monies are received quickly enough that a "Due from" receivable is not established.

ISSUANCE OF PURCHASE ORDERS

The recording of purchase orders is assumed to occur with one entry—for illustrative convenience. The library issued $33,450 worth of purchase orders during the fiscal year for books, periodicals, supplies, and repairs. Each encumbrance is assigned to a departmental account, based on the department responsible for originating the purchase order. The encumbrances are posted to the departmental accounts in the Appropriation-Expenditures subsidiary ledger.

August 15	ENCUMBRANCES	33,450	
	Administration	6,950	
	Reference Dept.	8,000	
	Children's Library	5,500	
	Circulation	9,000	
	Regional History	4,000	
	RESERVE FOR ENCUMBRANCES		33,450

Recording purchase orders issued during entire year

PRIOR-YEAR ENCUMBRANCES

There are $11,700 of outstanding encumbrances (orders) at the end of June 30, 20x0, and invoices for them are received, approved for payment, and paid during the year ending June 30, 20x1. The invoices are for a total of $11,900, or $200 more than the amount that was encumbered at the end of the previous year. The library has a policy of canceling unfilled encumbrances two months after the beginning of a new year, but all these encumbrances were filled by that time.

The following entries record the reversal of the encumbrances and the payment of the prior-year expenditures. The entry to close the expenditures of $11,900 is not made until the end of the fiscal year, and that closing entry is shown, as a combined entry, in the appendix to this chapter. It should be noted that in this case, $11,900 of 20x1's appropriations were approved to be used to satisfy encumbrances outstanding from 20x0.

August 1	ENCUMBRANCES—Prior Year		11,700	
	Reference			6,700
	Circulation			5,000
	UNDESIGNATED FUND BALANCE			11,700

Reversal of prior year's encumbrances

August 1	RESERVE FOR ENCUMBRANCES—			
	Prior Year		11,700	
	ENCUMBRANCES—Prior Year			11,700

Canceling prior year's encumbrances [The reserve account is left open at the end of each year.]

August 1	EXPENDITURES—Prior Year		11,900	
	Reference			6,700
	Circulation			5,200
	CASH			11,900

Payment of invoices on prior-year encumbrances

RECORDING THE PAYROLL

Unlike payments on purchase orders, the payroll is not encumbered, because the amount of the payroll is known at the beginning of the year and significant changes in this amount are not likely. Unlike a payroll expenditure, the amount encumbered under a purchase order is more likely to change between the time the purchase order is issued and the time the invoice is paid.

When the Fines Library pays its payroll, certain deductions must be made from employees' pay for social security, state and federal income taxes, insurance, and possibly a retirement plan. Such deductions are owed to the various agencies from the time the payroll entry is recorded. These amounts are considered liabilities from that date, and they need to be recorded as liabilities until they are paid.[3] The payroll for the H. K. Fines Library is $88,000 for the year, and it is assumed that deductions are made only for federal and state government liabilities.

June 20	EXPENDITURES	88,000	
	Administration	20,000	
	Reference Dept.	12,000	
	Children's Library	28,000	
	Circulation Dept.	20,000	
	Regional History	8,000	
	DUE TO FEDERAL GOVT—FICA		14,000
	DUE TO FEDERAL		
	GOVT—Income Tax		14,000
	DUE TO STATE		
	GOVT—Income Tax		10,000
	WAGES PAYABLE		50,000
	Recording the payroll		

In some library accounting systems, the payroll is handled by a local governmental agency, such as the city or county. This may occur even if the monies for the library payroll are provided by the library's resources. If this is the case, the library's accounting records would show the transfer of monies to the agency responsible for making the actual payment of the payroll as well as a credit to cash. When transaction such as these are handled by the city for the library, the city may bill the library a service fee.[4]

From the Library Desk: Treasury fees (for services) are charged as a percent of the total revenue received.

The State Board of Accounts charges us for audits.

Two anonymous survey respondents

The June entry is posted to the departmental accounts in the Appropriation-Expenditures subsidiary ledger. Just as the issuance of a purchase order is a reduction of the appropriation, the payment of a departmental payroll is also a reduction of the appropriation for wages. The liabilities owed to the federal government are composed of Federal Insurance Contribution Act (FICA) contributions (more commonly called social security taxes) and federal income taxes; the amount owed to the state is for state income taxes. Wages Payable records the employees' net pay.

The June 20 entry is recorded on the employees' payday. As employees cash their checks and the library starts to receive the canceled checks, the Wages Payable account is reduced and the Cash account is credited. Assuming all payroll checks had been cashed by June 25, the following entry would be made:[5]

June 25	WAGES PAYABLE	50,000	
	CASH		50,000
	Recording the cashing of payroll checks by employees		

EMPLOYER'S PAYROLL EXPENDITURES

In addition to tax deductions from an employee's gross pay, certain payroll taxes are charged directly against the library and must be paid to federal and state governments. One such tax is FICA for social security; the library must match the employee's FICA deduction.[6] The library must also pay an unemployment compensation charge to the state to support payments to qualified out-of-work wage earners. The rate charged the organization usually varies with the number of former employees of the organization who have made successful claims for unemployment compensation. In addition, the library has to make payments to an employee retirement and insurance plan. All these payments are the employer's payroll expenditures.

The FICA deduction from the employees' pay was $14,000; therefore, the library's FICA expenditure is also $14,000. The library makes a contribution to the employees' retirement and insurance plan of $6,700, and a payment to the state's unemployment compensation plan of $6,000. These amounts are recorded when the payroll entry for the employees is recorded on June 20.

June 20	EXPENDITURES	26,700	
	Administration	8,000	
	Reference Dept.	9,700	
	Children's Library	2,200	
	Circulation Dept.	5,100	
	Regional History	1,700	
	DUE TO FEDERAL GOVT—FICA		14,000
	DUE TO RETIREMENT AND		
	INSURANCE		6,700
	DUE TO STATE UNEMPLOYMENT		
	COMPENSATION PLAN		6,000
	Recording employer's payroll expenditures		

These employer expenditures are recorded in each of the subsidiary departmental ledger accounts. These charges are some of the additional costs of hiring an employee, above direct salary costs.

CURRENT-YEAR ENCUMBRANCES

Invoices for $32,000 were received on $30,000 of the current year's encumbrances of $33,450.[7] They were approved for payment but not immediately paid.

June 20	RESERVE FOR ENCUMBRANCES	30,000		
	ENCUMBRANCES		30,000	
	Administration			3,500
	Reference Dept.			8,000
	Children's Library			5,500
	Circulation Dept.			9,000
	Regional History			4,000
	Reversing encumbrances			

June 20	EXPENDITURES	32,000		
	Administration		3,500	
	Reference Dept.		9,000	
	Children's Library		5,500	
	Circulation Dept.		10,000	
	Regional History		4,000	
	VOUCHERS PAYABLE			32,000
	Recording current-year expenditures and recognizing them as liability			

In both the above entries for June 20, postings are made to the Appropriation-Expenditures Ledger. The first posting to the departmental account reduces the encumbrance, and the second posting records the actual expenditures. Notice that the expenditures approved for payment in the Reference and the Circulation departments are both $1,000 more than was encumbered. Before these expenditures could be approved, the Appropriation-Expenditures ledger would have to be checked to ensure that there is a sufficient departmental appropriation remaining to cover these additional expenditures. The Vouchers Payable account records the amount owed under the approved expenditures.

COLLECTION OF CASH FROM BOOK FINES AND BOOK SALES

During the 20x1 fiscal year, the library collected $2,700 in book fines and $2,800 in book sales revenues. The book sales revenues were collected by Friends of the Library. The entry to record these revenues is:

June 25	CASH	5,500		
	REVENUES		5,500	
	Book Fines			2,700
	Book Sales			2,800
	Recording collection of book fines and book sales			

PAID LIABILITIES

The library paid $32,000 of its payables:

June 25	VOUCHERS PAYABLE	32,000	
	CASH		32,000
	Recording the payment of liabilities		

Usually the Vouchers Payable account acts as a control account over the individual vendors to whom the $32,000 is owed. A subsidiary ledger is not used with this account in this illustration.

REIMBURSING PETTY CASH ACCOUNT

Many NFOs establish a Petty Cash account for small, miscellaneous expenditures such as delivery charges. When a payment is made from the Petty Cash account, a receipt and any supporting documents are placed in the fund's file, showing the reason for the expenditure and making it easy to assign the expenditures to object and program classifications. One person is usually made responsible for the Petty Cash account; if more than one person is involved in control of the account, it is difficult to assign responsibility for shortages.

The Petty Cash account should be thought of as a subdivision of the Cash account. This relationship is clearly shown in the entry by the library in initially establishing the Petty Cash account for $500:

July 4	PETTY CASH	500	
	CASH		500
	Establishing the Petty Cash account		

This entry should be made only when the account is established, and "reversed" only when the account is no longer needed. If it is decided to increase the amount in the Petty Cash account, Petty Cash is again debited and Cash is credited for the amount of the increase. Replenishment of the account does not increase the initial amount in the Petty Cash account ($500).

On December 17, the Petty Cash account was low and it was decided that the account should be replenished. Payments out of the fund were equal to $475 and the money in the Petty Cash drawer was equal to $25; so all the cash was accounted for, with no shortages in the account. If shortages had occurred, they would have to be recorded as expenditures of the period. The expenditures that were incurred, with payments from Petty Cash, should be assigned to the various departments in the subsidiary ledger in the same manner as other expenditures are handled. The entry to reimburse the Petty Cash account is a debit to Expenditures control account and a debit to the departmental accounts in the Appropriation-Expenditures subsidiary ledger. A credit is made to the Cash account, and that credit entry indicates that monies from the Cash account are being transferred into Petty Cash.

December 17	EXPENDITURES	475	
	Administration	350	
	Reference	15	
	Circulation	60	
	Regional History	50	
	CASH		475
	Reimbursing petty cash account		

INVENTORY OF SUPPLIES

The supplies inventory at the end of the year is determined through a physical count of the items in the inventory. Through this count, it is determined that there is $250 more inventory on June 30, 20x1, than there was on June 30, 20x0, the last time the inventory was counted.

If the ending inventory is more than the beginning inventory (the June 30, 20x0, ending inventory is the July 1, 20x1, beginning inventory), adjustment may be required. In this case, the inventory is not considered financially significant and no entry is made to record a prepaid inventory (asset), but the Reserve for Inventory of Supplies in the Fund Balance is increased. It needs to be increased by $250, and the Fund Balance—Undesignated is reduced by a comparable amount. As previously stated, this shows that this portion of the Fund Balance cannot be used for expenditures.

June 29	FUND BALANCE—Undesignated	250	
	RESERVE FOR INVENTORY OF SUPPLIES		250
	Recording increase in inventories and restricted reserve of fund balance		

The items in the inventory can be maintained on a departmental basis or by one person in Administration. If supplies are maintained in Administration, they are issued to the other departments on properly signed requisitions for supplies. In either case, control needs to be maintained over the supplies to prevent their unauthorized use. The best control is achieved when there is one central source for supplies, and they are not automatically distributed to departmental inventories. Control becomes more important with large stocks of inventory.

BUYING REPURCHASE AGREEMENTS

Repurchase agreements are purchased from a bank or broker for short-term investments of cash that otherwise would be idle. In a traditional repurchase agreement, the NFO provides cash to a broker or bank. In return, the broker or bank transfers securities to the NFO as collateral. At the maturity date of the transaction, the same securities are returned to the broker and the NFO receives its cash back along with an interest payment.[8]

In this example, after a period of up to three months, the bank returns the cash, with a premium. In other examples, the investments may be an overnight agreement. This is one method that can be used to invest the idle cash of the library and earn a return on it, but there is a risk of loss with these transactions.[9] The following entry illustrates the buying of the repurchase agreement:

May 1	REPURCHASE AGREEMENTS	25,000	
	CASH		25,000

Recording the investment in repurchase agreements

This transaction is interpreted as an investment (a buy and sell transaction) and not as a loan to a third party.[10] If it is known at the beginning of the year that idle cash is going to be invested in repurchase agreements, the amount of revenues expected to be received should be estimated and incorporated into the Estimated Revenues entry at the beginning of the year.

The interest premium on the repurchase agreement will be received on August 1. As a result, it will be received within 60 days of the year-end and considered part of this year's interest revenues. The entry to recognize $2,500 of interest premium received by August 30 follows:

June 30	REPURCHASE INCOME RECEIVABLE	2,500	
	INTEREST INCOME		2,500

Recording the accrual of revenues receivable on repurchase agreement

PAYING "DUE TO" ACCOUNTS

At periodic intervals during the year, the amounts owed to the federal government, the state government, and the retirement plan are paid. The H. K. Fines Library paid $18,000 owed on social security, $14,000 on federal income taxes, $10,000 on state income taxes, $3,000 on employment insurance, and the entire amount owed on the retirement and insurance plan, $6,700. The journal entry follows.

March 31	DUE TO FEDERAL GOVT—Income Taxes	14,000	
	DUE TO FEDERAL GOVT—FICA	18,000	
	DUE TO STATE GOVT—Income Taxes	10,000	
	DUE TO RETIREMENT AND INSURANCE	6,700	
	DUE TO STATE UNEMPLOYMENT		
	COMPENSATION PLAN	3,000	
	CASH		51,700

Recording payment of liabilities on payroll

RECEIPT OF UNRESTRICTED BEQUEST

The estate of Estes Parson was recently settled. In her will, Ms. Parson left $2,300 to the library to be used for the general operations of the library, without restrictions on its use. The library has been notified of the bequest, and it is awaiting the payment from the trustee bank. The entry to record the bequest in the general journal is as follows:

June 1	DUE FROM ESTATE OF E. PARSON	2,300	
	REVENUE—Contributions and Bequests		2,300
	Recording the receipt of a bequest		

The "Due from" account is a receivable, recognized on the books until the cash is actually collected from the trustee bank. The "revenue" is an item that will be recognized on the SREF as of June 30, 20x1. In some cases, this revenue may be recognized under a revenue subclassification called Other Financing Sources.

The journal entry for this type of bequest is a relatively straightforward entry, but it is not always this simple. If the library is aware of the possible receipt of a bequest, but the actual amount is unknown (because the estate has not been settled), the situation is a little more complex. In such a case, an entry cannot be made until the amount receivable from the estate is determined. Therefore, a description of the events should be made as a note to the Library's Balance Sheet. A note of this nature would resemble the following:

The estate of the late Sybil Lawrence, currently being settled, has bequeathed an 11 percent interest in such estate to the H. K. Fines Library. The exact amount of this interest is not known at the present time. Trustees for the estate have indicated that they estimate it to be between $275,000 and $550,000.

This note to the Balance Sheet provides an indication that an amount is collectible from an estate. If a range of the amount collectible can be estimated with reasonable probability, it should be stated in the note; otherwise, the amount should be omitted.

RENTALS ON EQUIPMENT

A photocopy machine has recently been rented from ABC Business Machines Company by the library. The machine is located in the administrative offices of the library, but it is available for all departments to use. A system has been established so that a department's use of the machine can be charged against that department's appropriation. This departmental charge is used to pay the rental contract. The rental charge is part of the Administration's original budget appropriation, and afterward it was assigned to departments based on usage rates. Rental on the machine is $700 a year, and the charges to the various departments are as follows: Reference Department, $202; Children's Library, $178; Circulation, $189; and Regional History, $89. The journal entries to record the signing of the contract and the transfer of monies within the departments follow.

May 1	ENCUMBRANCE		700	
	Administration			700
	RESERVE FOR ENCUMBRANCES			700
	Recording the signing of the machine rental contract			
May 10	RESERVE FOR ENCUMBRANCES		700	
	ENCUMBRANCES			700
	Administration			700
	Reversing encumbrances			
May 10	EXPENDITURES		700	
	Administration			700
	CASH			700
	Recording the receipt of the invoice			
June 30	EXPENDITURES		658	
	Reference			202
	Children's Library			178
	Circulation			189
	Regional History			89
	EXPENDITURES			658
	Administration			658
	Recording transfer of expenditures from Administration to other departments, based on usage records			

The effect of signing the rental contract is the same as the issuance of a purchase order. Even though this rental contract is not a purchase of supplies or books, it is recorded as an encumbrance at the time of the signing. This entry is shown on May 1. The May 10 entry records the reversal of the encumbrance and the recording of the expenditures; this entry occurs when the ABC Business Machines Company bills the library. Notice that the entire contract price is charged to Administration's subsidiary account because the expenditures had originally been part of Administration's appropriations.

The June 30 entry charges the various departments that have been using the photocopy machine for the copies they have run on the machine. At the same time, it reduces the charge of $700 to Administration by $658. This system has been established to control the use of the photocopier. Each department knows that it will be charged for its usage of the machine, and this knowledge (it is hoped) will help to control costs.[11] This is especially true if the machine has been used for a number of years and comparisons of usage costs can be presented to each department, illustrating the trend of costs over several periods.

LEASE PAYMENTS

Leases can be of two basic types: an "operating lease" or a "capital lease." Only the operating lease is considered here. The main difference between the operating lease and the capital lease is that the latter type is a purchase arrangement whereby the lessee assumes the risks of ownership. Unlike the capital lease, the operating lease is simply a means of allowing the lessee the right to use the property over a period of time without transferring the rights of ownership.

The H. K. Fines Library has entered into a lease for a small building as a branch library. As demand for a library in this community is uncertain, it was decided to rent building facilities rather than purchase them. The lease has been signed for a three-year period, with no rights to purchase the building at the end of that time (this is a characteristic of an operating lease). The lease payments are $6,000 for each of the first two years, and $6,700 in the third year. The first payment was made on July 31, 20x0, for a twelve-month period. At the time of payment, the following entry was made.[12]

```
20x0
July 31    RENT EXPENDITURES              6,000
               Administration                     6,000
                   CASH                                    6,000
           Recording one-year payment on lease
```

In addition to this entry, another entry restricts a portion of the Fund Balance for the amount of the unexpired lease payment at the end of the year.[13] This restriction indicates to a reader of the Balance Sheet that the amount restricted for leases is not available for appropriations. The journal entry that places this restriction in the Fund Balance is recorded as an adjusting entry on June 30:

```
June 30    FUND BALANCE—Undesignated         500
               RESERVE FOR LEASES                     500
           Recording a restriction or reserve of the Undesignated Fund Balance
```

COLLECTION OF RECEIVABLES

The H. K. Fines Library collected several receivables during the 20x1 fiscal year for $23,200: a state grant for $16,000 and pledges for $7,200. The entry to record these collections is as follows:

```
August 10    CASH                               23,200
                 STATE GRANT RECEIVABLE              16,000
                 PLEDGES RECEIVABLE                    7,200
             Recording the collection of receivables
```

As shown on the library's Balance Sheet in figure 6-3, the pledges receivable are recorded at their net amount. This means that the pledges are recorded at the amount that is actually expected to be collected, even if that amount is different from the amount initially pledged. The initial entry to record the pledges, along with the uncollectible amount, was recorded in the entry:

PLEDGES RECEIVABLE	8,000	
PLEDGE REVENUE		7,200
ESTIMATED UNCOLLECTIBLE PLEDGES		800

Recording the receivable on pledges

The amount on the 20x0 Balance Sheet in figure 6-3, $7,200, is shown net of the $800, which is expected to be uncollectible. From past experience, it is anticipated that 10 percent, or $800, of the pledges will not be collected. The uncollectible portion should not be allowed to increase revenues or influence estimated revenues; and without the credit to the Estimated Uncollectible Pledges account, an increase in revenues and estimated revenues would be based on a gross rather than a net forecast. As a specific pledge becomes uncollectible, it is written off as a receivable and the Estimated Uncollectible Pledges account is debited in the following manner.

ESTIMATED UNCOLLECTIBLE PLEDGE	xxx	
PLEDGES RECEIVABLE		xxx

Writing off an uncollectible pledge

In a subsidiary ledger, or as information supplemental to the accounting records, the actual names of the individual uncollectible pledges also are written off. If, at the end of the year, there is a balance in the Estimated Uncollectible Pledges account, it means that the amount estimated to be uncollectible is different from the actual amount written off. Furthermore, it means that the rate used to estimate uncollectible accounts, 10 percent, may have to be changed. There are two ways to adjust for this difference, depending on whether the pledge process is a yearly event or a less-than-yearly program.

If the pledge process occurs less frequently than once a year, the Estimated Uncollectible Pledges credit balance should be closed to the Pledge Revenue account. The credit balance means that the uncollectible pledges (written off) were less than the amount estimated. If the pledge process occurs with less frequency than every year and a *debit* balance exists in the Estimated Uncollectible Pledges account, the balance should be closed to an expenditures account, such as Uncollectible Pledges Expenditures, or to Pledge Revenue. A debit balance in the Estimated Uncollectible Pledges account means that there were more uncollectible pledges during the year than had been estimated. These situations are illustrated in the two following journal entries.

ESTIMATED UNCOLLECTIBLE PLEDGES   xxx
    PLEDGE REVENUE   xxx

Closing credit balance in Estimated Uncollectible Pledge account to
revenue account

UNCOLLECTIBLE PLEDGE EXPENDITURES   xxx
    ESTIMATED UNCOLLECTIBLE PLEDGES   xxx

Closing debit balance in Estimated Uncollectible Pledge account to an
expense account

If the seeking of pledges by an NFO is a yearly event, the debit or credit balance in Estimated Uncollectible Pledges is handled in a different manner. Regardless of a debit or credit balance in the account, the account is brought up to the 10 percent uncollectible balance that should exist in the Estimated Uncollectible Pledge account after the pledge period is over. For example, if the pledges receivable after the pledge period are equal to $1,000 and the uncollectible rate is still 10 percent, there should be a $100 balance in the Estimated Uncollectible Pledges account. If there is a $100 balance in the account, no entry needs to be made. If there is a $300 credit balance in the account, an entry is required to change the $300 credit balance to a $100 credit balance. The entry to record the proper amount in the uncollectible account when there is already a $300 credit balance in the account is as follows:

ESTIMATED UNCOLLECTIBLE PLEDGES   300
    PLEDGE REVENUE   300

Closing uncollectible pledges to revenue account

PLEDGES RECEIVABLE   1,000
    ESTIMATED UNCOLLECTIBLE PLEDGES   100
    PLEDGE REVENUE   900

Recording current year's pledges

The effect of these journal entries is a kind of "catch-up" adjustment because in the prior year the pledges that were written off were not equal to the estimated amount; that is, actually written-off pledges were less than the amount estimated to be uncollectible. Therefore, the Estimated Uncollectible Pledges account had a credit balance. This credit balance is reduced, and the net effect is that a total of $1,200 in pledge revenues is recognized.[14]

If the Estimated Uncollectible Pledge account had a debit balance of $200, the adjustment would be just the opposite of that described above. The reason for a $200 debit balance is that more pledges were written off as uncollectible than had been estimated to be uncollectible in the prior year. Again, if $1,000 in pledges is receivable in the current year and uncollectibility is estimated at 10 percent, there should be a $100 credit balance in the Estimated

Uncollectible Pledges account. The following entries are necessary journal adjustments for a $100 credit balance to exist in the account:

PLEDGE REVENUE	200	
ESTIMATED UNCOLLECTIBLE PLEDGES		200

Closing uncollectible account to revenue account

PLEDGES RECEIVABLE	1,000	
ESTIMATED UNCOLLECTIBLE PLEDGES		100
PLEDGE REVENUE		900

Recording current year's pledges

In every case, it is important to make the best possible estimate of uncollectible pledges because a difference between the amount that is estimated and the amount that actually becomes uncollectible may mean that the revenues estimated for the period are either under- or overstated.

A final point about pledges is related to the period in which the pledge revenue should be recognized. If a donor had designated a portion of his or her pledge for the NFO's use in the subsequent year, the portion of the pledge designated for the subsequent year should not be recognized as revenue until it is available for use. Until it is recognized as revenue, it is recognized in the accounts as a deferred revenue, which is a liability.

MISCELLANEOUS ENTRIES

The outstanding balance in the Vouchers Payable account in the Fines Library's Balance Sheet (figure 6-3) is reduced with a cash payment of $10,375. In addition to this transaction, cash of $8,000 was received from photocopying revenues during the year. Both of these transactions are recorded in the accounts as follows:

July 21	VOUCHERS PAYABLE	10,375	
	CASH		10,375

Recording cash payment on Accounts Payable

June 29	CASH	8,000	
	REVENUE		8,000
	Photocopying Revenue		8,000

Recording photocopying revenue for year

In addition to these two entries, a final entry in the unrestricted account group relates to action the board took during the year. The board removed the $4,945 portion of the Fund Balance that was designated for the purchase of office equipment. Originally, this portion of the Fund Balance had been designated for the purchase of certain office equipment, including a new copy machine, but this equipment was donated to the library by a local office equipment manufacturer. Accounting for an equipment donation does not affect the General Fund, and this type of transaction is discussed in a later chapter.

The board of directors has a right to designate a portion of the Fund Balance for specified purposes. This is a discretionary type of restriction and not a legal one; therefore, the monies can be transferred back to the unrestricted portion of the Fund Balance by board action. The entry to record this transfer back to the unrestricted portion of the Fund Balance is as follows:

June 30	FUND BALANCE—Designated	4,945	
	FUND BALANCE—Undesignated		4,945

Transferring the designated portion of the Fund Balance back into the undesignated portion

This entry closes the Designated Fund Balance for the purchase of office equipment and transfers $4,945 back into the undesignated portion of the Fund Balance account. This transfer makes an additional $4,945 available for use in the general operations of the library through additional appropriations.

EXERCISE 7-1   The General Fund

1. The Sexton Library has just ended its 20x7 fiscal year, on June 30. The bookkeeper is uncertain how to handle several transactions and has come to you, as director of the library, to ask your advice on handling these transactions. Tell the bookkeeper how the following transactions should be recorded in the books.

   a. There were prior-year encumbrances from the previous year for $15,200 that had not been reversed. Invoices had been received for $14,700. These invoices had been approved and paid. They represented $14,000 of issued purchase orders from the previous year. The remainder of the previous year's outstanding purchase orders had not been filled or canceled as of the end of the 20x7 fiscal year. Assuming that the entries at the end of the previous fiscal year had been properly made, but no entries had been made relating to these transactions during the 20x7 fiscal year, journalize the proper journal entries.

   b. The Petty Cash Fund, which was established with a $400 balance, needs to be replenished. The receipts and supporting documents showed $315 had been used for expenditures from the monies in the fund. At the present time, there is $75 in cash in the fund.

   c. The lease that the library entered into on a yearly basis, beginning December 1, 20x6, is renewable for each of the next three years at $3,600. Record the correct entry for June 30, 20x7.

d. During March, April, and May, a pledge campaign was conducted. This is a yearly campaign for funds. Pledges had been received for $7,500 at the end of the pledge period, and a 5 percent uncollectability rate exists for pledges. Record the proper entry as of June 30, 20x7. As of that date, it is known that $120 of these pledges is uncollectible.

e. The board has decided to designate $9,000 of the Fund Balance for the purchase of a van. The board's action has not been recorded in the books. If an entry is necessary, record it.

SPECIAL REVENUE—STATE GRANT PROGRAM

Under this state grant program, $15,000 is to be received to provide expenditure support for a program to bring reading materials to handicapped individuals who are unable to use the library's facilities. The grant was awarded on June 18, but the monies receivable under the grant have not yet been received. Before receipt of the monies, the library expended $7,500 of cash from the General Fund's resources for purposes which would qualify under the grant. These expenditures were made in anticipation of receiving the grant and to allow the program to start prior to the actual receipt of the monies. The entries to record these payments are the following:

General Fund

June 10	EXPENDITURES	7,500		
	Administration		7,500	
	VOUCHERS			7,500
	Invoice is approved for payment			
June 13	VOUCHERS PAYABLE	7,500		
	CASH			7,500
	Recording payment of invoice			

The June 10 and 13 entries record the expenditures incurred before receipt of the grant. The monies expended were taken from the General Fund's Cash account, and are reimbursable to the General Fund from the Special Revenue Fund after the grant is received. The General Fund is reimbursed for an expenditure it made for the Special Revenue Fund. On June 18, when it is learned that the grant has been awarded, the entry in the General Fund should recognize a receivable from the Special Revenue Fund and a reduction in expenditures. The entry is:

General Fund

June 18	DUE FROM SPECIAL REVENUE FUND	7,500	
	EXPENDITURES		7,500
	Administration		7,500

Recording a receivable from the restricted account group

Usually monetary transfers between funds are recorded in "Transfer to" or "Transfer from" accounts, but in the case of reimbursable expenditures, the expenditures must be recorded in the accounts. Also, this expenditure must be a charge against the proper fund. When cash is transferred from the reimbursing fund to the reimbursable fund (General Fund), or a receivable is recognized in the fund to be reimbursed, the expenditures in the reimbursable fund should be reduced. The entry on June 18 is such an entry, and it records a receivable and a reduction in the expenditures of the General Fund.

Shortly after the June 18 notice of the award is received, the Special Revenue Fund—State Grant recognizes an expenditure and a liability to the General Fund with the following entry:

Special Revenue—State Grant

June 20	EXPENDITURES	7,500	
	State Grant—Handicapped Services		7,500
	DUE TO GENERAL FUND—		
	Reimbursement		7,500

Recording the increase of expenditures previously incurred

This June 20 entry records $7,500 of previously incurred expenditures in the Special Revenue Fund where the state grant will be used. The liability and receivable between the two account groups will be canceled when cash is transferred from the Special Revenue Fund's Cash account to the General Fund's Cash account.

As previously stated, on June 18 the library received notice that it had been awarded the grant from the state, and the following entry is made in the Special Revenue Fund on June 20:

Special Revenue—State Grant

June 20	STATE GRANT RECEIVABLE	15,000	
	DEFERRED RESTRICTED CON-		
	TRIBUTIONS—Grant		15,000

Recording liability under grant

June 20	DEFERRED RESTRICTED		
	CONTRIBUTIONS—Grant	7,500	
	REVENUE—State Grant		7,500

Recognizing support equal to amount previously expended

The first entry on June 20 records the receivable from the state. The second entry recognizes as earned support the amount that had already been expended on the handicapped program out of the General Fund's monies on June 15 and recorded as an expenditure in the Special Revenue Fund on June 20. It is proper to record the reduction of a liability such as Deferred Restricted Contributions when money has been expended for the specific purposes of the grant before receipt of the grant. This is especially true when the expenditures are made in anticipation of receipt of the grant.

Receipt of the grant monies on June 28 requires the write-off of the receivable from the state and recognition of an increase in cash:

Special Revenue—State Grant

June 28	CASH	15,000	
	STATE GRANT RECEIVABLE		15,000
	Recording the receipt of state grant monies		

SUMMARY

This chapter has presented an overview of typical entries in the General and Special Revenue Funds. Some of these entries were highlighted in earlier chapters, but additional explanation of these entries, as well as the ones that were introduced for the first time, is helpful to the reader in understanding these funds. The importance of the General Fund and Special Revenue Funds cannot be overemphasized as the majority of journal entries in an NFO occur in these funds. Additional illustrations are provided in the appendix to this chapter, where the 20x0 financial statements for the H. K. Fines Library are brought up-to-date by incorporating the *dated* entries (only) in this chapter.

Finally, it should be noted that in order for accounting information to serve its intended purpose of helping managers make decisions, it must be provided on a timely basis. In some cases, reporting lags far behind the point where a decision must be made.

From the Library Desk: Our main problem is lack of timely information. It is now 24 July, for example, and the most recent information I have from accounting is from March. And we thought automation would facilitate the process!

Anonymous survey respondent

EXERCISE 7-2   The Special Revenue Fund

1. On June 19, 20x5, notice was received that a $2,000 federal grant had been awarded to the Morganville Library, but as of June 30, 20x5, the year-end, it had not been received. The grant was awarded for the purchase of ethnic materials for the Regional History Collection. In anticipation of receiving the grant, a $500 purchase had been authorized and paid for out of Regional History monies on June 10, 20x5. Record in general-journal form the correct entries between the General Fund and the Special Revenue Fund—Regional History.

2. Prepare the trial balance for the Special Revenue Fund in this chapter for the period ending June 30, 20x1.

APPENDIX: THE FINANCIAL STATEMENTS

The financial statements for the H. K. Fines Library have been prepared for the fiscal year ending June 30, 20x1, using all the dated transactions in this chapter, and the financial statements prepared in figures 6-2 through 6-4, as well as the Notes to the Financial Statements in figure 6-5. It is recommended that T accounts be opened for the accounts in the financial statements for the period ending June 30, 20x1, and the dated entries from this chapter be posted to these T accounts. A trial balance of the balances in these T accounts should be taken before the financial statements are prepared.

Libraries that are part of a city or state government, as is the H. K. Fines Library, are considered to be component units of the primary government, i.e., state, city, etc. As such, the financial statements of the H. K. Fines Library will appear in the city's or state's comprehensive annual financial report (CAFR). As a library's financial statements may be considered of secondary importance to a city or county manager, these abbreviated financial reports may be limited in usefulness to the library manager. At any rate, there are likely to be variations in the manner in which a city's component units are reported. The library's financial statements may be presented as a totally separate set of financial statements distinct from the CAFR, but this situation would be unlikely in most cases. In other cases, a library may be considered a Special Revenue Fund rather than a component unit, and consequently the financial reports would be more limited.

In this case, the following financial statements for the H. K. Fines Library are assumed to appear as separate statements within the primary government's CAFR. Although the library itself may have a different set of its financial reports available for use within the library, official statements are issued as part of the CAFR.

After the statement shown in Figure 7A-1 is completed, the following closing entries are made. For understanding the progression of the financial statements, it is better to make these entries at this time.

**FIGURE 7A-1   Combined Statement of Revenues, Expenditures, and Changes
in Fund Balance**

H. K. FINES LIBRARY
Combined Statement of Revenues, Expenditures, and Changes in Fund Balance
For the Year Ended June 30, 20x1

	General Fund	Special Revenue	Memo Totals
Revenue:			
Intergovernmental	$173,500	—	$173,500
Interest Income	2,500	—	2,500
State Grant	—	$7,500	7,500
Contributions and Bequests	2,300	—	2,300
Total Revenue	$178,300	$7,500	$185,800
Expenditures (Note 4):			
Program Services:			
Reference	$ 37,617	—	$ 37,617
Children's Library	35,878	—	35,878
Circulation	40,549	—	40,549
Regional History	13,839	—	13,839
Handicapped Services	—	$7,500	7,500
Total Program Services	$127,883	$7,500	$135,383
Supporting Services Administration	$ 37,892	—	$ 37,892
Total Expenditures	$165,775	$7,500	$173,275
Excess (Deficiency) of Revenue over Expenditures	$ 12,525	—	$ 12,525
Fund Balance at Beginning of Year	51,575	—	51,575
Fund Balance at End of Year	$ 64,100	—	$ 64,100

June 30	FUND BALANCE Undesignated	12,525	
	REVENUES	178,300	
	Intergovernmental:		
	City of Fines	68,000	
	Backlog County	66,000	
	State Grant	26,000	
	Interest Income	2,500	
	Contributions and Bequests	2,300	
	Book Fines	2,700	
	Book Sales	2,800	
	Photocopying	8,000	
	EXPENDITURES		165,775
	Reference		37,617
	Children's Library		35,878
	Circulation		40,549
	Regional History		13,839
	Administration		37,892

Recording the closing of expenditures and revenues for the fiscal year 20x1

June 30   FUND BALANCE—Undesignated   8,950
           APPROPRIATIONS   168,000
               ESTIMATED REVENUES   173,500
               ENCUMBRANCES   3,450
                   Administration   3,450

           Recording the closing of the budgetary entries and the outstanding
           encumbrances for the fiscal year 20x1

In reviewing the H. K. Fines Library's financial statements in Figures 7A-1, 7A-2, and 7A-3, several factors should be clear. First, these financial statements are combined statements and as such, they do not eliminate interfund transactions. Furthermore, combined statements such as these are unlikely to be issued to the public as part of the government's CAFR by the government of which the library is a component part. Instead the component unit's financial statements are found in a column within the primary government's financial statements, possibly aggregated with the financials data on other component units. Yet the information in these three separate statements is very useful for library managers and others who are trying to determine the financial condition of the library. From this perspective, Figure 7A-1 shows how the excess or deficit changed the Fund Balance for the year. Figure 7A-2 can be used to analyze the relationship between the library's assets and liabilities as well as determining the availability of new appropriations in the Fund Balance. Figure 7A-3 shows how effectively budget guidelines were followed.

Administration transferred $658 of photocopying costs to the other departments in the library by making them pay a usage charge. This method may not be effective in controlling the efficiency of use, but it is effective in reducing the expenditures charged to Administration during the year. Without those additional charges, Reference and Circulation would have lower unfavorable variances on the above schedule. Librarians should be aware of whether the charges made to their departments increase the efficiency of the library's overall operations or if these charges are simply being used to transfer expenditures away from one department to another.

The note shown in figure 7A-4 incorporates the necessary changes that have occurred during the fiscal year only. It would appear as an addition to the notes shown in figure 6-5.

NOTES

1. Allotments and detailed control of spending below the general NFO appropriations fit into a traditional management style that closely controls the decision making of professional managers, but these methods do not fit well with more empowered management styles.

2. There must also be at least $7,000 of cash available in the Cash account for this to occur.

FIGURE 7A-2 Combined Balance Sheet for the General Fund and Special Revenue Fund

H. K. FINES LIBRARY
Combined Balance Sheet—General Fund and Special Revenue Fund
June 30, 20x1

	General	Special Revenue	Memo Totals
Assets:			
Cash, including interest bearing			
savings account	$17,550	$29,700	$ 47,250
Petty Cash	500	—	500
Repurchase Agreement	25,000	—	25,000
Repurchase Premium Receivable	2,500	—	2,500
Due from Special Revenue—State Grant	7,500	—	7,500
Due from Estate of E. Parson	2,300	—	2,300
Investments (Note 2)	23,750	—	23,750
Total Assets	$79,100	$29,700	$108,800
Liabilities and Fund Balance:			
Vouchers Payable:	$ 2,000	—	$ 2,000
Due to State Unemployment	3,000	—	3,000
Due to Federal Government—FICA	10,000	—	10,000
Due to General Fund—reimbursement	—	$ 7,500	7,500
Deferred Revenue (Note 3)	—	22,200	$ 22,200
Total Current Liabilities	$15,000	$29,700	$ 44,700
Fund Balance:			
Reserved for:			
Encumbrances	$ 3,450	—	$ 3,450
Inventory	7,000	—	7,000
Leases	500	—	500
Employee Retirement	4,945	—	4,945
Unreserved:			
Designated by Board	12,055	—	12,055
Undesignated	36,150	—	36,150
Total Fund Balance	$64,100	—	$ 64,100
Total Liabilities and Fund Balance	$79,100	$29,700	$108,800

3. There are strict quarterly payment guidelines that must be met by the employer for the payment of federal and state payroll deductions. The 1998 schedules for FICA and Medicare taxes were as follows: (1) Medicare taxes are 1.45 percent of all employee's wages earned; (2) social security tax is 6.2 percent on the first $68,400 of wages earned (or $4,240.80). The upper limit of wages taxed under social security continues to increase and raise the taxes paid by both the employer and employee.

FIGURE 7A-3   Statement of Revenues, Expenditures, and Changes in Fund Balance—Budget and Actual (Non-GAAP)

H. K. FINES LIBRARY
Statement of Revenues, Expenditures, and Changes in Fund Balance—
Budget and Actual (Non-GAAP)
For the Year Ended June 30, 20x1

	Budget	Actual	Variance, Favorable (Unfavorable)
Revenues:			
City of Fines	$ 68,000	$ 68,000	—
Backlog County	66,000	66,000	—
State Grant	26,000	26,000	—
Contributions and Bequests	—	2,300	$ 2,300
Book Fines	2,500	2,700	200
Book Sales	3,000	2,800	(200)
Interest Income	—	2,500	2,500
Photocopying	8,000	8,000	—
Total Revenues	$173,500	$178,300	$ 4,800
Expenditures:			
Reference	$ 33,500	$ 37,617	$(4,117)
Children's Library	37,000	35,878	1,122
Circulation	38,500	40,549	(2,049)
Regional Library	14,000	13,839	161
Administration	45,000	41,342	3,658
Total Expenditures	$168,000	$169,225	$(1,225)
Revenues over (under) Expenditures	$ 5,500	$ 9,075	$ 3,575
Fund Balance, July 1		$ 51,575	
Fund Balance, June 30		$ 60,650	

FIGURE 7A-4   Additional Note to the Financial Statements

NOTE 4. Current-Year Expenditures on Prior-Year Encumbrances

The amount encumbered at the end of the 20x0 fiscal year was $11,700. During the fiscal year ending June 30, 20x1, expenditures on these encumbrances totaled $11,900.

4. Service billings by one government agency against another is a common method to raise the resources for the billing unit and change restricted funding into discretionary monies.

5. In most payroll accounting, a separate Cash account is established for the payroll checks. All payroll checks are then cleared through this one account. After all payroll checks have been cashed by the employees, the balance in this account should be zero.

6. In order to avoid year-end payroll liabilities, the last payroll period for the year usually ends on June 30—the year-end. Even so, there may be wages owed to other than regular employees at the end of the year.

7. This means $33,450 was initially encumbered. On $30,000 of those encumbrances, bills for $32,000 have been received.

8. Reverse repurchase agreements occur when the government gives its securities as collateral for a loan and promises to repay cash and interest at the maturity date of the loan or repurchase date. Sometimes these transactions may return different securities from those in the original agreement. Reverse repurchase agreements create a liability for the library whereas repurchase agreements are an asset.

9. There are several steps to take to safeguard these investments. One important step is to be certain that the other party to the agreement is a financial institution or SEC-registered broker-dealer. These institutions are subject to strict regulatory oversight. Of course, if no securities are transferred, the NFO has agreed to an unsecured loan (or investment).

10. There is disagreement as to whether a repurchase agreement is an investment or a loan transaction.

11. The department needs a continuing tally of its charges throughout the year; otherwise, this expenditure may result in overexpending of a department's budget appropriations for an item such as current expenditures at the year-end.

12. Usually, prepaid amounts are not recorded under MAM.

13. The monthly rental is $500, and for the 20x1 period of eleven months, this is equal to a rental expenditure of $5,500. The remaining $500 of the rental fee that was paid in advance becomes a reserve of the Fund Balance.

14. This entry could also be recorded as follows, just as long as $1,200 in pledge revenue is recognized at the time the transaction is recorded.

PLEDGES RECEIVABLE	1,000	
PLEDGE REVENUE		1,000

Recording current year's pledges

ESTIMATED UNCOLLECTIBLE PLEDGES	200	
PLEDGE REVENUE		200

Adjusting Estimated Uncollectible Pledge account to the proper balance of $100

8

The Capital Projects Fund and the General Fixed Assets Account Group

THIS CHAPTER EXPLAINS HOW the Capital Projects Fund and the General Fixed Assets Account Group are used within a library. The Capital Projects Fund (CPF) is used when a library is constructing a new physical facility as for example a new building or annex. All appropriations and other funding available for the construction project are accounted for in the CPF.[1] Separate CPFs are established for each construction project and the funding designated for those projects. Only after the project is completed is the CPF closed. As a result, there may be no year-end closing entries for project appropriations until the project is finished.

The General Fixed Assets Account Group (GFAAG) is similar to a fund but it is an account group because it has no appropriation purpose. The GFAAG is established for the purpose of keeping records about the NFO's fixed assets.[2] Fixed assets include land, buildings, fixtures, machinery, furniture, some property improvements, and equipment.[3] In addition, construction-in-progress and leases used to purchase fixed assets are included in the GFAAG. Infrastructure assets such as curbs, sidewalks, and lighting systems are only optionally recorded in the books, and thus they are not usually recorded anywhere. In NFOs, when a building under construction is completed

178

its valuation is transferred to the GFAAG. Therefore, the CPF and the GFAAG are considered together in this chapter.

THE CAPITAL PROJECTS FUND

An NFO's largest fixed asset is usually the building it occupies. This asset may be acquired through purchase or by having it constructed either by government workers or by a private contractor. It may also be acquired through a lease purchase agreement between the NFO and the contractor. There are many variations on a lease arrangement with a for-profit contractor that allow the NFO to use its nonprofit status to reduce the tax liability to the contractor and thus save on construction costs.[4]

The funding for the library's capital project usually begins with the issuance of bonds, operating and residual equity transfers to the CPF from other funds, and grants from private donors or other government agencies. The CPF is established to demonstrate the manner in which these funds are expended. Such funding does not lapse at the end of the fiscal year as is typical of the General Fund.

There are a number of costs beyond the cost of materials and labor incurred in the construction of a building such as overhead charges, cost of capital used in the construction, and interest charges on the debt incurred to finance the project.[5] These charges may or may not be incorporated into the cost of the project.

Overhead charges are those costs that cannot be directly traced to the project such as general governmental clerical and administrative costs. These costs may or may not be charged against the construction project. If the project is funded entirely by the primary government, there is no advantage to charging overhead costs to the project. On the other hand, if the project is funded by an outside agency, these overhead charges should be reimbursed by the funding agency and therefore appear as a cost of the project. As a result, it would be expected that an internally funded building would cost less than an externally funded building with the same square footage and characteristics. The overhead charged to a library often appears as a management service fee calculated as a percentage of construction costs incurred. This service fee may be paid to the General Fund.

Cost of capital is the cost of using the organization's resources. This charge may be implemented to ensure that all managers in the NFO realize that the use of capital (resources) is not free. Since repayment of interest and principal on the incurred debt is not recorded in the library's accounting records, it may appear that capital resources are free.[6] Once cost of capital charges is instituted as a charge within budget lines against all the capital resources invested in buildings, equipment, and other fixed assets, it becomes apparent the cost of using capital is not free.[7]

Another cost in the construction of a fixed asset such as a building is the interest paid to bondholders for the use of their monetary resources to finance the construction. In most cases, these costs are not part of the cost of the new construction although the only reason they were incurred was because these monies are needed to finance the construction project.[8] Again, this makes it appear in the records that the new fixed asset is less costly than the full costs incurred to build it. This can also lead to misinterpretation of financial comparisons among different NFOs and governments.

GETTING THE FINANCING

The financing for a project can come from intergovernmental transfers and the incurrence of new debt. It is assumed that the Fines Library cannot incur its own debt and the primary government of which the library is a part must incur the debt and than transfer the funding to the library for the construction of a new building. Therefore, all funding for the project is essentially composed of intergovernmental transfers. The $750,000 transfer comes from the City of Fines through the issuance of new debt that had been approved through a tax referendum. Additional funding is available from state and federal government grants. All these transfers are recognized within the CPF. The state and federal grants go directly to the library.

```
20x0
July 1    DUE FROM THE GOVERNMENTS    950,000
              General Fund                           750,000
              State Grant                            100,000
              Federal Grant                          100,000
                  REVENUES                                      200,000
                  OTHER FINANCING SOURCES—General Fund         750,000
          Recognizing the receivables from various governmental sources
```

In this entry, the money transferred from the City of Fines' General Fund is an "other financing source" rather than revenue. These transfers are reported as Other Financing Sources because monies are not from operations but from a debt issuance where the liability is reported in a fund other than CPF.

In some cases, the transfer of monies to the Fines Library from the General Fund may be delayed or they may be transferred in installments to the library for payments to be made to the contractors. Here, it is assumed that the library maintains its own CPF, and payments are made to the library as the contractor bills the library.[9] Payments to the library may be delayed for a variety of reasons. For example, the state and federal grants may require the completion of paperwork and need various approvals before the monies are transferred. The city may invest the monies received from selling debt into cash-generating investments that pay a higher return than the interest paid out on the new debt issue.[10] Consequently, the city is not anxious to pass these monies on to the library. At this point, it should be noted that if the bonds are sold at a premium the additional monies received cannot be used for construction. These monies are used for debt repayment. Unfortunately, if the debt is sold at a discount, the reduced funding for the construction project must be made up from other sources or the size of the project is reduced.[11]

As it is important to start the project as soon as possible, the library may seek short-term financing to start the project.[12] Here, it will be assumed that the project's funding was received from all governments in time to start the project.

Once the funding is received the following entry is recorded. This entry shows that $200,000 from the two grants was actually received. It also shows that the monies from the General Fund are in a form of a draw-down cash allotment. An allotment means the library requests installments of the cash from the city as it is needed. The city is earning interest income on the library's monies so it requires the library to follow this procedure.

July 15	CASH	200,000	
	CASH ALLOTMENT	750,000	
	DUE FROM THE GOVERNMENTS		950,000
	General Fund		750,000
	State Grant		100,000
	Federal Grant		100,000

Recording the receipt of the funding for the capital construction project

BEGINNING THE CONSTRUCTION PROJECT

The building is to be constructed for $750,000 by a private contractor, ABC Contractors, and the following entries will illustrate the transactions that occur in that construction process. The city's workers also have a role in the completion of the project, and materials and supplies will be provided for the new building by the city. The city will receive $200,000 for its support.

In a large construction project, it is necessary to establish spending guidelines for the private contractor. These guidelines help ensure that the monies are being properly spent. Figure 8-1 provides an example of such a document called an Application and Certification for Payment. The budgeted values and items of work are listed in columns 1 and 2. These are amounts that are agreed upon by the contractor and the Fines Library. As the project will take a year to complete, the contractor will periodically submit the application as a means to receive progress payments for the work completed up to the date of application. Currently, the construction has not started, and there are no dollar amounts shown under "Work Completed." The items of work in Figure 8-1 include charges for landscaping, provision of dumpsters to remove construction trash, building insurance, general labor, a contractor's fee, and rentals for various types of equipment. All these costs would have been negotiated with ABC Contractors.

Under this system, if a change in the agreed upon work is needed, it will require a formal Change of Order Form, and this change will be reflected in the application as an increase, decrease, or transfer of monies among the cost lines in Figure 8-1. A Change of Order Form is a document signed by the contractor and the library's representative indicating the cost of the change, the specific nature of the change, approximately when it will be made, and the effect on the overall cost of the project. This is a formal legal document.

Although it may appear that library personnel have many other duties to perform, the specialized nature of most new libraries requires that library personnel be closely involved in the construction process. Library personnel should note if changes need to be made and whether current construction is being satisfactorily performed. Leaving the oversight functions to others outside the library will not necessarily ensure that the new facility is properly constructed.

Further, if the tracking and review of the construction of the building are carried out by the primary government, i.e., the City of Fines, a service fee may be incurred. The charge for providing these services would be deducted from the funding available for the construction of the library building. A fee of this nature might be equal to 1 percent of all construction costs including those supplies, materials, and labor provided by the city.[13] In our example, the City of Fines charges a service fee of 1 percent of construction costs or $9,500 (.01 × $950,000). This fee will be deducted from construction monies available, and as a result, the number of computers installed in the library's new building for public use will be reduced.

The journal entry that supports the signing of the contract with ABC Contractors and the providing of supplies, materials, and miscellaneous labor from the city follows:

July 10	ENCUMBRANCES	950,000		
	ABC Contractors		750,000	
	City of Fines		200,000	
	RESERVE FOR ENCUMBRANCES		950,000	
	ABC Contractors			750,000
	City of Fines			200,000

Recording the signing of the contract and the encumbrances with the City of Fines and ABC Contractors

It is anticipated that all monies will be used for the project. If the entire $950,000 is not used, unused monies will be transferred out of the CPF to help

FIGURE 8-1 Certification for Payment for a Construction Budget

Application and Certification for Payment

Application Date:
Period From: To:

Item of Work	Budgeted Value	Work Completed			Total Completed to Date	Percentage of Completion	Retainage
		Previous Expenditures	Work in Progress				
			Work in Progress	Stored Materials			
Supervision	$ 28,000.00						
General Labor	35,000.00						
Bldg Mat. Allowance	172,000.00						
Rentals	7,000.00						
Landscape Allowance	13,000.00						
Dumpsters	4,000.00						
Temporary Facilities	1,500.00						
Retaining Wall	5,000.00						
Carpentry Material	7,000.00						
Metal	6,000.00						
Handicap Ramp	8,000.00						
Electrical	80,000.00						
Roof	50,000.00						
Sidewalks	12,000.00						
Base and Carpet	15,000.00						
Painting	31,000.00						
Duct Work	20,000.00						
Drywall	9,000.00						
Miniblinds	3,500.00						
Cleaning Labor	5,500.00						
Plumbing Allowance	112,000.00						
Contractor Fee	10,000.00						
Insurance and Bond	15,600.00						
Total Contract Price	$750,000.00						

pay off the bonds issued by the city to finance the project. Although it is unlikely that the funds would not be used in their entirety, it could occur. If it did, a question arises as to whether prorated portions of the grants should be returned to the state and federal government. For example, if 95,000 (or 10 percent) of the total funding was not used should 10 percent of the state and federal grants be returned? Unless the grants are specifically written to provide for this contingency, it is unlikely that monies will be returned to the granting agencies.

INCURRING EXPENDITURES IN THE CONSTRUCTION OF THE BUILDING

As the construction of the building starts, ABC Contractors begin to submit certifications of work progress and requests for progress payments. Figure 8-2 provides an example of the certificate submitted on September 30, 20x0. The Certification is submitted with supporting invoices. The invoices and other billings are reviewed to ensure that they are valid and reasonable charges. After the invoices are checked, the percentages of completion are reviewed to determine that these percentages are reasonable and correctly computed. The percentages show the level of total budgeted amounts that have been expended. For example, with Supervision, 25 percent of the total budgeted value of $28,000 has been spent. In the case of Supervision, the level of expenditures should be closely related to the overall construction completed. As the building is 30 percent completed (see totals in figure 8-2), it is reasonable to pay 25 percent of the requested supervision charges. Once approved, the Certification charges are used to record the proper journal entries. The Certification in figure 8-2 indicates that this is the first request for payment from the contractor since the work started on the building. For this reason, there are no dollar amounts in the column headed "Previous Expenditures."

The totals at the bottom of the Certification provide the information to record the journal entries in the ledger. The total cost of construction completed to date is $226,600. This includes materials purchased and placed on site. Obviously, not all these materials are incorporated into the new building itself. It is prudent not to pay for materials until they are physically incorporated into the structure of the building as they could be destroyed or stolen. As such, these amounts become a retainage for the H. K. Fines Library. A retainage is the amount of billings that are purposely withheld from payment by the library. This amount is shown as $120,000 in figure 8-2. The $120,000 of retainage is related to the $181,000 of materials stored on the construction site. Out of the $226,600 of completed work, a check for $106,000 will be sent to the contractor, and the remainder is recognized as a retained amount payable to the contractor.

FIGURE 8-2 Certification for Payment on Work Completed to Date

Application and Certification for Payment

Application Date: September 30, 20x0
Period From: July 1   To: September 30, 20x0

Item of Work	Budgeted Value	Work Completed Previous Expenditures	Work in Progress	Stored Materials	Total Completed to Date	Percentage of Completion	Retainage
Supervision	$ 28,000.00		$ 7,000.00		$ 7,000.00	25%	
General Labor	35,000.00		5,000.00		5,000.00	14	$100,000.00
Bldg Mat. Allowance	172,000.00		—	$150,000.00	150,000.00	87	
Rentals	7,000.00		1,000.00		1,000.00	—	
Landscape Allowance	13,000.00		—		—	14	
Dumpsters	4,000.00		1,500.00		1,500.00	38	
Temporary Facilities	1,500.00		500.00		500.00	33	
Retaining Wall	5,000.00		—		—	—	
Carpentry Material	7,000.00		3,000.00		3,000.00	43	
Metal	6,000.00		—	6,000.00	6,000.00	100	6,000.00
Handicap Ramp	8,000.00		—		—	—	
Electrical	80,000.00		2,000.00		2,000.00	3	
Roof	50,000.00		—		—	—	
Sidewalks	12,000.00		—		—	—	
Base and Carpet	15,000.00		—		—	—	
Painting	31,000.00		—		—	—	
Duct Work	20,000.00		—		—	—	
Drywall	9,000.00		—		—	—	
Miniblinds	3,500.00		—		—	—	
Cleaning Labor	5,500.00		—		—	—	
Plumbing Allowance	112,000.00		10,000.00	25,000.00	35,000.00	31	14,000.00
Contractor Fee	10,000.00		—		—	—	
Insurance and Bond	15,600.00		15,600.00		15,600.00	100	
Total Contract Price	$750,000.00		$45,600.00	$181,000.00	$226,600.00	30%	$120,000.00

September   EXPENDITURES   226,600
                VOUCHERS PAYABLE   106,600
                CONTRACTS PAYABLE—Retainage   120,000

        Journalizing the partial payment on the contractor's certification for
        payment dated September 30

                                                 226,600
        RESERVE FOR ENCUMBRANCES
                ENCUMBRANCES   226,600

        Reversing the encumbrances on the contract with ABC

It is often wise to set a retainage based on the entire contract price, in order to ensure the satisfactory completion of the project. In this project, $95,000 will be retained until the building is approved and accepted by the Fines Library. Therefore, once the $120,000 of materials are physically incorporated into the building's structure, the contractor will be reimbursed $25,000 ($120,000 − $95,000) in order to retain the proper percentage in Contracts Payable—Retainage. If possible, this amount should be held back from the first progress payment as this will keep the monies already received for construction invested in interest-generating investments for the longest period. In this case, the City of Fines will receive these revenues, because they are keeping interest revenue earned on the remaining invested bond proceeds. The outstanding voucher from October 1 is paid.

October 15   VOUCHERS PAYABLE   106,600
               CASH   106,600

        Paying vouchers payable

In figure 8-3, a second progress payment request is made by ABC Contractors for additional construction on the project. In this example, the previous progress payments made are all shown under the "Previous Expenditures" column. The work in progress is equal to $272,500 and all previously stored materials have been incorporated into the structure of the new building. The building is 67 percent complete as of December 31 and $95,000 of the payable construction costs (shown under the column "Retainage") are retained by the library to ensure that the building is satisfactorily completed. The journal entries corresponding with this certification follow:

December 31   EXPENDITURES   272,500
              CONTRACTS PAYABLE—Retainage   25,000
                   VOUCHERS PAYABLE   297,500

              RESERVE FOR ENCUMBRANCES   272,500
                   ENCUMBRANCES   272,500

        Journalizing the partial payment on the contractor's certifi-
        cation for payment dated December 31 and $25,000 of
        retainage [The encumbrances for the progress payments
        of $272,500 on the contract with ABC are reversed.]

After the vouchers are approved they are paid. The grant monies have been spent first, and they were in the Cash Account ($200,000 − $106,600 − $93,400). All other funding is provided by the General Fund through the Cash Allotment account. In this transaction, $204,100 of the cash allotment is used.

January 10	VOUCHERS PAYABLE	297,500	
	CASH		93,400
	CASH ALLOTMENT		204,100

Journalizing the payment to ABC Contractors

Additional progress billings for construction in progress will be filed as the building reaches completion. Figures 8-2 and 8-3 are representative of certifications filed by a contractor. Once the building is completed, the "Percentage of Completion" column will show that 100 percent of the expenditures have been made. After the last certification is submitted and the retainage released to the contractor, any shortcomings in the building will be resolved in court proceedings. For this reason, it is important that library managers closely inspect the building prior to making the last payment to the contractor.

There would probably be at least two more certifications for payment from the ABC Contractors. They are not shown here, but the final payment for $250,900 is shown ($750,000 − $499,100). It is assumed here that the contract for the building is completed on June 15, 20x1. By the end of the year June 30, 20x1, the retainage has not been paid to ABC Contractor as final inspections of the building are still continuing.

June 15	EXPENDITURES	250,900	
	VOUCHERS PAYABLE		250,900
	RESERVE FOR ENCUMBRANCES	362,900	
	ENCUMBRANCES		362,900
	VOUCHERS PAYABLE	250,900	
	CASH ALLOTMENT		250,900

Journalizing the final payment on the contractor's certification
for payment dated June 15, reversing the encumbrances on
the contract with ABC Contractors, and making the payment
on the approved vouchers

Although the building is completed, the materials, supplies, and labor still must be added to the internal features of the building. Furthermore, the final inspection has not been completed and the retained payable of $95,000 will not be paid until the building is found to be completely satisfactory. It will be assumed that the retainage is outstanding at the end of the fiscal year June 30, 20x1. Based on these assumptions, the financial statements for the CPF are shown in figures 8-4 and 8-5.

FIGURE 8-3 Certification for Payment on Work Completed to Date

Application and Certification for Payment

Application Date: December 31, 20x0
Period   From: October 1   To: December 31, 20x0

Item of Work	Budgeted Value	Previous Expenditures	Work Completed Work in Progress	Work Completed Stored Materials	Total Completed to Date	Percentage of Completion	Retainage
Supervision	$ 28,000.00	$ 7,000.00	$ 13,000.00		$ 20,000.00	71%	
General Labor	35,000.00	5,000.00	20,000.00		25,000.00	71	
Bldg Mat. Allowance	172,000.00	150,000.00	22,000.00		172,000.00	100	$95,000.00
Rentals	7,000.00	1,000.00	4,000.00		5,000.00	71	
Landscape Allowance	13,000.00	—	—		—	—	
Dumpsters	4,000.00	1,500.00	1,500.00		3,000.00	75	
Temporary Facilities	1,500.00	500.00	500.00		1,000.00	67	
Retaining Wall	5,000.00	—	4,000.00		4,000.00	80	
Carpentry Material	7,000.00	3,000.00	3,000.00		6,000.00	86	
Metal	6,000.00	6,000.00	—		6,000.00	100	
Handicap Ramp	8,000.00	—	8,000.00		8,000.00	100	
Electrical	80,000.00	2,000.00	50,000.00		52,000.00	65	
Roof	50,000.00	—	50,000.00		50,000.00	100	
Sidewalks	12,000.00	—	10,000.00		10,000.00	83	
Base and Carpet	15,000.00	—	—		—	—	
Painting	31,000.00	—	—		—	—	
Duct Work	20,000.00	—	15,000.00		15,000.00	75	
Drywall	9,000.00	—	4,500.00		4,500.00	50	
Miniblinds	3,500.00	—	—		—	—	
Cleaning Labor	5,500.00	—	2,000.00		2,000.00	36	
Plumbing Allowance	112,000.00	35,000.00	65,000.00		100,000.00	89	
Contractor Fee	10,000.00	—	—		—	—	
Insurance and Bond	15,600.00	15,600.00	—		—	100	
Total Contract Price	$750,000.00	$226,600.00	$272,500.00		$499,100.00	67%	$95,000.00

THE FINANCIAL STATEMENTS FOR THE CPF

The Statement of Revenues, Expenditures and Changes in Fund Balance (figure 8-4) shows that $200,000 of unexpended appropriations remain. This is technically true even if the cash is allotted through General Fund accounts.

FIGURE 8-4 **The Statement of Revenues, Expenditures, and Changes in Fund Balance for the Capital Projects Fund in the H. K. Fines Library**

H. K. FINES LIBRARY
Capital Projects Fund—Library Building
Statement of Revenues, Expenditures, and Changes in Fund Balance
For the Year Ended June 30, 20x1

Revenues:	
State Grant	$100,000
Federal Grant	100,000
Other Financing Sources—General Fund	750,000
Total Revenues and Other Financing Sources	$950,000
Expenditures:	
ABC Contractor	750,000
Excess of Revenues over Expenditures	$200,000
Fund Balance, Beginning of 20x0	—
Fund Balance, End of 20x1	$200,000

The expenditures are for $750,000 even though $95,000 of the agreed-upon contract price is still owed to the ABC Contractors. Once the building is approved, the final payment of $95,000 will be made, but all building expenditures have been recognized at this point.[14] After the payment on Contracts Payable is made, $200,000 will remain in the CPF to pay for internal expenditures on the building. There will also be a $9,500 service fee deducted from the grant balances and paid to the City of Fines for assistance in the construction of the building.

The Balance Sheet, in figure 8-5, shows $295,000 of remaining cash. This is composed of $200,000 in the two unused grants, and $95,000 that is owed to ABC Contractors. There are also encumbrances outstanding for services and materials to be delivered from the City for $200,000.

The Fund Balance shows the year-end encumbrances for $200,000. In some cases, funding may have been received but not encumbered. Any encumbered appropriations should be recognized in the Fund Balance in a separate section from unencumbered appropriations. For the H. K. Fines Library all construction appropriations are encumbered.

**FIGURE 8-5   The Balance Sheet for the Capital Projects Fund
in the H. K. Fines Library**

H. K. FINES LIBRARY
Capital Projects Fund—Library Building
Balance Sheet
June 30, 20x1

Assets:	
Cash	$295,000
Total Assets	$295,000
Liabilities:	
Contracts Payable—Retained Percentage	$ 95,000
Fund Balance:	
Appropriated:	
Reserve for Encumbrances	200,000
Total Liabilities and Fund Balance	$295,000

EXERCISE 8-1   The Capital Projects Fund

1. What is a Change of Order form and why is it important?
2. What are progress payments?
3. When should progress payments be retained?
4. Why are the CPF's unexpended or unencumbered appropriations not closed at the end of the fiscal year like the General Fund's appropriations?

GENERAL FIXED ASSETS ACCOUNT GROUP

In the NFO, purchases of fixed assets are recorded as expenditures in the General Fund, and expenditures are closed at the end of the fiscal year. As a result, there is no record in the NFO's General Fund regarding the assets owned such as land, buildings, equipment, or books. In order to have a record of the general fixed assets owned by the NFO, the valuation of fixed assets is recorded in the General Fixed Assets Account Group (GFAAG). This is the only record that shows the cost of the entity's fixed assets.[15] Although an NFO may maintain off-the-books accounting records of its fixed assets, without the use of a GFAAG, the accounting records are not in conformity with GAAP. The GFAAG does not record the inflow or outflow of funds as do the other governmental funds such as the General Fund. The GFAAG is simply a record of the fixed assets owned by the NFO along with a listing of the sources that provided funding for the purchased assets. Further, it should be noted that in nongovernmental NFOs but not in governmental NFOs[16] depreciation is recorded on all fixed assets except land.

TYPES OF GENERAL FIXED ASSETS

The general fixed assets of a library include land, library buildings, computers, expensive software packages, bookmobiles, copy machines, construction-in-progress, the base stock of the circulating collection, and inexhaustible collections. It is optional whether infrastructure such as sidewalks, outside lighting, and gutters is recorded in the GFAAG. Other costs that make an asset more efficient or extend its life may be added to the asset's book value. When these expenditures are added to the asset's value, they are said to be "capitalized." Figure 8-6 illustrates the GFAAG for the H. K. Fines Library on June 30, 20x0, with comparative data for the previous year.

Figure 8-6 is a comparative schedule because it presents information for two years. Most NFO financial reports do not present information on a com-

FIGURE 8-6   Comparative Schedule of General Fixed Assets Account Group for the H. K. Fines Library

H. K. FINES LIBRARY
Comparative Schedules of General Fixed Assets—By Source
June 30, 19x9 and 20x0

	19x9	20x0
General Fixed Assets:		
Land	$ 445,000	$ 450,000
Buildings	5,000,000	5,125,000
Equipment	880,000	880,000
Collections:		
Inexhaustible	—	—
Circulating	200,000	200,000
Integrated Computer Library System:		
Hardware	375,000	395,000
Software	250,000	250,000
Bookmobile	95,000	95,000
Total General Fixed Assets	$7,245,000	$7,395,000
Investment in General Fixed Assets by Source:		
General Fund	$3,500,000	$3,500,000
State Grants	250,000	400,000
Federal Grants	900,000	900,000
Capital Projects Fund	2,000,000	2,000,000
Donations and Gifts	595,000	595,000
Total Investment in General Fixed Assets	$7,245,000	$7,395,000

parative basis because the number of funds represented in a single report can lead to confusion if comparative information is also added. With the GFAAG, it is possible to prepare comparative statements. The upper part of the schedule shows the type of assets owned by the library, and the lower portion shows how the money to purchase them was raised. If assets are sold, the cash received is returned to the fund providing the original financing. It should be noted that the assets listed in figure 8-6 would be supported with additional subsidiary records. For example, the classification Equipment needs subsidiary accounts to classify the specific equipment that composes the Equipment asset total of $880,000.

An example of such a subsidiary record is shown in figure 8-7. This is a partial subsidiary account for the Equipment account recording information about five items in the equipment classification for the library. At a minimum, this subsidiary record shows the type of equipment, date of purchase, funding source for the purchase, an inventory control number that is physically tagged onto each equipment item, and the purchase price or other valuation at which the equipment was added to the library's accounts.

**FIGURE 8-7   A Subsidiary Record for Equipment Owned
by the H. K. Fines Library**

General Account: Equipment				
Type	Date Purchased	Funding Source	Inventory Control	Purchased Price or Valuation
Copier	11/97	General Fund	001738	$7,800
J. Deere tractor	8/98	General Fund	001739	$11,500
Snow blade	10/99	General Fund	001740	$780
Computers	7/97	State Grant	001700	$125,000
Bookmobile copier	7/96	Federal Grant	001736	$6,000

Other schedules can be prepared to show the assignment of general fixed assets by department, activity, or function depending on the reporting needs of the NFO. Current additions and deductions to fixed assets by department, activity, or function also should be prepared. This information shows which departments are adding or dropping fixed assets from their operations. Such a schedule helps to identify the level of investment each department needs in order to provide services, and from a managerial perspective it helps to determine the growth in fixed-asset purchases among departments. This is discussed more fully later in the chapter.

VALUATION OF GENERAL FIXED ASSETS

Before any asset valuations are assigned, it is important for the library to have an asset-capitalization policy. One characteristic of an asset-capitalization policy is the use of a cutoff cost as a basis for recording general fixed assets in the GFAAG. For example, a library may have a policy that only assets having a valuation of more than $750 should be recorded in this account group. All assets costing less than this amount are considered expenditures in the fund that made the purchase. The H. K. Fines Library capitalizes only assets that cost more than $1,000. Once a capital asset cutoff is determined, the valuation methods can be considered.

The valuations of general fixed assets in the GFAAG are based on the following three valuation methods:

1. Cost
2. Estimated cost
3. Fair market value

The first of the three valuation methods, cost, is not always simple to determine. The cost of an asset includes its historical cost, which is usually its purchase price and certain charges to place the asset into operation. These may include sales tax, freight and transportation charges, installation costs, architectural fees, demolition cost, land-preparation costs, and closing costs. Therefore, in most cases the cost of an asset includes more than its purchase price (cash discounts for early payment of the amount owed should be deducted from the cost of the asset). An accurate valuation assists in establishing the level of insurance coverage needed for these fixed assets.

The term "inexhaustible collection" refers to valuable books, works of art, and other similar items that do not lose their value through the passage of time. In fact, they may become more valuable as they become older. It is understandable that placing a cost on these collections is difficult—if it is possible at all. Therefore, asset values for such collections need not be recorded at a specific dollar value in the accounting records; in fact, no value may be shown for these collections. If no value is recorded for a collection, it is recommended that the collection be listed under an asset classification "Inexhaustible Collections," without any dollar value recorded for it. In addition, a reference note should be included as to the policy that is being followed with the inexhaustible collection. The note should disclose that the NFO has not recorded a dollar value on the collection. The note may also disclose an estimated high and low range in value for the inexhaustible assets. Although a collection may be insured for a specific dollar value, the collection may not be recorded at a specific value in GFAAG because it is in fact priceless.

The circulating collection refers to books that are continually in circulation among the public. These books wear out rapidly, have short-term interest value among the public, and are relatively inexpensive. The books in the circulating collection are considered to be exhausted within one year. A base stock valuation is used to value this portion of the collection in the GFAAG. The base stock is considered to be the minimum dollar amount needed to maintain a viable circulating library for the community. For the H. K. Fines Library, the cost valuation is $200,000 as shown in figure 8-6. The base valuation on the circulating collection is not changed unless it becomes apparent that the base stock needs to be increased or decreased in order to meet the community's needs adequately. A reference note should explain the policy the library is following with its circulating collection. A subsidiary account for the Circulating Collection is used and periodically checked to ensure that the collection is being adequately maintained.

When it comes to recording values for the fixed assets of an NFO, many organizations face difficulties because no value has ever been recorded for their fixed assets, and there are no remaining records of the original cost of these assets. Therefore the second method of valuing general fixed assets is based on estimated cost. Such estimations can be based on the partial records that are available. Of course, the best answer is to use historical cost of the original asset, if that can be ascertained. Possible alternatives include appraisals or reverse price-level adjustments from comparable assets purchased at today's prices. If it is not possible to value each asset separately, it may be necessary to use valuations of groups of assets.

It may appear that recording values for fixed assets is not worth the difficulty it presents; but before this decision is reached, several factors should be considered. First, it is difficult to be sure that easily removed assets will not be stolen. If no asset records are kept, it is easy for departing employees to depart with some of the less conspicuous assets. Second, without some type of control over assets, it is difficult to establish a maintenance program for them. Some assets may be purchased with a maintenance contract, but those that are not should also be maintained on a regular basis. At the minimum, recording asset values increases awareness of the need for an asset-maintenance policy. Third, fixed assets without documented valuations are difficult to insure.

Fourth, without a record of the assets owned by an NFO, it is difficult to plan for the replacement of assets as they wear out. For employees simply to request new equipment when old equipment wears out is not a satisfactory policy of asset replacement. Such a system does not provide for replacement

---

From the Library Desk: At the present, we have three out of six buildings with leaking roofs and inside damage to buildings. Each year library maintenance has had to be cut to allow for other expenses.

Anonymous survey respondent

of assets in a consistent and systematic manner. Finally, the financial statements do not present a true financial picture unless they show the dollar value of the fixed assets held by the organization and without an accounting record of assets owned by an NFO, the organization cannot receive an unqualified audit opinion.

Another fixed asset valuation method is fair market valuation. Fair market value is the price an asset could be purchased for in an arm's-length transaction between unrelated parties. Assets that are acquired through a gift or donation from an outside party are always placed in the GFAAG at their estimated fair market value at the time of receipt. If the fair market price of the asset is not determinable, it may have to be appraised.

ACQUISITION OF GENERAL FIXED ASSETS

When assets are purchased by the NFO, the expenditure is recorded in the fund making the purchase, and if the asset is used for general governmental operations, it is also recorded in the GFAAG as follows:

July 8	EQUIPMENT	12,000	
	INVESTMENT IN GENERAL FIXED		
	ASSETS—General Fund		12,000
	Imaging Equipment		12,000
	The purchase of equipment by the General Fund		

The July 8 entry shows the General Fund provided the money for the purchase.[17] The entry is recorded at its historical cost. This entry is the most commonly occurring one in the GFAAG. The entry also records the new purchase in a subsidiary account called Imaging Equipment under Investments in General Fixed Assets. A subsidiary record for each specific asset in the GFAAG should be maintained under the Equipment or Investment account.

Of course, general fixed assets can be constructed. The first portion of the chapter illustrated the entries for the construction of a building by the Library. The construction of the building increased the general fixed assets in the GFAAG. As the building is constructed, it is recorded as construction-in-progress in the GFAAG, and those entries follow. The three entries match the corresponding entries in the CPF. They also show that the monies for construction came from the General Fund through the CPF.

September 30	CONSTRUCTION-IN-PROGRESS	226,600	
	INVESTMENT IN GENERAL FIXED		
	ASSETS—CPF: General Fund		226,600
December 31	CONSTRUCTION-IN-PROGRESS	272,500	
	INVESTMENT IN GENERAL FIXED		
	ASSETS—CPF: General Fund		272,500

June 15   CONSTRUCTION-IN-PROGRESS   250,900
           INVESTMENT IN GENERAL FIXED
               ASSETS—CPF: General Fund   250,900
           The three entries recording the construction of the building
           in the CPF, and at the same time, increases in the Construction-in-
           Progress account in the GFAAG

At the end of the fiscal year, the building is not completed. Once the building is finished, the Construction-in-Progress account will be eliminated and an account titled "Building" will record the completed cost of the construction. In addition to the building itself, the assets within the building will be separately recorded in the GFAAG. The library currently has $200,000 remaining in its Capital Project Fund to purchase equipment, materials, and furnishings for the internal areas of the building. Those fixed assets costing more than the library's cutoff classification of $1,000 will be separately recorded in the GFAAG.

Other additions to the general fixed assets of the library this year included donations. The library received land and a rare book published in the 1500s. The land has an estimated fair market value of $23,000, and the book's fair market value is estimated between $14,000 and $50,000. The book will be kept in the library's rare book collection. The following entries record the receipt of the land.

Jan 15   LAND   23,000
          INVESTMENT IN GENERAL FIXED
              ASSETS—Gifts   23,000
          Recording the fair market value of the land in the GFAAG

The book will become part of the library's inexhaustible collections, and the library keeps a record of the value of these works and discloses the estimated value of the collection in the footnotes. Because of the wide range in estimated value for most of these works, the library does not place a definitive value for the inexhaustible collection in the GFAAG.

Additional methods of acquiring assets are through lease-purchase arrangements. In these agreements the asset is not purchased until the final payment is made, but the asset is recognized in the books for the present value of the minimum lease payments over the life of the lease. This entry is made at the time the lease is signed. Present value calculations are beyond the scope of this book, but the entry for the recognition of a leased asset is similar to those already illustrated.

DISPOSAL OF GENERAL FIXED ASSETS

General fixed assets may be disposed of in a variety of ways. They may be written off the books because they no longer have a value, they may be traded in on new assets, they may be sold to an external party or given to another internal governmental unit. If the asset is written off the books and the asset scrapped, the entry for its removal is a reversal of its original entry in the GFAAG. The equipment in the following illustration was originally purchased for $5,700. In the subsidiary account, Printing Press, the specific equipment is removed from the books.

February 10	INVESTMENT IN GENERAL FIXED			
	ASSETS—General Fund	5,700		
	Printing Press		5,700	
	EQUIPMENT			5,700
	The disposal of equipment			

In the next example, the oldest portion of the computerized library hardware used in the library's integrated computer system is traded in for an upgraded model costing $90,000. The old hardware received a trade-in value of $15,000, and it had an original cost of $65,000. In the GFAAG, the disposal of the old equipment must properly take into account the trade-in value of $15,000 for the old equipment. Both the new and the old equipment were paid for through the General Fund. The net cash outlay for the new equipment is $75,000.[18] The new hardware with the trade-in is worth $90,000, but the estimated fair market value of the new hardware is $75,000, the cash selling price. The fair market value should be recorded in the GFAAG.

March 15	INVESTMENT IN GENERAL FIXED		
	ASSETS—General Fund	65,000	
	INTEGRATED COMPUTER SYSTEM		
	Hardware		65,000

Recording the write-off and trade-in of the old hardware with a cost of $65,000

March 15	INTEGRATED COMPUTER SYSTEM—Hardware	75,000	
	INVESTMENT IN GENERAL FIXED		
	ASSETS—General Fund		75,000

Recording the purchase of the new hardware for the computer system

Some would argue that the actual cash outlay for the new hardware was $75,000, and an additional $15,000 (trade-in) of value was originally provided by general fund. As a result, the new hardware should be valued at $90,000 not $75,000. Here, it is believed to be better to record the asset at its fair market value.

If an old asset is sold to a third party rather than being traded in for a new asset, the cash that is received for the old asset goes to the fund that originally provided the monies to purchase the original asset. The GFAAG does not receive any of the cash from selling the asset.

This is one reason it is important to keep a record of which fund provided the original resources for purchasing the asset. Once the asset is sold, it is simply written off in the GFAAG. Assume computer equipment originally purchased for $1,000 was sold for $150.

March 18	INVESTMENT IN GENERAL FIXED			
	ASSETS—General Fund	1,000		
	Computer		1,000	
	EQUIPMENT			1,000

The sale of an old computer to a third party[19]

Besides being written off, traded in, or sold, general fixed assets can be transferred to other governmental units. If an asset is given to another governmental unit (not sold), the general fixed asset is written off the books in the GFAAG as has been illustrated.

RENEWAL OF GENERAL FIXED ASSETS

In order to keep the library's general fixed assets in working order, it is necessary to maintain them. Maintenance costs can consist of minor and major repairs. Minor repairs keep the asset working as it was before the repair was made. Major repairs extend the life of the asset and thus tend to renew the asset. Examples of major repairs are the replacement of a roof or the replacement of a motor in a bookmobile. A distinction needs to be made between minor and major repairs, and they need to be accounted for in a different manner. Expenditures that are made to extend the life of the asset should be added to the asset's value in the GFAAG; otherwise, the maintenance costs for minor repairs are recognized in the fund making the payment as expenditures. The primary government is usually responsible for making either type of payment for the library or transferring the appropriation to the library to make the payment. In the case of appropriation transfers, the entries are made in the library's books, and it is clear whether expenditures or increases in the capitalized value of general fixed assets are occurring. If the payment is recorded in the General Fund, there may be no way of knowing when an increase in the valuation of a fixed asset has taken place. As a result, the library's capitalized assets may be understated in their GFAAG and improperly insured.

Another result of not properly capitalizing asset improvement costs that extend the life of an asset is that is these costs are classified as expenditure, and as such, they are not recognized in the books beyond the current year.[20] Therefore, the library has no record of capital improvements. From a budgetary perspective, this procedure makes it easier to reduce maintenance on the general fixed assets because without proper records on all fixed assets such costs are easier to ignore. Further, when all these costs are put in the records as "expenditures" rather than long-term capital improvements that maintain the facilities in working order, it can be argued that the best way to save budget dollars is to reduce these "expenditures."

> *From the Library Desk:*   We've always had a problem with funding for maintenance. This has caused us a problem with having to be reactive to situations rather than proactive. (We wait until the basement floods and then try to figure out why, rather than make sure the gutters are in good shape, etc.)
>
> Anonymous survey respondent

THE GFAAG'S FINANCIAL SCHEDULES

Several financial schedules and accompanying footnotes are prepared for the GFAAG. These reports are called "schedules" as they are not financial statements. They include:

1. Comparative Schedules of General Fixed Assets—By Source
2. Schedule of Changes in General Fixed Assets—By Department
3. Notes to the Schedules

The information in these schedules helps managers determine how fixed assets are being used by activity or function in the library. It also helps library decision makers decide where fixed asset purchases need to or do not need to be made. Figure 8-8 updates the general fixed assets on a comparative basis in the H. K. Fines Library for the dated entries in the chapter through June 30, 20x1. As in figure 8-6, all general fixed assets are shown along with the sources for financing such as the General Fund, state and federal grants, capital projects fund, and donations. All the accounts shown in figure 8-8 would have subsidiary accounts disclosing specific assets within general fixed-asset classifications on the schedule. Subsidiary accounts are not shown here.

Another schedule that is usually prepared for the GFAAG is the Schedule of Changes in General Fixed Assets. This schedule, shown in figure 8-9, can classify general fixed assets by function, activity, or department, or a mixture of these methods depending on the needs of the NFO. Here, a department classification is used. It should be noted that sometimes it is difficult to determine how to assign the increases and decreases in general fixed assets to a specific department. For example, how should an equipment purchase used by all departments be assigned or allocated? How should expenditures for a new building be assigned to each department? To prevent the overassignment of general fixed assets to any one department a "General Use" classification is adopted in figure 8-9. The library's land and construction-in-progress assets are classified as "general-use" fixed assets.

Although the classification of general fixed assets to departments may not seem important, it could reflect on each department manager's performance. Economic value is the value created by a manager above a set percentage of

**FIGURE 8-8   Comparative Schedule of General Fixed Assets Account Group
for the H. K. Fines Library**

H. K. FINES LIBRARY
Comparative Schedules of General Fixed Assets—By Source
June 30, 20x0 and 20x1

	20x0	20x1
General Fixed Assets:		
Land	$ 450,000	$ 473,000
Buildings	5,125,000	5,125,000
Equipment	880,000	885,300
Construction-in-Progress	—	750,000
Collections:		
Inexhaustible	—	—
Circulating	200,000	200,000
Integrated Computer Library System:		
Hardware	395,000	405,000
Software	250,000	250,000
Bookmobile	95,000	95,000
Total General Fixed Assets	$7,395,000	$8,183,300
Investment in General Fixed Assets by Source:		
General Fund	$3,500,000	$4,265,300
State Grants	400,000	400,000
Federal Grants	900,000	900,000
Capital Projects Fund	2,000,000	2,000,000
Donations and Gifts	595,000	618,000
Total Investment in General Fixed Assets	$7,395,000	$8,183,300

the valuation of the general fixed assets assigned to that manager. Managers who create more value than this cost percentage are themselves more valuable to the organization. Although this may appear to involve profit objectives, such performance measures are sometimes used in NFOs. In such a system, the department manager who is arbitrarily assigned a larger dollar valuation of general fixed assets will have more difficulty in achieving a satisfactory performance evaluation.

In figure 8-9, the totals of $7,395,000 and $8,183,300 correspond with the totals in figure 8-8. The latter schedule shows how the change between this year's and last year's totals ($788,300) took place. Notes should accompany the two schedules to provide additional explanations about the accounting policies followed with the library's general fixed assets. Here, notes are provided in figure 8-10 to explain the valuation methods used and how the collections are recorded.

FIGURE 8-9 Schedule of Changes in General Fixed Assets—By Department for the H. K. Fines Library

H. K. FINES LIBRARY
Schedule of Changes in General Fixed Assets—By Department
For the Year Ended June 30, 20x1

	General Fixed Assets June 30, 20x0	Additions	Deductions	General Fixed Assets June 30, 20x1
Reference	$ 377,500	$ 75,000	$65,000	$ 387,500
Children's Library	212,500	—	1,000	211,500
Circulation	777,500	12,000	—	789,500
Regional History	332,500	—	5,700	326,800
Administration	120,000	—	—	120,000
General Use	5,575,000	773,000*	—	6,348,000
Total	$7,395,000	$860,000	$71,700	$8,183,300

*Includes land $23,000 and construction-in-progress $750,000

FIGURE 8-10 Notes to the General Fixed Asset Financial Schedules

NOTE 5. Fixed Assets

Fixed assets of the Library are recorded in the general fixed assets account group at historical cost or estimated cost if purchased or constructed. Donated fixed assets and fixed assets obtained through trade-ins are recorded at their estimated fair market value. These assets are not depreciated and interest incurred during construction is not capitalized. Infrastructure such as sidewalks is not capitalized. Incurred costs that extend the assets' lives are added to the general fixed asset account group.

NOTE 6. Inexhaustible Collections and Books

The values of the existing inexhaustible collections, including research books, are not readily determinable and the Library has not capitalized them. It is estimated that the materials in the inexhaustible collections have a current value ranging from $175,000 to $500,000. The circulating collection is exhaustible, and it is capitalized and included in the schedule at a base stock valuation of $200,000. This valuation is the estimated amount required to provide satisfactory book services for the community. Accessions and deaccessions during 20x0 and 20x1 were not significant.

SUMMARY

The chapter has treated the Capital Projects Fund and the General Fixed Assets Account Group used by a library. This fund and account group are covered together because fixed assets constructed in the CPF are normally transferred to the GFAAG after they are completed. Therefore, there is a close relationship between this fund and account group.

Library managers need to be familiar with the CPF and the accounting methods that are followed when a fixed asset is acquired. Although it would be expected that all monies that the library obtains from outside agencies for a construction project are entirely used in the construction of the new asset or its purchase, this is not always the case. If the primary government unit of which the library is part needs additional resources, it may attempt to divert monies obtained by the library for its own purposes. As explained in the chapter, this can be done through the charging of fees and other costs to the library for "services" from the primary government.

EXERCISE 8-2   The General Fixed Asset Account Group

1. The director of the Stile Public Library has been discussing the possibility of establishing an equipment replacement policy in the library. Under the proposed policy, 4 percent of the monies received annually from the General Fund would be retained for future purchases of assets. Comment on the director's proposal.

2. The Hansel-Comings County Library has used its library building for 25 years. During the current year, a new loading dock was added to the back of the building. The loading dock cost $11,000. Record what, if anything, needs to be recorded in the GFAAG. Assume the funding was provided by a state grant.

3. Describe the difference in the manner of handling exhaustible and inexhaustible collections in the GFAAG.

4. Why is the value of land, an inexhaustible asset, recorded on the books while the value of inexhaustible collections is not recorded?

5. The Martin County Library has sold a portion of its office equipment for $1,800. These assets were originally purchased with general fund monies. The original cost was $7,500. Record the sale of the office equipment in the GFAAG and the General Fund.

6. Why is depreciation usually not recorded in the GFAAG?

NOTES

1. The indebtedness incurred to construct a new building is accounted for in a General Long-Term Debt Account Group, and the payment of interest and principal on that debt is recorded in the Debt Service fund. As most libraries are

not allowed to incur long-term debt, these funds are not dealt with here. In most cases, long-term debt is incurred by the library's primary governmental entity, which may be a city, county, or state government.

2. In some NFOs the values assigned to the long-lived assets are recorded in the Plant Fund rather than a General Fixed Assets Account Group. The distinction is based on which professional accounting group's rules of financial reporting are being followed. Under the state and local government accounting procedures described in this book, four separate funds or account groups replace the Plant Fund.

3. As we saw in chapter 6, fixed assets may be depreciated over time but this is not a requirement in governmental NFOs, where concern is for the flow of funds.

4. Usually only the primary government and not the library is allowed to incur debt or lease obligations. Therefore, this topic is not considered here.

5. The cost of capital and the interest rate on the debt are not necessarily equal. The cost of interest on the debt is the cost of borrowing those specific funds. The cost of capital is an organizational cost that applies to the overall rate paid for borrowing (or using capital) by the entire organization.

6. The Debt Service Fund records the payment of interest and principal. The primary government's General Long-Term Debt Account Group keeps track of the outstanding debt incurred to fund the project.

7. In the United States this cost of capital charge is related to value-added concepts. In other countries, it is called capital charging. See G. Stevenson Smith and Martin Lally, "Capital Charging and Asset Revaluations: New Choices in Governmental Financial Reporting," *The International Journal of Accounting* 32 (1997) 45–62, and G. Stevenson Smith and Kerry Jacobs, "New Zealand: The Dynamics behind a Reinvented Government," *The International Journal of Public Administration* 22, no. 2 (spring 1999) 347–79.

8. When governmental NFOs operate enterprises similar to businesses, interest costs on construction of facilities are included in the completed cost of the fixed asset rather than as a current expenditure. This approach is used if full costs are to be reimbursed, but in the CPF this is not of accounting importance, and as a result, interest costs are not capitalized.

9. In other cases, the primary government will maintain all record keeping for the construction project. If the library has no choice, it must relinquish control, but under ideal circumstances, the library should maintain close control over the project and the resources of the project.

10. This is known as "arbitrage" and can result in unfavorable tax consequences such as fines for the government.

11. Premiums and discounts are related to the face value of the bond. For example if a $1,000 bond is sold for $980, it is sold at a discount of $20, or less than the face value of the bond. If it were sold for $1,100, it is sold for $100 premium. Usually, the market interest rates influence the amount of the premium or discount.

12. A library may be allowed to borrow monies on a short-term basis. However, it may need to borrow at a higher short-term interest rate in order to obtain temporary funding to start the project.

13. In some cases, a service fee may not be acceptable to the granting agencies, but if it is not specifically ruled out, such a fee can be used to transfer monies from designated purposes to discretionary spending. Here, it would be used to transfer monies that are supposed to be used for building construction to the General Fund for discretionary spending. This tactic is commonly used in NFOs and state and local governments. Although one might question why the city would charge a 1 percent fee against monies it is already giving to the library, it needs to be remembered that these transferred monies are designated to be used for building construction. Once the fee is collected, the same monies are no longer designated and are thus available for discretionary spending by the city rather than the library.

14. The closing entries related to the Statement of Revenues, Expenditures and Changes in Fund Balance's expenditures and revenues are shown here. These entries should be made prior to preparing the Balance Sheet.

REVENUES	950,000	
EXPENDITURES		750,000
ENCUMBRANCES		200,000

The encumbrances will be reopened at the beginning of the next year. In some cases, these budgetary transactions may not be made or the encumbrances may be kept open and not closed as all expenditures in the CPF are related to one construction project.

15. If a library has a profit-generating enterprise within its operations, such as a bookstore or gift shop, all assets of that profit-generating unit are maintained within the library's fund records and not in the GFAAG. The GFAAG is for the general fixed assets of the government and not those that might be used to generate profits.

16. In recognizing depreciation, the cost of an asset (i.e., its value) is assigned to yearly time periods in the asset's estimated life. For example, if an asset with an original cost of $1,000 has an estimated life of five years, $200 of its cost is recognized as depreciation in each of the next five years. This is determined by dividing the cost, $1,000, by the estimated life of five years. This is not a cash allocation method for the replacement or renewal of assets, but simply a method to allocate the benefits received from the use of the asset over the asset's life. No cash is involved when depreciation is recognized. The $200 of depreciation expense is recognized as an expense of the current fiscal period, and it reduces the recorded value of the asset in nongovernmental NFOs. If depreciation is recognized in governmental NFOs, it is not recognized as an expense but as a deduction from Investments in General Fixed Assets account. Depreciation of this nature is recognized in internal service and enterprise funds within governmental NFOs. Depreciation expense is also recognized in cost reimbursement grants or awards.

17. The initial entry in the General Fund would be as follows:

    EXPENDITURES   12,000

       VOUCHERS PAYABLE   12,000

If the encumbered amount was also for $12,000, it would be reversed at that amount. Later, the Vouchers Payable account is reduced when a cash payment is made. This journal entry is not added to the combined financial statements in chapter 7; it is presented here to illustrate interfund accounting transactions.

18. The expenditure is recorded in the General Fund as follows:

      EXPENDITURES—Computer Hardware   75,000

        CASH   75,000

      Purchase of hardware by the General Fund

This journal entry is not added to the combined financial statements in chapter 7; it is presented here to illustrate interfund accounting transactions.

19. The entry in the General Fund (which is not placed in the H. K. Fines Library's accounts but done here simply for illustrative purposes) is:

    CASH   150

       REVENUES   150

    The cash sale of an old computer and the receipt of the cash by the General Fund

20. Expenditures are closed at the end of each year, whereas capitalized costs remain as part of the fixed asset until the asset is removed from the records.

9

Endowment and Agency Funds

THIS CHAPTER DEALS with two NFO funds, the endowment fund and the agency fund. The endowment, or "trust," fund is used for the maintenance of NFO investments such as cash, debt, and possibly stocks that have been either contributed to the organization by a donor or designated by the board as an endowment. These contributions are called the *principal* of a trust fund, and a common characteristic of the principal is that its value must be maintained into perpetuity. When donors contribute such assets to a trust fund, their intention is that the assets will be maintained intact by the organization.

The principal of a trust fund is usually composed of securities that earn income in the form of interest. The interest is usually made available for donor-designated spending purposes, but in some cases, this income may have to be reinvested into the principal of the fund. Another characteristic of a trust is that there may be restrictions on the type of investments that can be made. For example, no investments may be made in the stock market. These legal restrictions may or may not exist, but any restrictions on acceptable investments need be recognized.

In the last part of the chapter, the agency fund is discussed. This fund is used by libraries that act as a fund transfer agent for other libraries. For example, a regional library may be responsible for transferring state monies to local community libraries. In those cases, an agency fund is used to record such transfers. An agency fund may also be used by a library that transfers operating monies to its branch libraries.

These two funds are considered together because they are both *fiduciary* funds. Fiduciary funds place the NFO in the role of acting as a trustee or custodian responsible for the administration of assets given to the NFO for a specific purpose other than its general operations.

THE TRUST FUND: AN OVERVIEW

When the principal of a trust fund is contributed to the NFO for maintenance and not for spending purposes, it is called a *nonexpendable* trust fund. If the income from a trust's assets can be expended, such income is transferred to an *expendable* trust fund. Just as the purpose of the nonexpendable trust fund is to maintain assets into perpetuity, the purpose of the expendable trust fund is to be able to demonstrate that expendable income is spent on the designated activities.

As we have seen, the principal of the typical trust fund cannot be used by the NFO, and it must be maintained intact; that is, it cannot be spent. A "term" trust or endowment is slightly different because at the occurrence of a future event or future date, the principal becomes available to the NFO for spending purposes. This event may be the death of the donor or that of an heir to the donor. Another trust that may expend its principal is called a *quasi* trust or endowment, and may be established by the board of the NFO. In such a trust, the NFO uses the assets of the organization to establish a trust fund. These assets form the trust's principal, but this principal does not have to be maintained intact. This trust is based on discretionary decisions of the board, which can be reversed without great difficulty. It is a simple matter for the board to change its policy and remove the assets from the trust for use in normal activities of the organization.

The principal in any trust may be administered by the NFO or by a trustee, such as a bank. The donor may have stipulated, as a condition of the contribution, that the principal is not to be transferred to the organization, but rather it is to be maintained by a specific trustee with only its income forwarded to the organization. In that case, only the investment income would be transferred to the NFO's expendable trust for spending.

Regardless of who administers the principal of a trust, the expected result is the generation of income, as well as gains and losses from the sale of investments, and these are the next considerations. The income of an endowment is usually considered to be the dividends and interest earned on the principal; and this amount is usually made available for some prespecified use. Such spendable income is recorded in an expendable trust fund. If the income should be available for the general, daily operations of the organization, it is recognized as revenue in the General Fund.

Although the income from a trust is clearly the dividends and interest earned on its principal, the concept of income can be broadened to include realized gains and even unrealized gains.[1] Such a "total-return" concept is another way of defining trust income. Under this concept of income, all appreciation on the securities in the trust's principal is considered to be part of the endowment's income. This view considers appreciation, unrealized and realized, as available for spending, just as dividends and interest are available for spending. As part of this approach, a "spending rate"—the portion of the total return that can be used for spending purposes—has to be set by the board. In other words, it is the total of dividends, interest, and appreciation that can be spent. Before this method can be adopted for an endowment, the NFO must obtain the advice of legal counsel to determine whether this method is acceptable. When the total-return concept is followed, net gains and (in some cases) net unrealized gains are expended by the trust to achieve the spending rate set by the board.

The NFO may set a policy that all unrealized net gains can be expended by the trust. This amount is determined by netting the unrealized gains and losses against each other and making the result (which is assumed to be a net gain) available for expenditures.[2] This procedure may raise the question as to how unrealized gains can be used when they have not been realized. One answer is that unrealized gains become usable once the trust sells the marketable securities with an unrealized gain for cash. The endowment's investments are readily marketable, and they can be quickly sold. This policy requires the conversion of marketable securities to cash in order to turn unrealized net gains into realized net gains. In effect, this is a policy which forces the realization of an unrealized gain through a sale if the endowment's cash balance is insufficient to cover the expenditures based on net unrealized gains.

If the cash in the trust's Cash account is equal to or more than the amount of the unrealized net gain, this cash can be transferred to an expendable trust fund without realizing the "paper" profits on the investments. This is a second approach for using unrealized gains. The net effect of this cash withdrawal is a reduction in the endowment's principal. Later, when the unrealized gain becomes a realized gain, it will replenish the principal. Of course, withdrawal of cash without the sale of the securities equal to the unrealized gain is a risky policy, as an unrealized gain can quickly disappear with decreases in market prices. Once this occurs, the principal will be permanently reduced, as the unrealized gain will never be realized.

Although the principal of the trust may not be legally spendable by the NFO, it may be available to be borrowed by the NFO. This approach essentially allows the NFO to use the endowment's principal. If these loans are made out of the endowment's principal to the NFO, it is almost the same as the spending of the principal, especially if the loan is never repaid. In these cases, the interest rate charged to the loan should be competitively determined and close to the market rate. It is expected that the principal and the interest will be repaid to the trust at predetermined dates and the loan will not become a revolving loan with only interest paid on the borrowed principal that is never repaid. When trust funds are accounted for by the NFO's trust manager, the manager may not be in a position to turn down the organization's request for a loan from the principal.

Another characteristic of trust funds is that the assets of the organization's various trusts may be combined into one investment pool, which allows for more efficient decision making in the investment process. Also, if the invested amounts are large enough, it can result in lower commission charges. The effect of the pooling process is a reduction in the risk of a bad investment to an individual trust by spreading the risk among all the trusts in the pool. When investments are pooled in this fashion, it is still necessary periodically to distribute the income and realized gains to the various trusts in the pool. This is a simple record-keeping task when the trusts are separately maintained, but when they are combined into a pool, it becomes more complex.

One method that can be used to distribute the income and realized gains and losses of the pooled investments is called the "market-unit method," which uses the market value of the investments as the basis for establishing a per share allocation procedure. This method is used to determine each trust's balance in the pool and the number of shares received upon the contribution of additional securities or cash to the pool. (This allocation procedure is explained in detail later.) It is based on a percentage distribution of all gains and losses to the trusts in the investment pool.

A final characteristic of trusts that should be noted is that they do not use appropriations, estimated revenues, or other budget entries. The reason is that the nonexpendable trust is not involved in spending the income earned on its principal, and therefore no need exists for these accounts. With the expendable trust, there are very limited purposes for which monies can be expended; therefore, budget entries are not necessary. As a result, the major accounting questions surrounding trusts relate to the handling of income, as well as realized gains and losses on the trust's principal.

TRUST FUND FINANCIAL STATEMENTS

NONEXPENDABLE ENDOWMENT

Financial statements for the H. K. Fines Library's nonexpendable trust funds are relatively straightforward documents as compared to the General Fund's financial statements. The financial statements for a nonexpendable endowment consist of a Statement of Support, Revenue, and Expenses and Changes in Fund Balance (SREF), a Balance Sheet, and a Statement of Cash Flows. The accounting concept used with a nonexpendable trust fund is the income concept (accrual accounting) rather than a funds flow concept as used in the General Fund. These three financial statements for the year ending June 30, 20x0, are illustrated in figures 9-1, 9-2, and 9-3, respectively, for the H. K. Fines Library.

The SREF (figure 9-1) prepared for the H. K. Fines Library's three trust funds is a financial statement like those prepared for a corporation. For example, note the use of the term "expenses" rather than "expenditures." The investment income recognized in the statement includes income received as cash as well as accrued income, i.e., income earned but not yet received. The term "other financing sources" is used to record realized gains and operating transfers. Other financing sources are those sources of revenue other than revenues earned from operating activities.

The use of capital additions on the statement needs to be explained. Capital additions can include revenue or income on investments, but they are usually only the gains (or losses) on the trust's investment that become part of the principal of the trust. This means that these amounts are not expended; rather, they become additions to the "capital" of the trust fund. With Trust C in figure 9-1, both revenues and all gains are added to the Fund Balance of the trust, and they become part of the trust's principal. With Trusts A and B, revenues and net realized gains are transferred to the expendable trusts.[3] Capital additions can also include gifts, grants, or bequests that become part of the principal of an existing trust.

Trust A's income and its net realized gains are designated for scholarship grants for students in library science at the local university. For this fiscal period, Trust A has a realized loss of $2,000, and no dividend or interest revenue was received. Thus, no scholarship grants were made. Trust B also expends all its investment income and its net realized gains, and its expendable monies are designated for the purchase of "computer-assisted reference" materials. In the current year, $35,000 of spendable monies were transferred to an expendable trust by Trust B. Trust C requires that all revenues and net realized gains on the investments, shown as $15,000, be returned to the trust as capital additions. Trust C is a term endowment, and it was contributed to the library with the condition that no expenditures are to be made from it until the donor's death. At that time, the entire principal becomes expendable. The net gains and investment income of $15,000 are shown as a Capital Addition and an increase in the Fund Balance in Trust C. At this point, the library has not pooled its investments, and each nonexpendable trust is accounted for separately in the library's books.

The Trust Fund Balance Sheet (figure 9-2) consists of a listing of the assets of the funds. These assets are usually composed of debt securities, as well as cash. The accounts listed on the Balance Sheet are control accounts, and the detailed information on each specific investment is in a subsidiary ledger. The method of valuing these investments is disclosed in the notes to the financial statements in figure 9-4.

Finally, it should be noted that Trust A had a $2,000 decrease in its investment portfolio due to a realized loss. Assuming the original principal in the endowment was $100,000, then there has been a reduction of the trust's prin-

FIGURE 9-1 Statement of Revenues, Expenses, and Changes in Fund Balance for Nonexpendable Trust Funds

H. K. FINES LIBRARY
Nonexpendable Trust Funds
Statement of Revenues, Expenses, and Charges in Fund Balance
For the Year Ended June 30, 20x0

	Trust A	Trust B	Trust C	Total
Revenue:				
Net Investment Income	—	$ 25,000	—	$ 25,000
Other Financing Sources:				
Net Realized Gains	$ (2,000)	10,000	—	8,000
Total Revenue (Loss) and Other Financing Sources	$ (2,000)	$ 35,000	—	$ 33,000
Expenses	—	—	—	—
Income (Loss) before Transfers	(2,000)	$ 35,000	—	33,000
Other Financing Uses:				
Operating Transfers to Expendable Trust	—	35,000	—	35,000
Increase (Decrease) in Fund Balance	$ (2,000)	0	—	$ (2,000)
Fund Balance, Beginning of Year	100,000	$725,000	$150,000	975,000
Capital Additions:				
Investment Income	—	—	5,000	5,000
Net Realized Gain (or Loss)	—	—	10,000	10,000
Fund Balance, June 30, 20x0	$ 98,000	$725,000	$165,000	$988,000

FIGURE 9-2 Balance Sheet for Nonexpendable Trust Funds

H. K. FINES LIBRARY
Nonexpendable Trust Funds
Balance Sheet
June 30, 20x0

	Trust A	Trust B	Trust C	Total
Assets:				
Cash	—	$ 40,000	$ 25,000	$ 65,000
Investments (Note 2)	$98,000	700,000	140,000	938,000
Total Assets	$98,000	$740,000	$165,000	$1,003,000
Liabilities and Fund Balance:				
Due to Expendable Trusts	—	$ 15,000	$165,000	$ 15,000
Fund Balance	$98,000	725,000	—	988,000
Total Liabilities and Fund Balance	$98,000	$740,000	$165,000	$1,003,000

cipal. In contributing the monies to the library, the donor included a binding legal stipulation that the principal needs to be maintained intact. To make up for this "deficit" in the fund's principal and ensure the endowment is meeting its legal obligations, the General Fund is prepared to make a $2,000 contribution to the fund in the following fiscal year. The contribution may not be necessary, of course, if market gains in the next year make up for the $2,000 "deficit."

The Balance Sheet for the H. K. Fines Library shows that the Fund Balance and liability totals are equal to the total of cash and investments. The information in the Balance Sheet in figure 9-2 should not be considered alone, but in conjunction with the information in the Notes to the Financial Statements in figure 9-4.

Figure 9-3 is the Statement of Cash Flows for the three trusts. A statement of cash flows shows information that is not available on accrual-based income statements and balance sheets. Cash flow statements show the inflow and outflow of actual cash in an organization. As an example of how the cash flows are different from revenues recognized on the income statement, consider a situation in which revenues owed to the NFO from another government have not been fully received. If $100,000 of revenues are owed to the NFO, then $100,000 is recognized as revenues on the income statement, but if only $50,000 has been received in cash, then a statement of cash flows will show $50,000 as the cash received from operating revenue activities. Many analysts view a statement of cash flows as providing a better basis for evaluating an organization's financial condition than the income statement.

In figure 9-3, cash inflows are from investing activities. They arose from the sale of securities and other investments, and the receipt of interest and dividends on investments. These inflows were partially used (as cash outflows) to purchase new investments. The top of the statement lists cash inflows and outflows from operating activities. Currently, there are no entries in this section of the statement, but there could be outflows for commissions paid on the purchase of investments and inflows from cash contributions and gifts. Also note that the ending cash balances in figure 9-3 are equal to the balance in Cash account on the Balance Sheet.

The Notes to the Financial Statements in figure 9-4 consist of supplemental notes. They are specifically related to the Balance Sheet in figure 9-2, but they are not the complete notes for the entire organization. The information that needs to be disclosed in the notes about these investments is:

1. Total cost and total market value of securities for each Balance Sheet date presented
2. The method used to determine cost of the securities and any permanent losses in valuation of the securities for each period in which an income statement is presented

FIGURE 9-3 Statement of Cash Flows for the Nonexpendable Trust Funds

H. K. FINES LIBRARY
Nonexpendable Trust Funds
Statement of Cash Flows
For Year Ended June 30, 20x0

	Trust A	Trust B	Trust C	Total
Cash Flows from Operating Activities	—	—	—	—
Cash Flows from Investing Activities:				
Proceeds from Sale of Investments	$18,000	$30,000	$30,000	$93,000
Purchase of Investments	(18,000)	(10,000)	(25,000)	(53,000)
Interest and Dividends Received	—	20,000	10,000	30,000
Net Cash from Investing	0	$40,000	$15,000	$70,000
Operating Transfers to Expendable Trusts*	—	(20,000)	—	(20,000)
Net Increase in Cash and Cash Equivalents	0	$20,000	$15,000	$35,000
Cash and Cash Equivalents, Beginning of Year	0	20,000	10,000	30,000
Cash and Cash Equivalents, June 30, 20x0	0	$40,000	$25,000	$65,000

*Trust B will transfer $35,000 to Trust E, but only $20,000 in cash has currently been transferred

FIGURE 9-4   **Notes to Financial Statements Relative to the Nonexpendable Trust Fund**

NOTE 1. Summary of Significant Accounting Policies

Trust Funds represent the type of funds that are subject to restrictions requiring in perpetuity that the principal be invested and the income only can be used. For Trusts A and B, income includes net realized gains.

NOTE 2. Investments

Investments are presented in the financial statements in the aggregate at the lower of cost (amortized, in the case of bonds) or fair market value.

	Cost	Market
Trust A	$ 98,000	$ 98,000
B	700,000	726,000
C	140,000	161,000
	$938,000	$985,000

Investments are composed of the following:

	Cost	Market
Corporate Bonds	$790,000	$790,000
U.S. Government Securities	138,000	186,000
Municipal Bonds	10,000	9,000
	$938,000	$985,000

The determination of fair market value is made by aggregating all current marketable securities. At June 30, 20x0, there was unrealized gain of $47,000 pertaining to the current portfolio. The portfolio had a cost basis on June 30, 19x9, of $920,000 and a market value of $950,000.

A net realized gain of $8,000 on the sale of marketable equity securities was included in the determination of the Increase in Fund Balance for 20x0. The cost of the securities sold was based on a first-in, first-out method in both years.

The method of security valuation that is described here should be consistently applied to all the organization's investments, regardless of their fund classification. In the case of the H. K. Fines Library, the marketable equity securities are valued by using the lower of cost or market, and the debt securities are valued by using the lower of amortized cost or market value. This is described in note 2. Also, in note 2, the amount of unrealized and realized gains is disclosed. The loss in Trust A is not considered a permanent loss at this point, and it is not disclosed in the notes.

These methods of recording investments usually result in two separate valuations. One is based on the market value of the security and the other is based in the value that is recorded in the books. This second valuation is called the *carrying value* of the security. The difference can be attributed to a variety of factors, including differences between the market price and the original purchase price.

EXERCISE 9-1   Characteristics of Endowment Funds

1. Explain the following terms:
   a. Capital additions
   b. Total-return concept
   c. Quasi-trust
   d. Spending rate
   e. Investment pool

EXPENDABLE ENDOWMENT

The expendable trust is established to spend all the monies it receives. The designated purpose for spending expendable monies is usually established by the donor. In most cases, the nonexpendable endowment transfers spendable monies to the expendable endowment. In the current year, nonexpendable Trust B transfers $35,000 of its spendable resources to Trust E.[4] Although there is usually a close accounting relationship between a nonexpendable and expendable endowment, single *expendable* endowments may be separately established when a donor contributes monies that allow for the spending of the entire principal and earnings on a specified purpose. The H. K. Fines has one endowment that allows the principal to be spent: Trust F.

The bases of accounting in an expendable and nonexpendable endowment are different. A funds flow concept, as applied in the General Fund, is used with expendable endowments because the focus is on the expenditure of monies rather than the maintenance of the fund's principal balance. Thus, the financial statements for the expendable endowment are different from those prepared for the nonexpendable endowment. The expendable endowment's financial statements are the Statement of Revenues, Expenditures, and Changes in Fund Balance and the Balance Sheet. The Statement of Cash Flows is not used. Budgetary entries may be established in this fund, but usually they are not because the trust's monies are spendable only for clearly defined purposes such as books, artwork, or scholarships, for example. If it is important to exercise more control over spending, budgetary accounts may be used.

Figures 9-5 and 9-6 show the Statement of Revenues, Expenditures, and Changes in Fund Balance and the Balance Sheet respectively, for the expendable trusts in the H. K. Fines Library. It should be noted that the term "expenditures" is used rather than "expenses." This change is due to the change in the basis of accounting from accrual to modified accrual. In

FIGURE 9-5 Statement of Revenues, Expenditures, and Changes in Fund Balance for the Expendable Trust Funds

H. K. FINES LIBRARY
Expendable Trust Funds
Statement of Revenues, Expenditures, and Changes in Fund Balance
For Year Ended June 30, 20x0

	Trust D	Trust E	Trust F	Total
Revenue:				
Donations	—	—	$66,000	$66,000
Total Revenue	—	—	$66,000	$66,000
Expenditures	$ 10,000	$17,000	3,000	30,000
Excess of Revenues or (Expenditures)	$(10,000)	$(17,000)	$63,000	$36,000
Other Financing Sources:				
Transfers from Nonexpendable Trusts	—	35,000	—	35,000
Increase (Decrease) in Fund Balance	$(10,000)	$18,000	$63,000	$71,000
Fund Balance, Beginning of Year	10,000	10,000	—	20,000
Fund Balance, June 30, 20x0	—	$28,000	$63,000	$91,000

217

FIGURE 9-6 The Balance Sheet for the Expendable Trust Funds

H. K. FINES LIBRARY
Expendable Trust Funds
Balance Sheet
June 30, 20x0

	Trust D	Trust E	Trust F	Total
Assets:				
Cash	$2,000	$15,000	$10,000	$27,000
Investments (Note 2)	—	—	56,000	56,000
Due from Nonexpendable Trusts	—	15,000	—	15,000
Total Assets	$2,000	$30,000	$66,000	$98,000
Liabilities and Fund Balance:				
Accounts Payable	$2,000	$ 2,000	$ 3,000	$ 7,000
Fund Balance:				
Unreserved	—	28,000	63,000	91,000
Total Liabilities and Fund Balance	$2,000	$30,000	$66,000	$98,000

figure 9-5, donations are shown as revenues. Trust F has received a donation from a library patron for $66,000 which is to be used in its entirety for the purchase of artwork for the library. Trust E records the transfers-in from its respective nonexpendable trust, Trust B, for $35,000. The transfer is considered to be an Other Financing Source rather than revenue on the statement. Because the transfers have not been entirely made, a Due from Nonexpendable Trust account for $15,000 is recognized in the Balance Sheet in figure 9-6.

The assets, liabilities, and fund balances are shown on the balance sheets in figure 9-6. The notes to these financial statements are in figure 9-7. They are used to explain the purpose of the expendable trusts. Notes should accompany these two financial statements explaining the nonexpendable trust funds' objectives and providing information about the investments held by Trust F. In the notes to the financial statements, it is disclosed that the gift contributed to the library included $55,000 in corporate stocks. Such investments are not permitted under the city's statutes. As a result, they will be sold as market conditions permit. Currently, the stocks have a market value of $56,000, and as they are donations, they are listed on the books at their fair market value.

FIGURE 9-7   Note Disclosures for the Expendable Trust Funds

NOTE 1. Summary of Significant Accounting Policies

The expendable trust funds are accounted for in the same manner as other governmental funds using a fund flows basis of accounting. Trust D is for scholarships for students in library science. Trust E is for the purchase of computer-assisted reference materials. Trust F is for the purchase of artwork.

NOTE 2. Investments

Investments are presented in the financial statements in the aggregate at the lower of cost (amortized, in the case of bonds) or fair market value.

	Cost	Market
Trust F	$55,000	$56,000

Investments are composed of corporate stocks. The determination of fair market value is made by aggregating all current marketable securities. The cost of the securities sold was based on a first-in, first-out method in both years. As of June 30, 20x0, there was an unrealized gain of $1,000 pertaining to this investment.

These stocks were received as part of a $66,000 gift to the library. Legally authorized investments by the City of Fines and its component units do not include capital stock. The library intends to sell these securities as market conditions permit.

TYPICAL ENTRIES FOR TRUST FUNDS

NONEXPENDABLE ENDOWMENTS

In the new fiscal year, the City of Fines has established an investment pool for all its nonexpendable endowments and other invested monies of the city. The city is requiring all its component units, of which the H. K. Fines Library is one, to put all excess monies and endowments' investments into the investment pool formed by the city. As of July 1, 20x0, the library has transferred all its nonexpendable endowments (cash of $50,000 and investments valued at $938,000 with a market value of $985,000) to the city's investment pool.

The library will receive quarterly reports from the managers of the investment pool showing the changes in the investment portfolio. These quarterly reports show unrealized gains and losses, realized gains and losses, earnings from dividends and interest as well as disclosing the investment activity during the quarter.

As a result of this change, the library will not record any transactions in its nonexpendable endowments during the current year. It will record transfers from the investment pool into its expendable endowments, and information about the investments in the pool will be disclosed in the notes to the financial statements.[5]

Figure 9-8 provides an illustration of a quarterly report that is sent to the library from the city's investment pool. As the report in figure 9-8 is prepared as an illustration, it is an annual report rather than a quarterly or monthly report. All updating nonexpendable journal entries are taken from this statement. It should be noted that even though the investment results are shown for Trusts A, B, and C in figure 9-8, all these investments are commingled within the investment pool. Therefore, the investment pool manager may be reluctant to report financial data by separate trust accounts. Yet, it is important for the library manager to have income and net realized gains separately reported for each trust. Without this separate reporting, it is difficult to demonstrate that donor-sponsored activities are being properly funded.

Several aspects of this report need to be highlighted before the library's journal entries, based on the report, are formulated. First note that the term "cost or amortized cost" is used. This concept was explained in chapter 6. But the concept of accrued interest has not been fully explained. Accrued interest changes the valuation of the investments in Part II of the report. Accrued interest on an investment is the amount of interest revenue earned due to the passage of time but not yet received. The accrual of interest occurs when, at the end of an accounting period, interest owed at that point in time is considered receivable and thus recorded in the records. Those investments upon which interest has accrued have been increased in value by the amount of accrued interest recognized to the end of June 30, 20x1, and investment interest income has also been increased. It is expected that such interest will be paid within a short period.

The report shows the amount of net unrealized gains and losses for each endowment. Although this amount is shown, it is not realized until the investments are sold in the market, and as a result, these amounts are usually not truly spendable. The market value column in Part II incorporates all unrealized gains (or losses) whereas the carrying value does not.

Data are provided about the library's investments to help judge the risk associated with these investments. For example, investments in commercial paper mean the library's portfolio includes short-term promissory notes issued by firms. These notes are based on the good name of the firm, and they are not backed by collateral for the loan. These investments are held by the dealer and not the city's agent. Dealer-held investments are likely to be riskier as they are further removed from the city's control. Additionally, there has been a $7,000 loss in the market value of these investments over the year. This could be due to changes in the interest rates.[6] The overall increase in the library's investment portfolio was $165,300 ($1,153,300 − $988,000) over the year. The net realized gain of $33,000 was reflected as a portion of this increase, and the rest of the increase came from the receipt of interest ($103,300) and unrealized gains ($29,000).

As indicated, Trusts A and B transfer all interest and realized gains to their respective expendable endowment. Those amounts are $94,000 and $19,800, respectively. Only Trust C transfers interest earnings of $17,500 and its realized and unrealized gains to its principal as capital additions. The only journal entries shown in the library's records would be the receipt of the monies in the expendable trusts and note disclosures about the investments in the city's investment pool. These entries showing the receipt of these monies are recorded in the following section and in the note disclosures in figure 9-11.

EXPENDABLE ENDOWMENTS

Because the nonexpendable investments have been transferred to the city's investment pool, the journal entries for the H. K. Fines Library's endowments are confined to the three expendable endowments. The entries in these endowments consist of the receipt of monies from the investment pool, endowment expenditures, and closing entries. The receipt of monies and endowment expenditures are shown together for the expendable trusts as year-end entries. In the following entry, all interest and net realized gains are recognized as cash transfers-in during the fiscal year.

June 30, 20x1
Trust:

	D	E	F
CASH	94,000	19,800	—
TRANSFERS-IN: Investment Pool	94,000	19,800	—

Recording the transfer-in of cash from the investment pool for Trusts D and E

FIGURE 9-8   The Investment Pool Report for the Library's Endowment Funds

CITY OF FINES
Investment Pool—Library Assets
Annual Summary
June 30, 20x1

PART I. Earnings

Trust	A	B	C	Total
Beginning Balance	$ 98,000	$725,000	$165,000	$ 988,000
Investment Returns:				
Interest	76,000	9,800	17,500	103,300
Dividends	—	—	—	—
Net Realized Gains and Losses	18,000	10,000	5,000	33,000
Net Unrealized Gains and Losses	6,000	12,000	11,000	29,000
Ending Balance	$198,000	$756,800	$198,500	$1,153,300

PART II. Investments*

	Carrying Amount	Market Value
Repurchase Agreements:		
Securities held by City's agent in city's name	$ 119,800	$ 127,500
U.S. Treasury Bills	376,850	388,850
Commercial Paper, uninsured and unregistered:		
Held by dealer	137,000	130,000
Corporate Bonds, registered	376,850	393,150
Total Investments	$1,010,500	$1,039,500

*Investments are shown at cost or amortized cost, plus accrued interest.

The earnings and net realized gains from the investment pool have to be separately assigned to the proper expendable trust fund because the monies from each are expendable for different purposes. If the monies are commingled, it cannot be shown that monies have been properly spent. Trust F is a totally expendable trust, and its stocks were converted into cash during the year, without a gain or loss, to allow expenditures to be made for its designated purpose of purchasing artwork for the library.

The following entries record the expenditures made by each of the trusts during the fiscal year. Although all are only shown as "Expenditures" each corresponding subsidiary ledger shows the detailed information about the purchases made. From those subsidiary accounts, it could be determined if the expenditures followed donor-designated purposes.

June 30, 20x1

Trust:	D	E	F
EXPENDITURES	98,000	17,000	60,000
ACCOUNTS PAYABLE	98,000	17,000	60,000
ACCOUNTS PAYABLE	100,000	19,000	63,000
CASH	100,000	19,000	63,000

Recording the expenditures of the three trusts for the donor-designated expenditures and the payment of accounts payable

The payments on accounts payable include this year's payables and those outstanding on the previous year's balance sheet (figure 9-6) of $2,000, $2,000, and $3,000 in Trusts D, E, and F, respectively.

In Trust D, a Fund Balance deficit of $4,000 has occurred because expenditures are higher than revenues. The deficit is apparent in figure 9-10. In order to cover the expenditures incurred by this trust fund and pay the accounts payable, $4,000 will be loaned to Trust D from the General Fund and recorded as an Advance. An advance is a form of short-term loan. The General Fund will be reimbursed as monies are received from the nonexpendable trust. As of the end of the year, this loan has not been completed and no entry is recorded.[7]

The closing entries for the three endowments differ slightly and each is considered separately. The effect on Trust D of the closing entries is a decrease in the Fund Balance by $4,000.

June 30, 20x1

Trust D	FUND BALANCE	4,000	
	OPERATING TRANSFERS-IN		94,000
	EXPENDITURES		98,000

Recording the closing entry for Trust D showing a decrease in the Fund Balance

For Trust E, expenditures did not exceed the transfers-in from the investment pool and its Fund Balance increased by $2,800. The effect of the following entry is seen in the Fund Balance in figure 9-9.

June 30, 20x1

Trust E	OPERATING TRANSFERS-IN	19,800	
	EXPENDITURES		17,000
	FUND BALANCE		2,800

Recording the closing entry for Trust E showing an increase in the Fund Balance

All the resources in Trust F are expendable; as a result its expenditures reduce the Fund Balance, and once all monies are spent the Fund Balance will be exhausted. At that time, the trust will be closed.

June 30, 20x1

| Trust F | FUND BALANCE | 60,000 | |
| | EXPENDITURES | | 60,000 |

Recording the closing entry showing a decrease in the Fund Balance equal to the amount of expenditures

The trusts' SREF and Balance Sheet for June 30, 20x1 are shown in figures 9-9 and 9-10, respectively. The SREF records the current year expenditures and transfers from the nonexpendable trust as well as the corresponding changes in the Fund Balance for the three trusts. The Balance Sheet shows the cash available for spending and the unreserved Fund Balance. The accompanying notes for the June 30, 20x1, period also need to be part of these financial statements. These notes about investments in the pool are closely related to the information in figure 9-8.

FIGURE 9-9 Statement of Revenues, Expenditures, and Changes in Fund Balance for the Expendable Trust Funds

H. K. FINES LIBRARY
Expendable Trust Funds
Statement of Revenues, Expenditures, and Changes in Fund Balance
For Year Ended June 30, 20x1

	Trust D	Trust E	Trust F	Total
Revenue:				
Donations	—	—	—	—
Total Revenue	—	—	—	—
Expenditures	$ 98,000	$ 17,000	$ 60,000	$ 175,000
Excess of Revenues or (Expenditures)	$(98,000)	$(17,000)	$(60,000)	$(175,000)
Other Financing Sources: Transfers from Nonexpendable Trusts	$ 94,000	$ 19,800	—	113,800
Increase (Decrease) in Fund Balance	$ (4,000)	$ 2,800	$(60,000)	$ (61,200)
Fund Balance, Beginning of Year	—	28,000	63,000	91,000
Fund Balance, June 30, 20x1	$ (4,000)	$ 30,800	$ 3,000	$ 29,800

FIGURE 9-10 The Balance Sheet for the Expendable Trust Funds

H. K. FINES LIBRARY
Expendable Trust Funds
Balance Sheet
June 30, 20x1

	Trust D	Trust E	Trust F	Total
Assets:				
Cash	——	$30,800	$3,000	$33,800
Total Assets	——	$30,800	$3,000	$33,800
Liabilities and Fund Balance:				
Accounts Payable	$ 4,000	—	—	$ 4,000
Fund Balance:				
Unreserved	$(4,000)	$30,800	$3,000	$29,800
Total Liabilities and Fund Balance	——	$30,800	$3,000	$33,800

FIGURE 9-11   Note Disclosures for the Expendable Trust Funds

NOTE 1. Summary of Significant Accounting Policies

The expendable trust funds are accounted for in the same manner as other governmental funds using a funds flow basis of accounting. Trust D is for scholarship grants for students in library science. Trust E is for the purchase of computer-assisted reference materials. Trust F is for the purchase of artwork. The library's nonexpendable trust assets are invested in the investment pool administered by the City of Fines. Unrealized gains (or losses) are retained by the investment pool for Trusts A and B. Interest, dividends, net realized and unrealized gains (or losses) are retained by the investment pool for Trust C.

NOTE 2. Investments

Investment pool investments are presented in the financial statements in the aggregate at the lower of cost (amortized, in the case of bonds) or fair market value.

	Cost	Market
Trust A	$ 107,500	$ 113,500
B	738,000	750,000
C	165,000	176,000
	$1,010,500	$1,039,500

Investments composed of the following:

	Cost	Market
Repurchase Agreements:		
Securities held by City's agent in city's name:	$ 119,800	$ 127,500
U.S. Treasury Bills	376,850	388,850
Commercial Paper, uninsured and unregistered:		
Held by dealer	137,000	130,000
Corporate Bonds, registered	376,850	393,150
Total Investments	$1,010,500	$1,039,500

The determination of fair market value is made by aggregating all current marketable securities. At June 30, 20x1, there was unrealized gain of $29,000 pertaining to the current portfolio. The portfolio had a cost basis on June 30, 20x0, of $938,000 and a market value of $985,000.

A net realized gain of $33,000 on the sale of marketable equity securities was transferred from the investment pool to the expendable trusts for 20x1. The cost of the securities sold was based on a first-in, first-out method in both years.

EXERCISE 9-2   Journal Entries for Endowments

1. The Cross Trust consists of a $500,000 nonexpendable quasi endowment that is not part of an investment pool. During the current fiscal year, the trust earned $30,000 in investment income and recognized a net gain of $27,000. The income is made available to the Forth Trust, an expendable trust, and the net gain increases the principal of the trust. Record the correct journal entries for both funds, as completely as possible with the available information. Assume the entries are recorded at the end of the fiscal year, on June 30, 20x2.

2. The Lord Harold Library has a nonexpendable endowment, the Carrie Trust, which has been established by the board with a $150,000 investment. All the gains and income from the trust are available to the Moe Trust, an expendable endowment. During the current year, $5,000 in net gains were received on the sale of $30,000 of securities, and $6,000 in income earned by the Carrie Trust as of the third quarter. Record all entries for the sale of the securities and the amounts transferred between the two trusts as of the end of the third quarter, on October 1, 20x1.

3. The Morelane Library Board has adopted the total-return concept with its Ross Trust, which consists of $250,000 in investments, at cost. The board adopted a spending rate of 10 percent of cost. The return from the trust was composed of net gains of $2,000, net income of $18,000, and unrealized gains of $8,000. Ten percent of the endowment was made available to an expendable endowment, the Lowe Trust. Record the correct journal entries in the Ross Nonexpendable Trust and the Lowe Expendable Trust for the transfer of cash on July 1, 20x3, only.

INVESTMENT POOLS

As has been indicated, it may be of advantage for the NFO to form or join an investment pool with its trust assets. An investment pool is formed when the investment assets of a number of trusts are merged into one large fund. The investment pool's portfolio is either managed by the organization itself or handled by a trustee outside the organization. In either case, at periodic intervals (perhaps monthly or quarterly), the amounts of realized gains and losses, as well as the income from the investments, are allocated to all the trusts in the pool. Each trust in the pool has a fund balance account on the investment pool's balance sheet.

As an example of how an investment pool allocates its returns, assume that the following investments and cash in the Woodward Library's three trusts are placed into an investment pool.

Trust X: $98,000 in investments: market value $99,000
Trust Y: $40,000 in cash and $720,000 in investments: market value $735,000
Trust Z: $150,000 in investments; market value $163,000

Furthermore, assume that a share in the investment pool is arbitrarily set at a value of $100. This amount is set arbitrarily when the pool is established. Once this share value is set, the number of shares held by each trust in the investment pool can be determined as follows:

No. of Shares

Trust X	999
Trust Y*	7,750
Trust Z	1,630
Total	10,370

*Cash plus market value of securities

If a new trust were placed in the investment pool at this point, the market value of its investments and cash would be divided by the market unit value of $100 to determine the number of shares it would have in the pool. For example, if a new trust were added to the investment pool and it had securities with a market value of $100,000, it would have a total of 1,000 shares in the investment pool. It is important that all calculations be based on market values.

Suppose, however, that the Too-Late Trust, with $100,000 in market value securities, were to join the investment pool after the investments held by the original three trusts have doubled in value. This doubling of investment values increases the market value of each share to $200. The result is that a new trust entering the investment pool with $100,000 in market value securities would receive only 500 shares in the investment pool, and would correspondingly receive a smaller proportion of any future gains, losses, and investment income. As purchases and sales of securities occur in the pool, realized gains and losses occur. These realized gains and losses should be netted against one another and the results distributed to the shares in the investment pool at periodic intervals.

As an example of how the distribution process is handled, assume that during the first quarter of a fiscal year, securities with a value on the books of $3,000 are sold for $3,500, which results in a realized gain of $500. To record this sale, the following entry should be made in the pool:

CASH	3,500	
RESERVE ON REALIZED GAINS AND LOSSES		500
INVESTMENTS		3,000

Recording the sale of investment pool securities by the investment pool

The credit to the control account, Investments, is tied in with a subsidiary ledger entry. (The subsidiary ledger contains all the detailed information on the securities sold.) The $3,000 credit causes a decrease in the securities in the subsidiary ledger by an equal amount. The account Reserve on Realized Gains and Losses acts as a holding account. The amount of gains is credited to this account, and the amount of losses is debited to it. After a certain time has passed, the amount accumulated in the account is allocated to the trusts on a per-share basis. Whenever a gain or loss occurs on the sale of a security, it is recorded in the Reserve account.

As an example of how the amount in the Reserve on Realized Gains and Losses is distributed to the trusts in the investment pool, assume that the balance in this account has accumulated to a $5,185 credit balance. (This balance includes the previous gain of $500.) This amount is to be distributed to Trusts X, Y, and Z, on the basis of the per share figures previously shown. By dividing the total number of shares (10,370) into the amount in the Reserve account ($5,185), the amount of gain attributed to each share is determined ($.50). When the $.50 per share amount is multiplied by the number of shares held by each trust, the total amount of gain allocated to each trust is calculated. The following table shows these results.

	Allocated Gain	Computation
Trust X	$ 495	990 × .50
Trust Y	3,875	7,750 × .50
Trust Z	815	1,630 × .50

These changes are recorded as an increase in the Fund Balance for each trust in the investment pool. The allocation procedure does not affect the percentage of shares allotted to each of the trusts, but it does increase the dollar value attributed to each of the shares in the pool. The results of the distribution are recorded as follows in the Fund Balance accounts of the investment pool:

RESERVE ON REALIZED GAINS AND LOSSES	5,185	
FUND BALANCE—Trust X		495
FUND BALANCE—Trust Y		3,875
FUND BALANCE—Trust Z		815

Recording the net gains allocated to each trust

This entry divides the net realized gains among the trusts. When the investment pool receives investment income, it is periodically divided among the trusts by the same procedure.

The total in the Fund Balance of each trust equals the amount that can be withdrawn from the investment pool. Assume the investments in the pool are valued at cost by the NFO and the NFO separately maintains its own investment records. When a trust's investments are withdrawn from the pool, there is a different withdrawal balance on the NFO's books than the amount shown in the pool's records. This situation occurs when two different sets of records are maintained on the valuation of the same investments in the pool. One is kept by the investment pool at market and another is kept by the NFO at cost.

As an example of these procedures, assume that the Kirwin Library has its investments in an outside investment pool, and it is going to withdraw from the pool. The investments are accounted for at cost on the books of the Kirwin Library, and market valuation is kept on the trust's investments by the investment pool. The trust's Fund Balance is equal to $120,000 in the NFO's records, and the market value of the trust's investments is $150,000. Obviously, the Kirwin Library will withdraw the market value of its investments ($150,000) from the investment pool. At that time, it would be necessary to record updating entries for the difference in Kirwin's accounting records.

EXERCISE 9-3   The Investment Pool

1. An investment pool has been formed by two trusts. Trust X has securities listed at a cost value of $89,000 (market value of $110,000). Trust Y has cash of $15,000 and securities with a cost value of $37,000 (market value of $57,000).
   a. The market unit value is set at $75. Determine how many shares each trust receives.
   b. Assume that at the end of the first quarter, investment income is equal to $17,000 and net gains have been $20,000. Allocate these amounts to the two trusts.

2. An investment pool is composed of four trusts. The investments are valued at cost on the books. The Fund Balance section on the NFO's Balance Sheet appears as follows:

	Cost Value	Shares
Fund Balance—Trust A	$125,000	500
Fund Balance—Trust B	78,000	400
Fund Balance—Trust C	48,000	600
Fund Balance—Trust D	67,000	500

It has been decided that Trust A will withdraw $59,000 (market value) from the investment pool. This withdrawal will reduce Trust A's shares by 200 shares. In terms of its cost value, this withdrawal is equal to $50,000. Journalize the withdrawal by Trust A on the books of (a) the investment pool and (b) the NFO.

3. Why are unrealized gains and losses automatically part of any market valuation of investment securities?

AGENCY FUNDS

The agency fund is a custodial fund that for most libraries holds cash to be distributed to other governmental units. Agency funds are similar to trust funds in that both have fiduciary responsibilities to outside parties, but the

NFO's involvement in trust fund activities entails more decision-making choices. With the agency fund, the NFO is responsible for ensuring that the monies with which it is initially entrusted are passed on to the proper authorities. Such an obligation is best reported under the funds flow concept for financial reporting. These financial reports are relatively simple as all cash is matched by liabilities owed to other funds. In libraries, agency funds may be used with pass-through grants, branch library fines, and possibly deferred compensation withholdings from its employee payroll.

An agency fund is used when the NFO acts as an agent for another governmental unit with the responsibility for passing on monies to the other unit, but with no responsibility for ensuring that the other unit correctly spends its monies. These monies are recorded as receipts and disbursements, not revenues or expenditures.

Another use for agency funds may be with library fines collected by branch libraries. If these amounts are to be periodically submitted to the main library and the branch library is the custodian of these monies until they are forwarded to the main library, an agency fund may be used to account for these fines. Of course, a separate checking account for fines collected may serve the same purpose.

A library may have a deferred compensation plan for its employees. Under such plans, usually related to an employee's pension contributions, withholdings from the employee's pay are deferred from liabilities for federal income taxes until a later date. The effect of these plans is to reduce the amount of federal income taxes paid by the employee. Such plans are available for governmental units under Internal Revenue Service regulations. An agency fund is used to record, hold, and distribute these monies to the proper governmental unit.

Figure 9-12 illustrates the Agency Fund's balance sheet for pass-through grants at the H. K. Fines Library. The library has been chosen by the state to act as a regional distributor of funding for the "Learn to Read" program. The Balance Sheet is the only financial statement prepared for the Library's Agency Fund because the fund records only assets and liabilities, never revenues or expenditures. With larger agency funds, it may be necessary to prepare a second report showing the changes in assets and liabilities for the fund during the year, but for this agency fund it is not necessary.

It should be noted that there is no Fund Balance in this Balance Sheet. The cash in the Agency Fund is to be completely distributed to county libraries and as a result, no extra monies are accumulated in a Fund Balance. During the fiscal year, the cash is paid out to the county libraries, and the agency fund is closed. The H. K. Fines Library does not check to ensure that the monies are properly spent by the other libraries. The responsibility to ensure that these monies are properly expended belongs to the granting agency. Of course, if the Fines Library does receive a share of these monies, it must

FIGURE 9-12   The Balance Sheet for the "Learn to Read" Regional Pass-through Grants

H. K. FINES LIBRARY
"Learn to Read" Agency Fund
Balance Sheet
June 30, 20x0

Assets

Cash $175,000

Liabilities

Due to County Libraries—Eastern Region $175,000

ascertain that *its* Learn to Read expenditures have been properly made. During the year, the following entry is recorded, and at that point, the Agency Fund is closed.

July 15, 20x0
DUE TO COUNTY LIBRARIES—Eastern Region   175,000
    CASH   175,000
Recording cash payments to the county libraries

SUMMARY

This chapter is concerned with fiduciary or custodial funds. The two funds of this nature are endowments (both nonexpendable and expendable) and agency funds. A nonexpendable trust is required to maintain a patron's donation intact. The donation is termed the *principal* of the trust fund, and this amount must not be spent. The principal of the trust is invested to earn a return, and within the fund, securities are bought and sold to earn gains. The accounting for the receipt of income, realized gains and losses, and the formation of investment pools is explained in the chapter. Expendable trusts are allowed to spend the monies they received for the purposes designated by the donor. Reporting for the expendable endowment must clearly show the purposes of all expenditures.

The H. K. Fines Library's financial statements for the library's nonexpendable endowments are presented as well as the Notes to the Financial Statements. The library's nonexpendable trusts are put into an investment pool after the June 30, 20x0 fiscal year. Therefore, financial statements are not prepared for them in the new fiscal period. Even without these financial statements for the nonexpendable trust, there is still a need for adequate disclosures about the investments in the investment pool.

Financial statements are presented for the expendable trust funds, also. In the chapter, the expendable trusts' financial statements and notes are updated for the accounting entries illustrated in the chapter. All the dated entries in the chapter have been used to update the financial statements to the period ending June 30, 20x1.

The last part of the chapter outlines the activities of the agency fund. This fund is also a custodial fund, like the trust funds, but its activities are usually restricted to the receipt and disbursement of monies by the NFO.

NOTES

1. Net realized gains are the difference between market gains and losses. Market gains occur when an investment is sold at a higher price than it was purchased. Market losses are the opposite. Unrealized gains are "paper gains" because they have not been realized through the sale of the investment.

2. The term "net" as used here refers to determining the difference between two numbers. For example, the difference between the revenues and expenditures is called "net income" rather than "income" and occasionally we are said to be "netting" the result.

3. As will be explained, Trusts A and B transfer their expendable monies to expendable Trusts D and E, respectively.

4. Normally, Trust A would transfer expendable monies to Trust D, but there are no transfers this year because of the $2,000 loss in Trust A.

5. In some cases, the monies received from the pool are put into separate Special Revenue Funds. Techinally, these monies are an expendable endowment and should be recorded in an endowment fund. In most cases, the only accounting effect is to hide the fact that the NFO has endowments. In either case, investment information must be fully disclosed in the notes.

6. If market interest rates increase, and the interest rate on a security held by the library stays fixed, then the only way that security can be sold is at a loss. This situation arises because no one will purchase a security that pays less interest income than can be earned on market rates, except at a lower price. The reverse of this situation occurs when market rates fall. With falling market rates, the value of a bond you already own rises. If you own a Treasury bond paying 7 percent and today's market rates are 6 percent, your bond is more valuable. If you wanted to sell it, you could sell it for a profit over your purchase price.

7. When the journal entry for the loan is made in Trust D, it will appear as follows:

CASH	4,000	
ADVANCE FROM THE GENERAL FUND		4,000

Recording a loan from the General Fund for the deficit in the trust fund

10

Combined Financial Statements and Analysis of the Results of Performance

THIS FINAL CHAPTER has three purposes. First, it will focus on the culmination of the previous chapters' work in developing financial statements for the H. K. Fines Library with the preparation of combined financial statements for the library. The second portion of the chapter consists of an analysis of financial statements to help determine how a library is performing. This evaluation is made from both a financial ratio and a broader goal performance perspective.

The combined financial statements illustrated in this chapter are part of the financial documents issued to the public to report on the financial condition of the library. The detail of information in the combined financial statements is aggregated more than the financial statements illustrated in earlier chapters. For the H. K. Fines Library, this aggregation of financial information is largely related to the endowment funds. As a result, it is easy to trace numerical amounts in individual fund financial statements to the combined statements in this chapter.

In accounting for the various funds in the previous chapters, separate accounts, such as Cash in the trusts and Cash in the General Fund, were used. Here, similar accounts in different funds are added to calculate the total Cash in the NFO. Also, when financial statements for the organization as a whole are combined, they show the General Fund, Special Revenue, Capital Projects, General Fixed Assets Account Group, and Trust Funds together on each combined financial statement. In preparing these combined statements all individual trust funds (three in the case of the H. K. Fines Library) are *combined* into a single financial statement for all trust fund accounts.

Note that the term *combined* financial statement is used and not *consolidated*. There is an important difference between these terms. "Combining" a statement simply involves adding amounts across account balances in the various funds. For example, if the liabilities in the General Fund are $110,000 and the liabilities in the Trust Funds are $114,000, a combined financial statement would show the total liabilities at $224,000. With a consolidated statement, the addition works differently. Assume that the General Fund owes $10,000 to the Capital Projects Fund and, in turn, the Plant Fund has a receivable from the General Fund for an equal amount. Under a "consolidated" concept, the $10,000 is netted out from the receivables and liabilities of the respective funds before a consolidated financial statement is prepared. If the total liabilities in both funds were equal to $224,000, this netting process would leave a total in the consolidated liabilities of $214,000, which is $10,000 lower than under a combined statement. Also with consolidations, $10,000 is deducted from the combined receivables balance in the two funds.

Use of a consolidated statement is supported in for-profit accounting because such an organization should not record monies owed to itself as liabilities in its financial statements, nor should that same amount be recognized as a receivable. In NFO accounting, the combined statement approach is more strongly supported because the funds in an NFO are a self-balancing set of accounts that, largely, are accounted for separately from one another. In NFO accounting, the parts of the organization are considered to be as important as the entire organization for reporting purposes. The view stems from the need to demonstrate that separate monetary sources are being used for the purposes for which they were appropriated. Obviously, there are significant differences between financial statements prepared under the combined and consolidated approaches.

In preparing financial statements, NFOs actually use both the combined and the consolidated approaches. In general, the combined approach is used with interfund transactions, but the consolidated approach is used with some intrafund transactions. That is, the combined approach is used, between separate funds (i.e., General and Endowment) consolidated approach is used within a fund group. The consolidated approach nets out any receivables and payables within a fund group, as between the separate trusts in the endowment funds of the H. K. Fines Library. This situation occurs when there is a subdivision of a major fund group, and with the H. K. Fines Library, the only multifund groups are the *expendable* endowment funds. If there are amounts owed between the nonexpendable and expendable endowment funds, these amounts should be shown in the statements and not netted out against one another. In this case, combining is a better policy because it discloses whether the NFO is using the nonexpendable trust's principal as a loan, and this information should be available to readers of the financial statements so that its legitimacy can be evaluated.

The combined financial statements represent the summation of all the accounting activities of the organization, from the source documents on up. A number of financial documents are prepared prior to preparing the combined financial statements. As one moves up this list of statements from the source documents to the combined financial statements, detail in each document becomes more aggregated. The following list illustrates this change of detail, from the specific at the bottom of the list to the more aggregated at the top.

1. Combined Financial Statements and Supplemental Schedules
2. Separate Fund Financial Statements
3. Special Reports
4. Trial Balances
5. Ledgers
6. Journals
7. Source Documents

The detail in each of these documents is based on the needs of the potential user of the report or document. For example, the general public is not interested in the detailed information available in source documents (vendors' names, invoice numbers, etc.), but the financial staff of the NFO is very interested in this information. Source documents have a specific audience orientation, and so do the other reports and documents. Figure 10-1 presents a matrix of potential users of the documents and reports generated by an NFO. In figure 10-1 it can be seen that the general public's attention is more focused on the combined financial statements, statistical schedules, and the audit opinion whereas a governmental agency providing monies to the NFO is likely to be more concerned with special reports on the usage of those monies, as well as supporting copies of source documents. The audit opinion is not part of any sequence of specific-generalized information, but is included in the matrix to show the type of users who are interested in it.

This chapter looks at the most aggregated statements in the list by illustrating the combined financial statements for the H. K. Fines Library. Then, technical analysis is used to evaluate the financial statements and other performance measures are reviewed.

COMBINED FINANCIAL STATEMENTS

The combined financial statements for the H. K. Fines Library are presented in figures 10-2, 10-3, and 10-4. It should be made clear that an NFO may well

FIGURE 10-1   Matrix of Users' Interest in Financial Documents

	User					
Statement	General Public	Higher Level Management	Financial Staff	Grant Providers	Donors	Creditors
Combined	✔	✔	✔		✔	✔
Separate Fund Financials		✔	✔	✔		
Trial Balance			✔			
Statistical Schedules	✔	✔	✔	✔	✔	✔
Ledgers/Journal Entries			✔			
Source Documents			✔	✔		
Audit Opinion	✔	✔	✔	✔	✔	✔

✔ Financial documents of major interest

prepare and issue *two* "financial packages." The first set is called the comprehensive annual financial report (CAFR), and it includes the combined financial statements, account groups, audit opinion, the notes, and usually the introductory section with a transmittal letter, and a final section with supplemental schedules of statistical information. Supplemental statistical information disclosing book accessions and deaccessions during the year, information about the library's patron usage statistics, changes in budget dollar over a ten-year period, number of staff and personnel costs as a percentage of total budget dollars over a five- or ten-year period, or information about grant monies received in terms of amounts and sources may be reported. The CAFR also includes the individual (as well as the combined) fund statements. These individual financial statements are called *combining* financial statements. Thus, it contains separate financial reports for each endowment or special revenue fund, for example.

The second financial package is called the general purpose financial statements (GPFS). This financial package is an abbreviated form of the CAFR. It is issued to those readers who do not need all the information in the CAFR. The GPFS would not include individual (combining) financial statements in each fund group nor would it include the account groups. The GPFS does not have to include the CAFR's introductory sections either. The GPFS includes only the combined financial statements, the notes, and the audit opinion. With larger NFOs, there can be a big difference between the CAFR and the GPFS, but not among medium-sized libraries.

Figure 10-5 presents the Notes to the Financial Statements. These notes are part of both the CAFR and the GPFS. The audit opinion, also a CAFR and GPFS document, is illustrated in figure 10-6. Although the audit opinion was explained in chapter 3, an audit opinion for the H. K. Fines Library's combined financial statements in the GPFS is included here. All financial data for the H. K. Fines Library are viewed from the GPFS perspective in this chapter unless otherwise noted.

The combined financial statements for the H. K. Fines Library are the SREF (GAAP-basis), SREF—Actual and Budget, and the Balance Sheet. If the H. K. Fines Library accounted for its own nonexpendable trust funds, instead of using an investment pool, a Statement of Cash Flows would be prepared. A review of the combined statements in this chapter makes it apparent that some minor changes have been made in the previously prepared financial statements for the separate funds in chapters 6, 7, 8, and 9. Finally, it should be remembered that all the closing entries shown in the previous chapters are made only after the combined financial statements have been prepared. Therefore, they should be ignored at this point. These closing entries were presented in earlier chapters to better illustrate the entire accounting sequence for the various individual funds.

COMBINED SREF (GAAP-BASIS)

The combined SREF, presented in figure 10-2, is basically a summation of the SREFs for the General Fund, Special Revenue Fund, Capital Projects Fund, and the expendable Endowment Fund. The first adjustment to the combined SREF which distinguishes it from the individual SREFs is that Other Financing Sources are listed before the Excess rather than after Revenues as was previously shown. Other financing sources can be shown in either location on the SREF.[1]

If the library's nonexpendable trusts were reported, they would be reported in *one* separate column in figure 10-2. In the City of Fines' SREF, where the library is considered a component unit, the nonexpendable trust would not be separately reported, but neither would it be shown as part of the city's fiduciary fund totals. Thus, it may be very difficult to analyze the library's financial operations by reviewing the city's financial reports. There is a need for separate fund reporting for the library. If these funds' columns are not reported upon, or shown only as one total column for the entire library, it is very difficult for the library's management to get an accurate picture of its financial status. Many times a city reports only totals for its component units such as a library, school district, or parks department.[2] There is no assurance that a library will have access to financial statements as shown in figures 10-2, 10-3, and 10-4.

The combined SREF for 20x1 presents its data in an aggregate format for all funds and does not show individual fund statements for the endowments. Depending on the level of aggregation, such data make it difficult for library managers to identify financial trends or changes. This argument favors the

FIGURE 10-2 Combined Statement of Revenues, Expenditures, and Changes in Fund Balance

H. K. FINES LIBRARY

Combined Statement of Revenues, Expenditures, and Changes in Fund Balance
For the Year Ended June 30, 20x1

	General Fund	Special Revenue	Capital Projects	Endowments	Memo Totals
Revenue:					
Intergovernmental	$173,500	—	—	—	$ 173,500
Interest Income	2,500	—	—	—	2,500
State Grant	—	$7,500	$100,000	—	107,500
Federal Grant	—	—	100,000	—	100,000
Contributions and Bequests	2,300	—	—	—	2,300
Total Revenue	$178,300	$7,500	$200,000	$—	$ 385,800
Expenditures (Note 4):					
Program Services					
Reference	$ 37,617	—	—	—	$ 37,617
Children's Library	35,878	—	—	—	35,878
Circulation	40,549	—	—	—	40,549
Regional History	13,839	—	—	—	13,839
Handicapped Services	—	$7,500	—	—	7,500
Supporting Services Administration	37,892	—	—	—	37,892
Other Expenditures:					
ABC Contractor Payments	—	—	$750,000	—	750,000
Endowment Expenditures	—	—	—	$175,000	175,000
Total Expenditures	$165,775	$7,500	$750,000	$175,000	$1,098,275
Less: Other Financing Sources					
General Fund	—	—	$750,000	—	$ 750,000
Nonexpendable Trusts	—	—	—	$113,800	113,800
Excess (Deficiency) of Revenue and Other Financing Sources over Expenditures	$ 12,525	—	$200,000	$(61,200)	$ 151,325
Fund Balance, Beginning of Year	51,575	—	—	91,000	142,575
Fund Balance, End of Year	$ 64,100	$—	$200,000	$ 29,800	$ 293,900

FIGURE 10-3 The Combined Balance Sheet

H. K. FINES LIBRARY
Combined Balance Sheet
June 30, 20x1

	General	Special Revenue	Capital Projects	Endowments	Memo Totals
Assets:					
Cash, including interest bearing savings account	$18,050	$29,700	$295,000	$33,800	$376,550
Repurchase Agreement	25,000	—	—	—	25,000
Repurchase Premium Receivable	2,500	—	—	—	2,500
Due from Special Revenue—State Grant	7,500	—	—	—	7,500
Due from Estate of E. Parsons	2,300	—	—	—	2,300
Investments (Note 2)	23,750	—	—	—	23,750
Total Assets	$79,100	$29,700	$295,000	$33,800	$437,600
Liabilities and Fund Balance:					
Vouchers Payable	$ 2,000	—	—	$ 4,000	$ 6,000
Due to State Unemployment	3,000	—	—	—	3,000
Due to Federal Government—FICA	10,000	—	—	—	10,000
Contracts Payable—Retained Percentage	—	—	$ 95,000	—	95,000
Due to General Fund—Reimbursement	—	$ 7,500	—	—	7,500
Deferred Revenue (Note 1)	—	22,200	—	—	22,200
Total Current Liabilities	$15,000	$29,700	$ 95,000	$ 4,000	$143,700
Fund Balance:					
Reserved for:					
Encumbrances	$ 3,450	—	$200,000	—	$203,450
Inventory	7,000	—	—	—	7,000
Leases	500	—	—	—	500
Employee Retirement	4,945	—	—	—	4,945
Unreserved:					
Designated by Board	12,055	—	—	—	12,055
Undesignated	36,150	—	—	$29,800	65,950
Total Fund Balance	$64,100	—	$200,000	$29,800	$293,900
Total Liabilities and Fund Balance	$79,100	$29,700	$295,000	$33,800	$437,600

241

FIGURE 10-4   Combined Schedule of Revenues, Expenditures, and Changes in Fund Balance—Budget and Actual (Non-GAAP)

H. K. FINES LIBRARY
General Revenue Fund
Combined Schedule of Revenues, Expenditures, and Changes in Fund Balance—
Budget and Actual (Non-GAAP)
For the Year Ended June 30, 20x1

	Budget	Actual	Variance, Favorable (Unfavorable)
Revenues:			
City of Fines	$ 68,000	$ 68,000	$ 0
Backlog County	66,000	66,000	0
State Grant	26,000	26,000	0
Contributions and Bequests	—	2,300	2,300
Book Fines	2,500	2,700	200
Book Sales	3,000	2,800	(200)
Interest Income	—	2,500	2,500
Photocopying	8,000	8,000	
Total Revenues	$173,500	$178,300	$ 4,800
Expenditures:			
Reference	$ 33,500	$ 37,617	$(4,117)
Children's Library	37,000	35,878	1,122
Circulation	38,500	40,549	(2,049)
Regional Library	14,000	13,839	161
Administration	45,000	41,342	3,658
Total Expenditures	$168,000	$169,225	$(1,225)
Revenues over (under) Expenditures	$ 5,500	$ 9,075	$ 3,575
Fund Balance, July 1		$ 51,575	
Fund Balance, June 30		$ 60,650	

preparation of separate financial statements for each of the funds. For the H. K. Fines Library, this is significant only for the expendable endowments, as they have been combined into one aggregated total in the financial statements. (In the CAFR, the separate endowment funds would be shown as combining statements. Remember that we are viewing these financial statements as GPFSs.)

COMBINED BALANCE SHEET

The Combined Balance Sheet (figure 10-3) is an aggregation of the accounts shown on the library's individual balance sheets from previous chapters. The only changes in the statement relate to the combining of Balance Sheet account balances. For example, the Cash and Petty Cash accounts were combined into one total. The reason for combining these accounts is to eliminate unnecessary detail, but no reports should be so abbreviated as to be misleading. In reviewing the financial statements, it can be seen that it would be helpful to use two-year comparative financial columns to allow for better financial comparisons, but usually comparative statements are not used.

COMBINED STATEMENT OF REVENUES, EXPENDITURES, AND CHANGES IN FUND BALANCE—BUDGET AND ACTUAL

The library's GPFS must also include the Combined Statement of Revenues, Expenditures, and Changes in Fund Balance—Budget and Actual (SREF2). The only governmental funds that used a complete set of budgetary journal entries were the General Fund and Special Revenue Fund. As a result, the SREF2 is the same financial statement that was prepared in chapter 7. If the Capital Projects Fund had recorded budgetary entries in its accounting records, as it could have, then it would be necessary to combine those amounts here and determine the variances from budgeted amounts. Please remember that in the Capital Projects Fund a budget was established with ABC Contractors, but those amounts were legal guidelines for the contractor to follow. They were not incorporated into the library's accounts. As a result figures 10-4 and 7A-3 are the same, but the SREF2 needs to be shown here as a representation of the H. K. Fines Library's complete financial report.

COMBINED NOTES TO THE FINANCIAL STATEMENTS

The combined Notes to the Financial Statements (figure 10-5) represent comprehensive notes to the financial statements. The notes in figure 10-5 combine the notes from the other funds' statements as illustrated in the previous chapters. Note 7 has been added to describe contingencies that are financially significant to the library. In this case, it describes the importance of grant monies to the library's operations. In addition, all funds and account groups used by the library are described in these comprehensive notes to the financial statements, and additional information is provided about the concept of fund equity. Finally, note 8 adds supplemental information about the employees' defined pension plan.

FIGURE 10-5   Notes to Accompany the June 30, 20x1 Financial Statements of H. K. Fines Library

H. K. FINES LIBRARY
Notes to the Financial Statements
June 30, 20x1

NOTE 1. Summary of Significant Accounting Policies

The H. K. Fines Library is part of the City of Fines. The Library operates under a Director and an appointed Board of Directors. The Library provides general library, reference, community resources, and administrative services. The accounting poli-

(Continued)

**FIGURE 10-5   Notes to Accompany the June 30, 20x1 Financial Statements
of H. K. Fines Library   *(Continued)***

cies of the H. K. Fines Library conform to generally accepted accounting principles
(GAAP) as applicable to local governments. The following is a summary of the
more significant policies.

A. Financial Reporting Entity

The Library's financial statements include all funds and account groups over which
the Board exercises oversight responsibility. Oversight responsibility includes such
aspects as the appointment of governing body members, designation of management, the ability to significantly influence operations and accountability for fiscal
matters.

The branch libraries at Cabin Creek and Moore Head are included within the
Library's reporting entity since the Library's Board is the governing body for each
branch library.

The Library is includable as a component unit with the City of Fines.

B. Basis of Presentation

The accounts of the Library are organized on the basis of funds or account groups;
each is considered a separate accounting entity. The operation of each fund is
accounted for within a set of self-balancing accounts composed of the Library's
assets, liabilities, fund balances, revenues, and expenditures. The various funds are
grouped by type in the financial statements. Account groups are used to record
transactions that do not directly change expendable financial resources.

Total columns on the combined statements are "memorandum only" totals to indicate that this data is not comparable to consolidated information and that the data in
these columns do not conform to generally accepted accounting principles. Interfund eliminations have not been made in aggregating the data in this column.

The following fund types and account groups are used by the Library:

Governmental Funds

The General Fund: To account for all financial resources except those required to be
accounted for in other funds. This fund is the general operating fund of the Library
and it is used to account for administration, library services, supplies, and maintenance of library building and collections.

The Special Revenue Fund: To account for the proceeds of specific revenue sources
(other than expendable trusts, debt service, or major capital construction projects)
that may be restricted by donors, administrative actions, or legal statutes.

The Capital Project Fund: To account for the construction of major capital construction projects.

The Endowment Funds: The expendable trust funds are accounted for in the same
manner as other governmental funds using a funds flow basis of accounting. Trust D

is for scholarship grants for students in library science. Trust E is for the purchase of computer-assisted reference materials. Trust F is for the purchase of artwork. The Library's nonexpendable trust assets are invested in the investment pool administered by the City of Fines. Unrealized gains (or losses) are retained by the investment pool for Trusts A and B. Interest, dividends, net realized and unrealized gains (or losses) are retained by the investment pool for Trust C.

The Agency Funds: To account for custodial monies that are temporarily held by the library in an agency capacity for another fund. Agency funds use the modified accrual method of accounting.

General Fixed Assets Account Group: To account for the fixed assets owned by the library.

C. Basis of Accounting

The accounting and financial reporting treatment applied to a fund is determined by its measurement focus. All governmental funds are accounted for using a current financial resources measurement focus. With this measurement focus, only current assets and current liabilities generally are included on the balance sheet. Operating statements of these funds present increases (i.e., revenues and other financing sources) and decreases (i.e., expenditures and other financing uses) in net current assets.

The modified accrual basis of accounting is used for all governmental and agency funds. Under this method, revenues are recognized when received, except for those accruable, which are recorded as receivable when measurable and available to pay current-period liabilities. The Library considers revenues available if they are collectible within 60 days of the year-end.

Expenditures are generally recognized under the modified accrual basis of accounting when the related fund liability is incurred.

The Library recognizes deferred revenues. Deferred revenues arise when resources are received by the Library before it can legally claim them, as when grant revenues are received before the qualifying expenditures are made. When the qualifying conditions of the grant are met, the deferred revenue is removed from the balance sheet liabilities and recognized as a revenue.

Encumbrance accounting, under which purchase orders, contracts, and other commitments for the expenditure of monies are recorded in order to reserve a portion of the appropriation, are used by the Library. Encumbrances outstanding at year-end are carried forward to the new fiscal year. These encumbrances are the equivalent of expenditures for budgetary purposes. Outstanding encumbrances are reported as reservations of fund balances on the balance sheet and represent commitments that will be honored in the subsequent fiscal year. All unencumbered appropriations lapse at the end of fiscal year.

D. Budget

The Library is required under City Ordinance 45(a)(7) to adopt an annual balanced budget by July 1 each year. The Board usually approves a preliminary budget in

(Continued)

FIGURE 10-5   Notes to Accompany the June 30, 20x1 Financial Statements of H. K. Fines Library   *(Continued)*

March or April for the fiscal year beginning July 1. The Board uses a legally adopted budget with actual data on a basis that includes encumbrances and is inconsistent with generally accepted accounting principles. A reconciliation between budgetary and generally accepted accounting principles is provided at the end of this paragraph. The budget is approved during a public board meeting and published in the paper as required by city ordinance. The Director is authorized to transfer budget amounts within line items, but supplemental appropriations that amend total appropriations of any fund require a Board passed resolution.

Reconciliation between Budgetary and GAAP Expenditures:

	Actual	−	GAAP	=	Difference (Outstanding Encumbrances)
Reference	$26,000	−	$25,000	=	$ 1,000
Children's Library	15,000	−	13,000	=	2,000
Circulation	34,700	−	32,000	=	2,700
Regional Library	15,000	−	11,000	=	4,000
Administration	26,000	−	24,000	=	2,000
					$11,700

E. Inventories

The cost of supplies are charged to expenditures as purchased in the year in which the expenditure is budgeted. Inventories of these items are immaterial at year-end.

F. Fixed Assets

Fixed assets used in governmental funds are accounted for in the general fixed assets account group rather than in the governmental fund, and no depreciation is recorded on general fixed assets. Donated fixed assets are valued at their estimated fair market value on the date of their donation. Library books are recorded as expenditures when they are purchased.

G. Retirement Plan

Pension costs are funded as they accrue. All funds that have employees transfer their share of such benefits to the employee benefits fund from which the costs are paid.

H. Comparative Data

Complete comparative data, with the presentation of prior year totals by fund type have not been presented in each of the statements since their inclusion would make the statements unduly complex and difficult to read.

NOTE 2. Pooled Cash and Investments

Investments in certificates of deposit, U.S. Government obligations, repurchase agreements, and other investments are recorded at cost or amortized cost except for donated investments and those in the City's pooled investment fund which are recorded at market value.

Investment pool investments are presented in the financial statements in the aggregate at the lower of cost (amortized, in the case of bonds) or fair market value.

	Cost	Market
Trust A	$ 107,500	$ 113,500
B	738,000	750,000
C	165,000	176,000
	$1,010,500	$1,039,500

Investments are composed of the following:

	Cost	Market
Repurchase Agreements		
Securities Held by City's Agent in City's Name	$ 119,800	$ 127,500
U.S. Treasury Bills	376,850	388,850
Commercial Paper, Uninsured and Unregistered		
Held by Dealer	137,000	130,000
Corporate Bonds, Registered	376,850	393,150
Total Investments	$1,010,500	$1,039,500

The determination of fair market value is made by aggregating all current marketable securities. At June 30, 20x1, there was unrealized gain of $29,000 pertaining to the current portfolio. The portfolio had a cost basis on June 30, 20x0, of $938,000 and a market value of $985,000.

A net realized gain of $33,000 on the sale of marketable equity securities was transferred from the investment pool to the expendable trusts for 20x1. The cost of the securities sold was based on a first-in, first-out method in both years.

NOTE 3. Fund Equity

The fund equity is the excess over liabilities and reserves. The reserved accounts indicate the portion of the fund balance which has been legally segregated for specific purposes and is not appropriable. The unreserved designated accounts indicate the portion of the fund equity set aside for future projects. The unreserved undesignated account indicates the fund balance available for future appropriations. Reserves of the fund balance are nonappropriable equity. Designations of the fund balance are fund balance amounts that have been designated for use by management.

In the current year, there was an excess of budgetary expenditures over revenues of $10,800 and actual expenditures over revenues of $5,315 in the General Fund.

(Continued)

**FIGURE 10-5   Notes to Accompany the June 30, 20x1 Financial Statements
of H. K. Fines Library   *(Continued)***

Although this was a planned level of spending, continued spending leading to an excess of expenditures over revenues could eventually lead to a deficit in the Fund Balance.

NOTE 4. Current-Year Expenditures on Prior-Year Encumbrances

The amount encumbered at the end of the 20x0 fiscal year was $11,700. During the fiscal year ending June 30, 20x1, expenditures on these encumbrances totaled $11,900.

NOTE 5. Fixed Assets

Fixed assets of the Library are recorded in the general fixed assets account group at historical cost or estimated cost if purchased or constructed. Donated fixed assets and fixed assets obtained through trade-ins are recorded at their estimated fair market value. These assets are not depreciated and interest incurred during construction is not capitalized. Infrastructure such as sidewalks is not capitalized. Incurred costs that extend the assets' lives are added to the general fixed asset account group.

NOTE 6. Inexhaustible Collections and Books

The values of the existing inexhaustible collections, including research books, are not readily determinable and the Library has not capitalized them. It is estimated that the materials in the inexhaustible collections have a current value ranging from $175,000 to $500,000. The circulating collection is exhaustible, and it is capitalized and included in the schedule at a base stock valuation of $200,000. This valuation is the estimated amount required to provide satisfactory book services for the community. Accessions and deaccessions during 20x0 and 20x1 were not significant.

NOTE 7. Commitments and Contingencies

The library receives a substantial amount of its support from federal, state, and local governments. A significant reduction in the level of this support, if this were to occur, may have an effect on the library's programs and activities.

NOTE 8. Pension Plan

The Library's employees participate in the City's defined benefit plant. All full-time employees are eligible to participate in the plan. Currently, the 25 employees participate in the plan.

THE AUDIT OPINION

The three financial statements, general fixed asset schedule, and the notes to the financial statements should be accompanied by an audit opinion from the independent certified public accountant who examined the financial statements to see if they have been prepared under generally accepted accounting principles. (For additional information about the importance of an audit opinion, refer back to chapter 3.) An example of an audit opinion to accompany the GPFS, prepared under generally accepted accounting principles, is shown in figure 10-6.

At a minimum, the audit opinion covers the three financial statements, general fixed asset schedule, and notes to the financial statements included in the GPFS. Such an opinion is illustrated in figure 10-6. If the audit opinion covers the CAFR, it also covers the combining financial statements for individual funds. If other supplementary information is included in the financial report, the audit opinion does not cover these supplemental statistical schedules.

FIGURE 10-6   Audit Opinion on the Library's Financial Statements

---

To the Board of Directors of the H. K. Fines Library   July 31, 20x1

We have audited the accompanying general-purpose financial statements of the H. K. Fines Library, a component unit of the City of Fines, as of and for the year ended June 30, 20x1. These general-purpose financial statements are the responsibility of H. K. Fines Library management. Our responsibility is to express an opinion on these general-purpose financial statements based on our audit.

We conducted our audit in accordance with generally accepted auditing standards. Those standards require that we plan and perform the audit to obtain reasonable assurance about whether the general-purpose financial statements are free of material misstatement. An audit includes examining, on a test basis, evidence supporting the amounts and disclosures in the general-purpose financial statements. An audit also includes assessing the accounting principles used and significant estimates made by management, as well as evaluating the overall general-purpose financial statement presentation. We believe that our audit provides a reasonable basis for our opinion.

In our opinion, the general-purpose financial statements referred to above present fairly, in all material respects, the financial position of H. K. Fines Library, City of Fines, as of June 30, 20x1, and the results of its operations for the year then ended in conformity with generally accepted accounting principles.

                                                    Certified Public Accountant

---

GENERAL FIXED ASSET SCHEDULES ACCOMPANYING
THE FINANCIAL STATEMENTS

These CAFR schedules provide the same information about the library's general fixed assets as in chapter 8, but it is important that they be repeated here.

FIGURE 10-7   The General Fixed Asset Account Group

H. K. FINES LIBRARY
Comparative Schedules of General Fixed Assets—By Source
June 30, 20x0 and 20x1

	20x0	20x1
General Fixed Assets:		
Land	$ 450,000	$ 473,000
Buildings	5,125,000	5,125,000
Equipment	880,000	885,300
Construction-in-Progress	—	750,000
Collections:		
Inexhaustible	—	—
Circulating	200,000	200,000
Integrated Computer Library System:		
Hardware	395,000	405,000
Software	250,000	250,000
Bookmobile	95,000	95,000
Total General Fixed Assets	$7,395,000	$8,183,300
Investment in General Fixed Assets by Source:		
General Fund	$3,500,000	$4,265,300
State Grants	400,000	400,000
Federal Grants	900,000	900,000
Capital Projects Fund	2,000,000	2,000,000
Donations and Gifts	595,000	618,000
Total Investment in General Fixed Assets	$7,395,000	$8,183,300

H. K. FINES LIBRARY
Schedule of Changes in General Fixed Assets—By Department
For the Year Ended June 30, 20x1

	General Fixed Assets June 30, 20x0	Additions	Deductions	General Fixed Assets June 30, 20x1
Reference	$ 377,500	$ 75,000	$65,000	$ 387,500
Children's Library	212,500	—	1,000	211,500
Circulation	777,500	12,000	—	789,500
Regional History	332,500	—	5,700	326,800
Administration	120,000	—	—	120,000
General Use	5,575,000	773,000*	—	6,348,000
Total	$7,395,000	$860,000	$71,700	$8,183,300

* Includes land $23,000 and construction-in-progress $750,000

LETTER OF TRANSMITTAL

Usually the financial statements and schedules are accompanied by a transmittal letter written by the director of the library. The letter is usually part of the CAFR, and it is included in an introductory section that incorporates a table of contents.[3] The letter is addressed to the general public and the board. The purpose of this letter is to highlight the financial environment the NFO is facing in the current year and in future years. The letter should point out that the responsibility for the financial statements rests with the management of the NFO, as the financial statements were prepared by management. In addition, it should be stated that the management of the NFO believes that all necessary information and disclosures have been made to make the statements both accurate and understandable. Also, the guidelines under which the statements have been prepared (i.e., generally accepted accounting principles) should be stated.[4] If any environmental factors are affecting the NFO now or in the near future, they should be disclosed. The letter should be signed by the director of the NFO. An example of a transmittal letter from the H. K. Fines Library is illustrated in figure 10-8.

The list of supplemental statistical data in the CAFR is not limited in any manner as its purpose is to provide additional information about the NFO. Obviously, those financial conditions vary from one organization to another. The format of the minimum financial package that is issued to the public about the financial operations of the NFO is illustrated in figure 10-9, where it can be seen that the transmittal letter heads up the report. Although the transmittal letter does not have to be part of the GPFS, it is recommended that it be included. The combined financial statements are included in the second section of the package. Included with the financial statements are Notes to the Financial Statements and the GPFS audit opinion.

If the CAFR is used, the order of the financial components begins with the transmittal letter, followed by the combined financial statements, notes to the financial statements, any combining financial statements, account group reports, the auditor's opinion, and ends with the various schedules of statistical information, as for example, statistics on patron usage and grant dollars received over the last five years.

EXERCISE 10-1   The Combined Financial Statements

1. Explain the difference between consolidated and combined financial statements. Which method is more likely to be used by an NFO?

2. Prepare a list of the financial information and financial statements prepared for the CAFR and the GPFS. Why are there differences between the lists?

**FIGURE 10-8   Transmittal Letter for the Financial Statements Written
by the Director of the Library**

To members of the public and the Board of Directors: August 15, 20x1

Enclosed herein is the financial report of the H. K. Fines Library as of June 30, 20x1. The accuracy, completeness, and fairness of this report is the responsibility of the management of the H. K. Fines Library. Every effort has been made to ensure that the reports are accurately prepared and that all the necessary disclosures have been made to make these financial reports complete.

The accompanying reports, which have been prepared under generally accepted accounting principles, consist of two sections:

1. The financial statements, notes to the financial statements, and the auditor's opinion.
2. The supplemental financial schedules which highlight specific financial information about the Library's operations

The Library is in sound financial condition as of the year ending June 30, 20x1, but there are several environmental factors affecting the Library which are of concern to its future functioning. In recent years, there have been cutbacks in the grants and funding available to the Library, especially from the Federal government. During the fiscal year ending June 30, 20x1, the Library has been fortunate to receive grant support from the State and Federal governments. It cannot be assumed that this support will continue. If an additional level of funding is not found from other sources in the future, the Library will be faced with making certain curtailments in its present level of services to the community. Every effort will be made to control costs prior to the curtailment of any of our programs.

A second factor affecting the Library's operations relates to the completion of construction on a new building for the Library. In order for construction to be completed on the building, certain variances from the City's building code need to be approved. At the present time, these changes are being considered by the City Council, and the Library anticipates that these variances will be approved and the building will be occupied by the Library on schedule.

Efforts have been made over the past year to upgrade the financial reporting of the H. K. Fines Library in order to provide better financial information to the City Council, and the citizens of the City of Fines and Backlog County. We hope that you will find the following financial statements useful in understanding your Library.

Sue Fines
Director
H. K. Fines Library

FIGURE 10-9   Components of an NFO's GPFS Package for Public Issuance

Introductory Material
    Director's Transmittal Letter (optional)
Audited Material
    Combined Financial Statements
        SREF
        Balance Sheet
        SREF2
        Statement of Cash Flows
        GPFS Audit Opinion

ANALYSIS OF THE FINANCIAL STATEMENTS

Financial statements prepared under GAAP represent an accepted method of accounting that is widely understood. This common foundation provides a basis for further analysis of these statements, and this analysis provides the NFO with information about its financial and performance trends.

The points of financial interest for NFOs are slightly different than those of profit-oriented corporations. For example, the groups interested in the financial performance of a corporation are the management, the stockholders, the creditors, and governmental agencies. The stockholders, a very influential group, are interested in high returns in the form of dividends and stock appreciation. This stockholder concern for dividends and stock appreciation translates into an intense push for high earnings by managers. The other two interest groups, creditors and governmental agencies, are concerned with different aspects of the corporation's performance. The creditors of a corporation are interested in the corporation's long-term earning power to repay its debt. The governmental agencies are interested in various regulatory and compliance aspects of the corporation's activities.

In an NFO, it is significant that no stockholder group is present. Although the interests of creditors and governmental agencies are unchanged, the replacement of stockholder groups with public service concerns changes managers' orientations. Yet, NFO management must still review organizational financial trends to determine the organization's financial ability to continue to meet its changing service goals.

It is important that the service orientation of an NFO be understood prior to analyzing its financial statements. Financial analysis of the NFO is not oriented toward rate-of-return considerations. The NFO is concerned with the viability of its programs, and this concern is related to questions about its cash position, its Fund Balance account, and the sources from which it receives support. In analyzing the financial reports of NFOs, it is important to take into account the central question about the NFO's ability to continue its programs successfully. Here, the analysis is directed first toward that question.

FINANCIAL RATIO ANALYSIS

Ratio analysis can be related to financial ratios or performance ratios. Financial ratios use past financial data, largely from the financial statements, to analyze trends and underlying relationships. Performance ratios are related to evaluating the effectiveness and/or efficiency of program performance through the activities of personnel. Performance ratios can be computed by using financial data, level-of-output information, or a mixture of both.

Financial ratios will be evaluated in this section and performance ratios in a later section.[5] A first consideration in using financial ratio analysis is the method of accounting that is used. With the financial ratios computed here, it is assumed a modified accrual method of accounting is used. If an organization is using the cash basis or governmental accrual, the computation and interpretation of these ratios will not have much significance. If cash-based financial statements are available, they need to be converted to modified accrual basis before any of the ratios described here can be accurately interpreted.

For ratios to have meaning, they must be compared over a historical period to analyze trends. Historical comparisons investigate ratio trends within one organization over consecutive time periods or between organizations of similar size (at the same period) to determine deviations. The primary purpose of this analysis is to determine how ratios have changed over the specified period and whether the organization's position has improved or deteriorated. The primary purpose of the second type of comparison is to determine how similar NFOs are performing at the same point in time. (The basis for "similar size" could be the dollars in the budget appropriation.) This would allow an organization to determine if it is seriously out of alignment in a particular financial area. At the present time, there is no set of referenced or available financial ratios data for different-size libraries with which comparison can be made. Therefore, it is usually necessary to make comparisons within one specific library to determine historical trends.

Many of the financial ratios that are explained in this section are directed at the organization as a whole rather than any specific fund. Several ratios are used to measure the financial flexibility of the NFO. For example, two NFOs may receive the same amount of revenue and support, and both could have approximately the same expenditures, yet one of these organizations would be able to have a flexible response to the changing requirements of its patrons whereas the other organization could not respond or is very slow to respond. Such a difference can often be attributed to the type of administration in the two organizations, but it can also be related to differences in their financial structure.

If an organization is to respond to the changing needs of its users, there must be sufficient funds for it to add or change programs. It is possible to apply financial ratio analysis to determine if any of the inaction is related to an organization's financial structure. In order for monies to be available for new programs, the administration must be able to make discretionary spending choices. Yet, in some NFOs expenditures may be heavily weighted toward mandated expenditures, which may be necessary under grant programs or other restricted conditions under which monies have been received.

Figure 10-10 shows a number of relevant financial ratios. Ratio 1 can be used to measure the financial flexibility of an NFO's General Fund. As the percentage of mandated expenditures and transfers becomes a larger percent of total revenue and support, the organization is less able to respond to the needs of its patrons with new programs or special activities. If this ratio is computed for two organizations, and for one it is 50 percent and for the other it is 89 percent, it is obvious that it would be hard for the second organization to respond to additional needs of its patrons with new spending or through the curtailment of old programs. An organization that has 89 percent of its programs mandated cannot respond very quickly to new needs. Thus, ratio 1, the Percentage of Mandated Expenses and Transfers, provides an indication of the NFO's financial flexibility.

"Mandated transfers" are required cash transfers from the General Fund to other funds. The ratio would not be computed for a fund in which all the spending was mandated for a specific purpose such as special revenue, expendable endowments, or capital project funds. For a transfer to be considered a mandated transfer, it would be required by more than NFO board action. Any transfers made under the action of a board are considered discretionary rather than mandatory. Although staff salaries are not transfers, they should be treated as mandated transfers if the staff cannot be terminated relatively quickly.

Another ratio of financial flexibility relates to "discretionary" balances in the organization's Fund Balance. A discretionary balance in the Fund Balance includes any portion of the Fund Balance that has been designated by the board for a specific purpose as well as any portion of the Fund Balance that is undesignated. The discretionary balance in the fund balances can be used for new programs and capital expenditures.[6] Therefore, increases in discretionary portions of Fund Balance totals are an indication of increases in financial flexibility. Ratios 2 and 3 in figure 10-10 are directed at detecting trends in the flexible portion of the fund balances. Ratio 2, Discretionary Fund Balance Changes, analyzes the change in the Fund Balance available for discretionary expenditures from one year to the next.

In ratio 2, the discretionary portion of the Fund Balance for the current year is divided by the discretionary portions of the Fund Balance total in the previous year. If the result of the computation is more than 100 percent, it

FIGURE 10-10 Financial Ratios

1. Percentage of Mandated Expenditures and Transfers $= \dfrac{\text{Mandated Expenditures and Mandatory Transfers}}{\text{Total Revenues and Support}}$

2. Discretionary Fund Balance Changes $= \dfrac{\text{Current Year Board-Designated and Undesignated Fund Balance Dollars}}{\text{Prior Year Board-Designated and Undesignated Fund Balance Dollars}}$

3. Fund Balance Ratio $= \dfrac{\text{Board-Designated and Undesignated Fund Balance}}{\text{Total Assets (not including fixed assets)}}$

4. Spending Ratio $= \dfrac{\text{Total Revenue and Support} + \text{Other Financing Sources}}{\text{Total Expenditures and Mandatory Transfers}}$

5. Excess/Deficiency Ratio (General Fund) $= \dfrac{\text{General Fund Excess (Deficiency)}}{\text{Total Revenue and Support} + \text{Other Financing Sources}}$

6. Governmental Support $= \dfrac{\text{Revenue and Support from Governmental Sources}}{\text{Total Revenue and Support} + \text{Other Financing Sources}}$

7. Rate of Return on Investments $= \dfrac{\text{Investment Income (unrealized and realized gains) on nonexpendable trusts}}{\text{Average cost of nonexpendable investments}}$

8. Deferred Maintenance Ratio $= \dfrac{\text{Maintenance Expenditures}}{\text{Total Plant and Equipment} \times .05}$

9. Cash Turnover $= \dfrac{\text{Total Expenditures and Mandatory Transfers}}{\text{Average Monthly Cash Balance}}$

indicates that there has been an increase in the Fund Balance available for discretionary spending. If the result is less than 100 percent, it means that the discretionary portion of the Fund Balances has decreased from the previous year and the financial flexibility of the organization is also likely to have decreased. A trend of continual decreases in the discretionary portion of the Fund Balance indicates decreases in the organization's ability to respond to any new needs of its patrons within a reasonable period of time. Another check on this trend is the relationship between the discretionary portion of the Fund Balance and total assets. If there is a continual decrease in the discretionary portion of the Fund Balance as a percentage of total assets, it would be expected that the financial flexibility of the organization would also tend to decrease. Ratio 3, the Fund Balance Ratio, measures this relationship by dividing the total assets of the NFO into the discretionary portion of the Fund Balance. A continual decrease in the Fund Balance ratio from year to year indicates that the organization's financial flexibility is probably decreasing.

These first three ratios are used to analyze the financial flexibility in an NFO and its internal ability to respond to new program and activity needs. The ability of an NFO to respond to legitimate needs of its patrons within a reasonable time period can be hampered by the organization's financial inflexibility.

The next three ratios, 4, 5, and 6, analyze trends in the revenue and support received by the NFO. These ratios are specifically directed at determining how well the expenditures of the current year stayed within the revenue and support received in the current year. They are also directed at determining the level of governmental support to the organization. Ratio 4, the Spending Ratio, shows whether the organization's expenditures stayed within the revenues received in the current year. Although these variances are apparent in comparing budget and actual expenditures, this ratio provides a concise number for the organizational analysis. All revenue and support is divided by total expenditures and mandatory transfers. The numerator in this ratio does not include additions to capital received during the year, but only revenue and support. Transfers that are not mandatory are not included in the denominator of the ratio. If the ratio is equal to 1, it means the organization broke even in terms of the relationship between revenue and support and expenditures and mandatory transfers. If the ratio is greater than 1, there was a surplus, and if the ratio is less than 1, a deficiency developed during the year. In the latter case, the organization could draw on a previous year's surplus available in the Fund Balance to finance its operations during the year. This type of deficit financing can only provide support for a short-term period.

The fifth ratio relates the excess or deficiency in the General Fund to the total revenue and support received by that fund during the current fiscal year. This ratio is called the Excess/Deficiency Ratio. The *excess* is the amount of revenues and support that remains after current-year expenditures have been deducted. Any prior-year expenditures deducted to compute the excess or deficiency should be added back to the excess before the ratio is computed, as this is a current year ratio. Mandatory transfers in and out should be deducted from the excess or added to the deficiency, respectively. This ratio shows a relationship between an adjusted excess and revenue and support that would highlight problems more quickly than the financial information on the SREF. If there is a deficiency, the Excess-Deficiency Ratio will be equal to a negative number. The major significance of a negative number is that a deficiency exists. This ratio provides a means of determining whether the General Fund's operations were financed from current-year revenues and support. When the ratio is viewed over a period of several years, it also provides a means to determine if the General Fund is tending toward continual deficiencies and whether those deficiencies are increasing or decreasing over time.

Another concern—beyond whether the organization is operating within the finances it receives in a year—is the sources of support. Ratio 6 investigates the percentage of revenue and support received from intergovernmental sources. Revenue received from intergovernmental sources includes all the monies received from the federal, state, city, and county governments, regardless of the form in which it is granted. The major source of revenue and support for many NFOs is other governments, and if this source of monies should decrease, it can have a major impact on the services offered. For this reason, decreases in the percent of revenue and support received should be further analyzed to determine the specific source that has been reduced. Ratio 6, Governmental Support Rate, is directed at determining the amount of revenue and support received from intergovernmental sources as a percentage of all revenue and support. Review of this ratio over a period of several years should provide a clear indication of the trend in this source of revenue and support, as well as the rate at which it is changing. By changing this ratio to include only one source of intergovernmental revenue at a time in the numerator, it is possible to isolate the trend for that single source of support. It is, of course, also possible to determine the percentage contributions of other sources to the total revenue and support of the organization. Another revenue source that needs to be analyzed is the percent of return on investments held by the organization. Ratio 7, Rate of Return on Investments, investigates this relationship by dividing the endowment's investment income (without unrealized or realized gains and losses) by the average cost of investments during the year. The investment income should be reduced by any commission and service charges the NFO is required to pay. The average cost of investments is found by adding the beginning and ending investment cost values and dividing the total by 2. The rate of return on investments can be based on a cost or market valuation, but the base needs to be consistent from year to year. This method is a common way of determining the rate of return. From this information, it can be determined whether the organization is earning an adequate rate of return on its investments for the amount of risk it is willing to accept. If the rate of return appears low, this may indicate that a change in portfolio management is needed.

It is important for the NFO to maintain its fixed assets (building and equipment) in good working order. This means incurring costs for preventive maintenance expenditures before a building or equipment arrives at such a state of disrepair that it can only be replaced. If these fixed assets are not being properly maintained, the NFO is incurring deferred maintenance costs that will turn small repair expenditures into large future expenditures. Ratio 8 provides a means to analyze the level of deferred maintenance in an organization. The current year's maintenance expenditures are divided by the total plant and equipment in the organization multiplied by 5 percent. Five percent is an arbitrary number based on the assumption that 5 percent of the cost of facilities would be a minimum amount to spend on maintaining the facilities in any one year. If it is necessary, the ratio can be separately computed for buildings and equipment. The purpose is to compare the amount of actual expenditures for preventive maintenance made by the NFO with a recommended level. If the ratio is less than one, it means that maintenance expenditures need to be increased to keep the level of deferred maintenance from increasing in the organization. This ratio is important because as budget cuts occur, maintenance expenditures are usually the first expenditures to be reduced.

The last ratio, ratio 9, is directed at determining how efficiently the cash of the organization is handled. The Cash Turnover Ratio attempts to determine the level of average monthly cash balances that are maintained in relation to the amount of yearly expenses and mandatory transfers. A high turnover ratio indicates that minimum cash balances are maintained in relationship to expenses and mandatory transfers. Holding excessive cash balances within the NFO reduces the earnings that can be received from investing cash into short-term investments. (The average monthly cash balance is computed by determining the cash balance at the end of each month and finding the average of this total.)[7] The Cash Turnover Ratio should be checked to determine if minimum cash balances are maintained, i.e., those balances that are minimum to meet the monthly payment needs of the organization.

The majority of the financial ratios highlighted here are directed at the viability of the NFO. Once these ratios are computed, they need to be compared (over several years) to produce trends and provide indications about changes, if any, in the NFO. The ratios illustrated here may be computed on a monthly, quarterly, or annual basis depending on the needs of the NFO. These ratios are important because although an organization may continue to exist, it may exist only with a curtailed level of patron services. Reductions in program activities may be made necessary by cutbacks in resources, but also by subtle changes in financial structure that become apparent through financial ratio analysis. It is important that these changes be recognized. In order to compute these ratios and perform the analysis described here, a library must have a good set of financial statements prepared under GAAP.

Analysis of financial ratios is important for evaluating the continuing viability of an organization, but other ratios are useful in providing information about how efficiently the organization is operating. These ratios are called *performance ratios*.

From the Library Desk: Financial information does not necessarily correlate/indicate quality of service. Need to analyze the worth of a service, project, or resource in relationship to expenditures.

Anonymous survey respondent

EXERCISE 10-2   Financial Ratio Analysis

1. Compute all nine financial ratios in figure 10-10 for the H. K. Fines Library, based on the combined financial statements and notes to the financial statements in figures 10-2, 10-3, 10-4, and 10-5 for the period ending June 30, 20x1, and the Comparative Schedules of General Fixed Assets in figure 10-7. Additional information:

    There are no mandatory transfers.
    Mandated expenditures total $274,568.
    Maintenance expenditures are equal to $250,000.
    The beginning cash balance is $376,050.

2. A series of financial ratios has been calculated for the Sandra Treble Library for the year ending June 30, 20x1. The results of the computation are shown below, and they need to be interpreted. You are to (a) interpret the results of the computations to the library's administration and (b) determine if additional information would help you understand the implications of these ratios.

Ratio	Results
1. Percentage of Mandated Expenses and Transfers	70%
2. Discretionary Fund Balance Changes	102%
3. Fund Balance Ratio	10%
4. Spending Ratio	1.2%
5. Excess/Deficiency Ratio (General Fund)	1%
6. Governmental Support	79%
7. Rate of Return on Investments	6%
8. Deferred Maintenance Ratio	60%
9. Cash Turnover	25 times

3. Financial ratio information for the Sandra Treble Library (question 2) has been collected for the June 30, 20x1 and 20x2 fiscal years, as well as for the 20x3 year-end. With this new data, reanalyze the financial situation facing the Treble Library in the year ahead.

		Results		
Ratio		20x1	20x2	20x3
1. Percentage of Mandated Expenses and Transfers		75%	73%	70%
2. Discretionary Fund Balance Changes		70%	65%	102%
3. Fund Balance Ratio		9%	8.2%	10%
4. Spending Ratio		.88	.98	1.2
5. Excess/Deficiency Ratio		−3%	.05%	1%
6. Governmental Support		87%	80%	79%
7. Rate of Return on Investments		4%	12%	11%
8. Deferred Maintenance Ratio		60%	55%	50%
9. Cash Turnover		10	18	25

4. It was said in the chapter that the computation of financial ratios lacks meaning if it is based on financial statements prepared under the cash basis rather than the modified accrual basis. Describe the changes that would occur in the following ratios if they were based on a cash system rather than a modified accrual method of accounting.
  a. Rate of Return on Investments
  b. Spending Ratio
  c. Deferred Maintenance Ratio

PERFORMANCE RATIO ANALYSIS

Although financial ratios have common meaning across many NFOs, performance ratios are more specifically related to the objectives of a particular NFO. The reason for the singularity of performance ratios is that the specific activity being measured may not be common among all NFOs. There is a greater conformity among governmental NFOs' financial statements, upon which the financial ratios are based, than among the activities performed within those organizations. Since the types of performance measures developed for NFOs will vary, this section will consider the two general performance measures that may be used to evaluate the efficiency and effectiveness of provided services. Additionally, the difficulty of implementing performance measures will be reviewed.

Performance analysis, as it is considered here, relates to the evaluation of the performance of departments, programs, and the individuals who are responsible for the functioning of those programs or departments. These evaluations of management performance are tied to efficiency or productivity and effectiveness measures. These two aspects of performance must be considered together (whenever possible) for a comprehensive evaluation of performance. Many but not all efficiency and effectiveness measures are dependent on the cost information reported in financial reports. Prior to considering these two types of performance measures, another question should be answered: Why use performance ratios?

There are a number of reasons for developing performance ratios within an NFO. The major reason is to develop some form of feedback to the administration and the public that goes beyond financial measures. Feedback of this nature is important if the NFO's administrators are to improve service delivery. Through use of these measurement procedures, it can be determined whether performance is improving or deteriorating. Such performance ratios can be used to evaluate whether services are being satisfactorily provided to the public. If performance ratios are established for specific achievement levels, it is easy to determine whether these objectives have been met. In effect, performance measures allow for better control over the activities of the organization and they provide a way to measure services provided to the NFO's patrons.

EFFICIENCY AND EFFECTIVENESS MEASURES

As previously stated, performance ratios may measure the efficiency or effectiveness of a function. When the efficiency of an operation is considered, an attempt is made to determine the relationship between the resources used and the results obtained from using those resources. In many cases, such relationships are evaluated using cost per unit of output measures. When there is a decrease in cost per unit of output, it is generally considered favorable from an efficiency or productivity viewpoint.[8] Figure 10-11 shows two performance ratios that illustrate efficiency measures. The first ratio, Cost per Item, puts a per-unit cost on each item added to the library's collection. This measure is computed by dividing the total program costs from the SREF by the number of accessions during the year. This is a measure of how much it costs to operate the entire library, and it indicates the cost of new material acquired for the library.[9] If it is clear that some of the yearly costs of operations in the library are not part of normal operations, they should be excluded from total

FIGURE 10-11   Efficiency Measures

1. $\text{Cost per Item} = \dfrac{\text{Total Program Expenses}}{\text{Accessions}}$

2. $\text{Maintenance Cost Ratio} = \dfrac{\text{Total Maintenance Costs}}{\text{Total Square Footage in Library}}$

program costs. An example of this type of cost might be a special grant for re-modeling the building.

An NFO normally establishes its yearly goals in terms of a particular per-formance measure, based partially on past performance and partially on the future needs of the organization. These yearly goals may be separated into monthly or quarterly targets. In all cases, goals are intended to be reachable. Such a goal might be to reduce the cost per unit of items added to a library's collection during the year by 5 percent. Of course, if the performance measure is a broad one, like the cost per unit of items added to the entire library, non-achievement of this goal leaves the administration of the library in a quandary. This situation arises because it is difficult to determine what actions need to be taken to improve such a broad per unit cost measure. Therefore, it is always better to have a cost-per-unit measure established by specific programs or de-partments, rather than on an entire library basis. If cost objectives of a particu-lar program or department are not satisfactorily met, it is easier to determine where to take corrective actions.

Another example of an efficiency measure that could be used to evaluate the NFO's cost of operations is the maintenance cost per square foot. Ratio 2, the Maintenance Cost Ratio, measures maintenance cost by dividing the num-ber of square feet in the organization's physical facilities into total mainte-nance costs for the fiscal year. Again, a goal can be established of reducing the cost per square foot of maintenance expenses by a specific percentage.

A problem with using cost-per-unit measures is how to deal with allocated costs. When efficiency ratios are based on per-unit cost information, some costs are directly related to the program functions but others are allocated overhead costs. These allocated (or assigned costs) are indirect overhead costs that are important to the functioning of the organization as a whole, but they do not directly contribute to the service function which is being evaluated on a unit cost basis. In addition, these costs are usually assigned on a basis that is outside the control of the person who is responsible for the particular ser-vice center. Therefore, in per-unit cost performance evaluations, it is not a good idea to include indirect or allocated costs as part of the total cost of a per-unit performance measure.

Another consideration when using per-unit cost information is the effect of inflation on the cost measure. There may be an increase in per-unit costs that does not reflect decreases in efficiency, but is simply attributable to the effects of increased inflation. Therefore, at times when inflation is considered serious, per-unit cost information should be downwardly adjusted for the ef-fects of inflation.

Both ratios in figure 10-11 are concerned with the efficiency of an NFO, but other measures need to be used to evaluate the effectiveness of program delivery. Effectiveness measures indicate how well a service is provided or how well an activity meets its established objectives. Effectiveness might mean reducing the time it takes to perform an activity while maintaining performance quality rather than directly reducing the cost per unit.

Yet another measure of effectiveness within an NFO is whether costs stay within budget guidelines. To determine whether budget guidelines are being followed, variances from budget appropriations should be investigated with a schedule such as a Statement of Comparison between Budget Appropriations and Actual Expenditures and Encumbrances (as illustrated in figure 10-12).[10] Although the SREF2 provides information of this nature, the Statement of Comparison between Budget Appropriations and Actual Expenditures and Encumbrances (SBAAE) provides this information in much more detail by department. Additionally, the SBAAE provides comparative financial information from the previous year (June 30, 20x0). As a performance objective, this analysis determines whether an NFO's administration is effective in controlling its costs of operation. The "actual encumbrances" in this statement, column two, are encumbrances that are still outstanding at the end of the 20x1 fiscal year. Note, however, that this statement does not measure how efficiently these resources were used.

In the SBAAE, the amounts shown under the Actual Expenditures and Encumbrances column are for expenditures in the current fiscal year; therefore, if any payments are for prior-year encumbrances, they need to be deducted. The "Budget Appropriation" column records the budget recognized at the beginning of the year.[11] Under each program classification there are a number of object expenditure classifications, such as supplies and automobile expenditures.

Looking at the statement for the Skyview County Library in figure 10-12, we can see that there are differences between the budgeted appropriations and the current expenditures and encumbrances. The difference is shown in the column headed Actual (Over) Under Budget. Some of these differences are over and some are under the budgeted amounts. Although it may appear that there is reason for concern only when the actual amounts are over the budgeted amounts, all significant differences should be reviewed to determine their cause. To be "under budget" is generally considered good, but if excessive amounts were approved initially, the budget itself is not necessarily "good." Therefore, if actual spending is significantly below budgeted amounts, we would need to determine why so much was initially allocated to this budget classification. This investigation evaluates the effectiveness of the NFO in administering its budget.

For example, in Circulation, Salary and Benefits expenditures were $2,600 under budget. This difference could be explained by personnel leaving the library in the latter part of the fiscal year and not earning the salary that had been allocated. In any case, if this difference is considered significant, it should be investigated. For the same reason, it may be necessary to investigate why actual expenses and encumbrances are $1,300 over the budgeted amounts for Salary and Benefits in Administration.

QUALITY MEASURES

There is yet another aspect to efficient and effective performance that needs to be considered. Although efficient performance indicates how cost-effectively a task is performed, efficiency measures alone cannot evaluate patrons' satisfaction with the service. It is conceivable that a task could be performed efficiently, yet generate little satisfaction among patrons who receive the service. Performance measures should not measure efficiency without evaluating customer satisfaction. Of course, it is more difficult to gauge patrons' satisfaction than to calculate a financial ratio or efficiency measures. But quality measures must also be collected because it cannot be assumed that increases in efficiency and effectiveness automatically guarantee increases in satisfaction among patrons. Patron satisfaction surveys should be used in conjunction with effectiveness and efficiency measures.

Performance measures of this nature measure such things as percentage of users satisfied with services, average response time to questions or calls, capacity levels at theater performances, and collection levels from pledges in a fund drive.

IMPLEMENTATION ISSUES

Another concern with performance measures is their successful implementation. In this regard, a first step is an expression of strong commitment from top-level administration for the establishment and use of performance measures. Clearly time and effort will be needed to implement the system; therefore, top-level administration should be supportive of this need for time. In organizations with strong hierarchical structures, it may be difficult for employees to take the commitment of higher-level managers seriously. In fact, persuading staff members of management's true commitment may be the most difficult step to implement. If this step is not correctly implemented, the program of performance evaluation will not work.

It is also important that the service centers to be evaluated be correctly identified. Usually this is fairly simple and is based on the organizational structure within the NFO. When service activities are divided between two organizational units, this step takes more planning. Once the service centers within an NFO are classified, the next step is to identify the services and activities provided by these units. The service activities vary with the NFO, but they can include such factors as the number of questions answered, the number of miles of street to be cleaned, the number of meals prepared, or the number of tickets sold. After the service activities are identified, efficiency and effectiveness measures are developed to evaluate the success with which these services are being provided to the public.

FIGURE 10-12 Statement of Comparison between Budget Appropriations and Actual Expenditures and Encumbrances

SKYVIEW COUNTY LIBRARY
General Fund
Statement of Comparison between Budget Appropriations and Actual Expenditures and Encumbrances
For the Year Ended June 30, 20x1

	Budget Appropriations	Actual Expenditures and Encumbrances	Actual (Over) Under Budget	June 30, 20x0 Actual Expenditures and Encumbrances
Administrative:				
Supplies	$ 1,000	$ 1,200	$ (200)	$ 1,500
Automobile Expense	3,000	1,300	1,700	1,000
Postage	4,000	3,000	1,000	2,500
Salary and Benefits	27,000	28,300	(1,300)	16,250
Equipment Rental	400	42	358	450
Building Rental	7,000	5,500	1,500	—
Travel	2,000	1,200	800	2,000
Miscellaneous	600	350	250	300
	$ 45,000	$ 40,892	$4,108	$24,000
Reference:				
Books	$ 5,700	$ 6,000	$ (300)	$ 5,000
Salary and Benefits	22,100	22,100	—	15,550
Telephone	1,750	1,000	750	1,250
Postage	2,325	1,000	1,325	1,500
Equipment Rentals	250	202	48	—
Travel	1,200	1,000	200	1,500
Miscellaneous	175	15	160	200
	$ 33,500	$ 31,317	$2,183	$25,000

Children's Library:				
Books	$ 4,300	$ 4,500	$ (200)	$ 2,500
Postage	1,020	500	520	1,000
Salary and Benefits	31,000	30,600	400	9,150
Telephone	300	350	(50)	200
Equipment Rentals	200	178	22	—
Miscellaneous	180	150	30	150
	$ 37,000	$ 36,278	$ 722	$13,000
Circulation:				
Records	$ 500	$ 400	$ 100	$ 300
Books	700	600	100	400
Salary and Benefits	28,000	25,400	2,600	18,550
Telephone	1,500	1,250	250	1,250
Periodicals	5,300	6,000	(700)	5,700
Equipment Rentals	400	189	211	—
Travel	2,000	1,750	250	—
Miscellaneous	100	60	40	100
	$ 38,500	$ 35,649	$2,851	$26,300
Regional History:				
Books	$ 3,000	$ 3,200	$ (200)	$ 1,000
Salary and Benefits	9,800	9,800		9,000
Postage	500	400	100	200
Telephone	475	400	75	200
Equipment Rentals	125	89	36	—
Travel	—	—		500
Miscellaneous	100	50	50	100
	$ 14,000	$ 13,939	$ 61	$11,000
Totals	$168,000	$158,075	$9,925	$99,300

Another step relates to development of the performance measures themselves, which can be done by a committee or by the administration of the NFO. Whatever method is chosen, the people who are going to be evaluated should make a serious contribution to the development of the measures. This participation is important if a commitment to performance is to exist among those individuals who will be evaluated. It is important that the performance measures be agreed upon as fair. Further, if a performance measure is not seen as clearly relating to the service function that is being performed, it is not likely to have much influence on the actions of the persons performing the service. The measures should be clearly and uniquely related to the type of service activities that are being performed. This will make it clear to staff members that their efforts are leading to better performance evaluations.

There is a danger that using only one or a limited number of performance ratios can lead to dysfuntional changes in behavior. This effect can be particularly obvious when a single performance ratio is used. Even if several performance measures are collected, one may be overemphasized by the evaluators. Suppose, for example, that response time appears to be the most important performance measure for a service center. As a result, the response time may decrease, but this lower response time may be achieved by a relatively large percentage decrease in *satisfactory* responses. To overcome this problem, response time should be interrelated to other measures, such as counting the number of questions or calls being answered. If the number of calls is decreasing, it may be because of unsatisfactory responses. Therefore, it is not good practice to use just one performance measure in one service center, as the personnel may concentrate on that aspect of service to the possible detriment of the organization's overall goals. Performance measures can be a powerful tool in encouraging behavior change if they are properly used, but care must be exercised to ensure that the new behavior is the type that is being sought.

The reporting system within the NFO should already lend itself to the collection of data for the development of performance measures. If possible, the use of performance measures should require development of only a minimum number of new forms for data collection. In addition, the personnel who are involved with the collection of the data should clearly understand how it is to be collected and how the ratios are to be computed. The performance measures for the various programs or departments in the NFO should be presented in a report that allows for easy comparisons. This presentation should include information on a prior period, whether monthly or quarterly, so that comparisons can be made with the current period. In addition, the objectives for a particular service area should be clearly stated on this report.

Once performance indicators are presented in report form, the last step in implementing and using a performance system includes setting achievable goals, taking corrective actions when performance does not meet set objectives, and providing the proper incentives for good performance. The implementation of a performance system is, in effect, the implementation of a feedback system, and one important reason for having a feedback system is to take the appropriate actions when feedback is received. Corrective actions will vary with the performance measure and the ability of the NFO to make changes when they are considered necessary. Not all variances from objectives will require corrective actions. Before any actions are taken, the magnitude of the variance from the objective needs to be considered, as well as the alternatives for corrective action available to the organization. When rewards are provided for good performance, it should be done in a way that makes it clear that efficiency and effectiveness are being recognized. An example of such a reward is merit pay for performance. Yet in too many organizations, merit pay is awarded for meeting unclear goals. When merit is determined in this fashion, it ceases to have positive motivational effects.

Finally, performance information should be timely. If it is not, the information collected may be too late for meaningful corrective actions to be taken. Praise for good performance levels should also be given promptly. Ideally, evaluations of performance should occur on at least a monthly basis.

Unlike financial ratios, which can be generated largely from reviewing the data in the accounts and on the financial statements, performance ratios require a commitment on the part of administrators in establishing agreed-upon performance objectives. Once these objectives are established, information must be collected to determine if these objectives are being met. If these performance measures are accepted and the objectives are not achieved, it means that lower evaluations may be necessary for those who are not performing at the agreed-upon levels. Although it is sometimes felt that the services provided by an NFO are unquantifiable, they can be quantified if consideration and thought is put into designing the evaluation measures.

EXERCISE 10-3   Performance Ratio Analysis

1. In recent years, the Harry Malone Library has been experiencing a decrease in governmental support. The director of the library has been aware of this trend and an attempt has been made to make up for the decrease with campaigns for pledges of financial support from the public. The total amount of pledges received has varied a great deal from year to year, and a large number of pledges have remained uncollected at year-end.
   a. Are there any performance measures that might be used so that the amount of variances in year-to-year pledges is apparent and more control is exercised over this variation?
   b. Suggest a performance measure that might be used to reduce the amount of uncollected pledges.

(Continued)

EXERCISE 10-3   Performance Ratio Analysis   *(Continued)*

    c. Can you think of any type of financial ratio that would help to determine whether the pledges are substituting for the funds lost from governmental sources?

2. The Morehead County Library has been experiencing an increase in the cost of building repairs and maintenance in recent years. In order to monitor the performance of the Custodial Department, which is responsible for the repairs and maintenance of the library, a performance measure was introduced. This performance ratio divided the number of square feet in the library into the costs of repairs and maintenance over the past three years. A goal was set in the current year to reduce the cost per square foot to one-half of its average over the last three years. The director emphasized to the Custodial Department the need to cut costs by achieving this goal, and the severe consequences if it was not attained. At the end of the current year, the goal had been achieved. The director was very happy with the results, and was about to explain to the board the success the library had achieved with reducing repair and maintenance costs, when the pipes from the lavatory above the boardroom burst and quickly ended the meeting. The director was embarrassed and decided never to use performance evaluation again. Comment on this situation and suggest ways to avoid problems such as this one when performance measures are used.

3. The difference between budget appropriations and actual expenses is considered a performance measure at the Whittfield Library. The Circulation Department at the Whittfield Library had been managed by Ms. Beth Wilson for twenty years. During that period, Ms. Wilson never exceeded her budgeted appropriations. Ms. Wilson retired at the beginning of the current fiscal year, and the Circulation Department was headed by Mr. Thomas Jones during the current fiscal year just ended. The Circulation Department's budgeted appropriations have just been compared with its total expenses in the current year, and the results show that expenses exceeded budgeted amounts by $1,000. Within the department, there were both positive and negative variances from budgeted amounts. The director of the library has just told Mr. Jones, "When Ms. Wilson was in charge, expenses were always under the budgeted amounts!" Should Mr. Jones be reprimanded for excessive spending? Why do you think Ms. Wilson's expenses were never over the budgeted amounts?

SUMMARY

This chapter illustrates the combined financial statements for the H. K. Fines Library. These combined financial statements are based on the financial statements that had been individually prepared for each of the funds in earlier chapters. The combined financial statements, notes to the financial statements, and auditor's opinion are the main financial documents in the NFO. In addition, an NFO may want to highlight certain aspects of its financial operations with supplemental statistical schedules. The supplemental schedules vary with the needs of the specific organization. Financial reports should be accompanied by a transmittal letter from the director of the NFO to accompany and introduce the organization's financial report. A combination of these financial documents can be presented to the public as either a comprehensive annual financial report (CAFR) or a general purpose financial statement (GPFS).

The second part of the chapter describes some of the ratios that may be used to analyze an NFO's financial statements. Here, financial ratio analysis is especially concerned with the continued viability of the NFO, and the ratios presented focus on this area. Financial ratios are useful for bringing to light trends that might otherwise go unnoticed. Another area of analysis is using ratios to measure the efficiency and effectiveness of operations. The examples in this chapter show how these ratios can be used to answer questions about whether program goals are being efficiently achieved. Financial ratios are more useful in making comparisons between organizations than are quality measures because financial ratios are based on financial statements that have common characteristics. Other, more quality oriented, performance measures will vary with the goals established for the individual NFO's programs. However all these ratios can be useful tools for managerial planning and decision making if used wisely.

NOTES

1. The City of Fines' General Fund made a transfer of monies to the library's Capital Project Fund from proceeds obtained in selling a bond issue. It should be noted that this was a transfer from the *city's* General Fund, not the library's. As financial data are aggregated upward from the library to the city, both transfers would appear on the same financial statement for the city and cancel one another in the totals column. This result occurs because one fund's transfer "in" is another fund's transfer "out," with a net result equal to zero, but that is not the case with component units such as the library. For this reason, the transfer remains in the library's "Memo Totals" column.

2. In the city's SREF, the library might be included in one column titled "component units." In that column, the library and the city's other component units are aggregated into one column. Obviously, little useful financial information is provided to the library from such an approach.

3. It would be acceptable to use this letter with the GPFS also.

4. If a cash or modified cash method is used, this needs to be stated.

5. The viewpoint taken here is to evaluate the separate performance of the library that is a component unit of a larger governmental organization. Obviously, the

viability of the larger unit significantly affects the financial health of its component units. If the financial analysis of the entire government were undertaken, different ratios and analysis would likely be required.

6. This assumes there is enough cash in the Cash balances to cover the expenditures that are eventually incurred.

7. If information is not available on a monthly basis, the beginning and ending cash balances for the fiscal year can be averaged by dividing their total by two.

8. Of course some organizations consider an increase in costs per unit as a good measures of quality. Most school systems believe an increase in the expenditures per pupil measures an increase in the quality of the education program. This creates a tendency toward higher and higher costs.

9. Accessions are not all book accessions. It is acceptable to count accessions other than books as equal to an equivalent number of books.

10. This schedule provides a basis for determining cost-per-unit efficiency measures also.

11. If the beginning budget appropriations were revised during the year, the revised amounts would appear in this column.

Answers to
the Exercises

CHAPTER 2

EXERCISE 2-1

1. A   =   L + FB
        = $35,000 + $40,000
        = $75,000

2. FB   =   A − L
        = $45,000 − $45,000
        =   Zero. The Fund Balance has a zero balance.

3. L   =   A − FB
        = $55,000 $15,000
        = $40,000

4. FB   =   A − L
        = $15,000 − $17,500
        =   −$2,500. The Fund Balance has a deficit. There have been more expenditures than there have been inflows of resources.

5. FB   =   A − L
        = $25,000 $15,000
        = $10,000. The Fund Balance should be equal to $10,000. The bookkeeper will have to check the books to find the error if the books are going to balance.

EXERCISE 2-2

1. Asset (Dr.); Asset (Cr.). Two asset accounts are affected.
   Equipment (Dr.); Cash (Cr.).

2. Asset (Dr.); Liability (Cr.).
   Cash (Dr.); Deferred Restricted Contributions (Cr.). The credit entry will vary depending on whether the NFO is classified as "governmental" or "nongovernmental."

3. Asset (Dr.); Liability (Cr.).
   Cash (Dr.); Loans Payable (Cr.).

EXERCISE 2-3

1. a. No. It creates a liability.

   b. No. This transaction is like a refund from a previous expenditure.

   c. Yes. User's Fee Revenues

   d. Yes. Interest Revenues

2. a. This is an expense or expenditure.

   b. This is not an expense but in governmental NFOs it is an expenditure.

   c. This is not an expense but in governmental NFOs it is an expenditure.

   d. This is usually not immediately an expense. It appears on the books as a prepaid asset; i.e., an asset that had been paid for ahead of its use. Once it is used, it turns into an expense. This method is acceptable with governmental NFOs, but many times these organizations record the expenditure as an expenditure also.

EXERCISE 2-4

1. Asset (Dr.); Revenue (Cr.).
   Cash (Dr.); Theatrical Revenues (Cr.).

2. Asset (Dr.); Revenue (Cr.).
   Cash (Dr.); Investment Revenue (Cr.).

3. Expenses (Dr.); Asset (Cr.).
   Xerox Rental Expense (Dr.); Cash (Cr.).

4. Expenses (Dr.); Liabilities (Cr.).
   Book Expenses (Dr.); Accounts Payable (Cr.).

   Although it may appear that books should be recorded as an asset, if these books are part of the circulating collections, they have an expected life of only one year, and they are an expense. Of course, if book purchases have an expected life of over one year, they should be recognized as an asset when they are purchased. In governmental NFOs, asset purchases are recorded as expenditures.

EXERCISE 2-5

1. a. Journalizing requires that entries be made in the General Journal.

   b. Posting requires the use of the General Journal and the General Ledger.

2. June 5 Office Supplies Inventory 725
         Accounts Payable   725
        Purchased office supplies

   June 7 Cash   85
         Deposits Payable   85
        Patrons' deposits

June 11	Delivery Expenses	7	
	Cash		7
	UPS delivery charge		

June 16	Deposits Payable	50	
	Cash		50
	A portion of deposits is returned		

June 27	Cash	75	
	Fines Revenue		75
	Total fines collected for the month		

June 27	Salary Expenses	7,500	
	Cash		7,500
	Employees' salaries for month		

June 27	Accounts Payable	725	
	Cash		725
	Paid for office supplies received on June 5		

3. a. T accounts needed to perform the analysis are shown here. Page 5 is recorded under the PR column.

Cash

Date	PR	Amount	Date	PR	Amount
June 5	5	$1,200	June 1	5	$250
			June 4	5	750
			June 6	5	50

Accounts Payable

Date	PR	Amount	Date	PR	Amount
June 1	5	$250	[In a "normal" situation there would be a credit balance in this account.]		

Salaries Payable

Date	PR	Amount	Date	PR	Amount
June 4	5	$750	[In a "normal" situation there would be a credit balance in this account.]		

Interest Revenue

Date	PR	Amount	Date	PR	Amount
			June 5	5	$1,200

Miscellaneous Expenses

Date	PR	Amount	Date	PR	Amount
June 6	5	$50			

b. The balance in the Cash account is $150. This is the difference between the debit of $1,200 and the total credits of $1,050 ($250 + $750 + $50 = $1,050).

4. The general ledger.

5. The posting reference, which is the account number, must be transferred to the general journal. Without this cross-reference, it is very difficult to trace transactions from the general journal to the general ledger.

6. It is possible to trace an entry from the general journal to the general ledger because the account number assigned to an account is posted to the post reference column in the general journal. This allows for a reference to the proper account in the general ledger. The same process works in reverse for tracing an entry from the general ledger to the general journal. The cross-reference key in the general ledger is the page number of the general journal and the date of the entry in the journal. Both the page number and the date are transferred to the general ledger in the posting process, and they allow for tracing entries back to the general journal. In a computerized system, the cross-referencing is automatically performed.

7. The answers are shown in figure 2-18.

CHAPTER 3

EXERCISE 3-1

1. a. No. Entries are made only when cash flows into or out of the NFO.

   b. Yes.

   c. Yes.

2. a. No. There is no cash inflow.

   b. Yes.

   c. Yes, if expected to be collected within 60 days; otherwise no.

3. a. No. There is no cash outflow.

   b. Yes.

   c. No. This is one of the differences between MAM and the accrual method.

4. a. An expenditure or disbursement

   b. A prepaid asset

   c. An expenditure, as there is no recognition of this type of prepaid item

5. The purchases method recognizes the expenditure for inventory items when they are purchased whereas the consumption method recognizes the expenditure when the inventory item is actually used. Under the second method, the expenditure is recognized at a later period.

EXERCISE 3-2

1. Journal entries for

   Question 2

   a. Cash: No entry.

   b. Accrual: PLEDGES RECEIVABLE   22,500
                    PLEDGES REVENUE   22,500

   The pledges receivable are recorded for only the amount that is estimated to be collectible. In some cases, an uncollectible account is established for the $2,500 estimated to be uncollectible.

   c. MAM: PLEDGES RECEIVABLE   22,500
                    PLEDGES REVENUE   22,500

   Question 3

   a. Cash: No entry.

   b. Accrual: June 30   INTEREST EXPENSE   7,000
                          INTEREST PAYABLE   7,000

   c. MAM: No entry.

   Question 4

   a. Cash: INSURANCE EXPENDITURES   250
                    CASH   250

   b. Accrual: PREPAID ASSETS   250
                    CASH   250

   c. MAM: INSURANCE EXPENDITURES   250
                    CASH   250

2. All three accounting methods use the same entry.

May 1	SUPPLIES EXPENSE OR EXPENDITURES	750	
	CASH		750

3. The entries follow:

Accrual and MAM:

May 1	INVENTORY OF SUPPLIES	750	
	CASH		750

Cash: The cash method recognizes only inflows and outflows of cash, and it does not use a consumption method.

May 1	SUPPLIES EXPENSE	750	
	CASH		750

EXERCISE 3-3

1. The Balance Sheet is a financial statement that provides a list and a dollar balance for assets, liabilities, reserves or restrictions as well as the total balance in the Fund Balance accounts. The Balance Sheet shows the balances in these accounts as of a specific date.

2. As compared with the accrual-based balance sheet,

   a. the cash-based statement does not list any liabilities.

   b. the cash-based accounting system does not recognize any reserves in the fund balance.

   c. in general, no prepaid assets are recognized on the cash-based balance sheet.

3. In the case of Receipts over Disbursements, a cash-based statement is being used. When this amount is described as "Net Assets," it is the terminology used in an accrual-based financial statement for a nongovernmental NFO. As such, it incorporates restricted grants and other funding that has a short time frame to becoming unrestricted assets of the NFO. Net assets also include those assets that are permanently restricted. Thus net assets are more expansive than the difference between cash inflows (receipts) and cash outflows (disbursements).

4. The major difference between these terms is that net assets included restricted resources that are considered liabilities when the traditional fund balance concept is adopted. The major difference therefore is in the accounting perspective as to the characteristics that a liability represents.

5. The major difficulty in using a cash-based balance sheet in making financial decisions is that no liabilities are listed. This makes it appear that all the cash is available for spending when this is usually not the case. In using a cash-based Statement of Receipts and Disbursements, the difficulty is that the expenditures/disbursements are not assigned to the periods in which they are incurred, and the revenues are not assigned to the periods in which they are earned. The overall result of this is a rather unclear financial picture for an NFO using a cash-based system.

EXERCISE 3-4

	Balance Sheet Prepared Under		
	MAM	Cash Basis	Accrual Basis
Cash	✔	✔	✔
Interest Income Receivable	✔		✔
Prepaid Insurance			✔
Reserve in Fund Balance	✔		
Accounts Payable	✔		✔
Temporarily Restricted Net Assets			✔*

---

*For nongovernmental NFOs

EXERCISE 3-5

OUTER BANKS PIRATE MUSEUM
Balance Sheet
June 30, 20x5

Assets		Liabilities	
Cash	$75,000	Salaries Payable	$3,700
Inventory of Supplies	500		
Grant Receivable	12,500		
		Total Liabilities	$ 3,700
		Net Assets	
		Unrestricted	$71,800[1]
		Restricted:	
		Temporarily Restricted	12,500
Total Assets	$88,000	Total Liabilities and Net Assets	$88,000

---

1. When the entire amount of estimated revenues is not entirely used for appropriations, the remainder will be put into net assets. It should be noted that the unrestricted portion of the net assets also includes a $500 balance in the supplies account that is unrestricted but unspendable.

CHAPTER 4

EXERCISE 4-1

a. ESTIMATED REVENUES	110,000	
APPROPRIATIONS		101,100
FUND BALANCE		8,900

b. ESTIMATED REVENUES   110,000

Investment Income	75,000	
Federal Awards	25,000	
Fund-raising Campaign	10,000	
APPROPRIATIONS		101,100
Personnel		75,000
Administrative Supplies		4,500
Craft Supplies		5,200
Utilities		10,100
Staff Development		1,100
Publicity		1,200
Repairs and Maintenance		4,000
FUND BALANCE		8,900

c. Without departmental expense information, it is very difficult to control the level of spending. The major reason is that responsibility for overexpending resources cannot be traced to a single department or individual. The accounting system must provide sufficient information to assign this responsibility. This information can be developed by assigning account numbers to the expense accounts in each department.

d. ESTIMATED REVENUES   110,000

Investment Income	75,000	
Federal Awards	25,000	
Fund-raising Campaign	10,000	
APPROPRIATIONS		101,100
Craft Education		50,550
Personnel		37,500
Administrative Supplies		2,250
Craft Supplies		2,600
Utilities		5,050
Staff Development		550
Publicity		600
Repairs & Maintenance		2,000
Exhibits		
Personnel		37,500
Administrative Supplies		2,250
Craft Supplies		2,600
Utilities		5,050
Staff Development		550
Publicity		600
Repairs and Maintenance		2,000
FUND BALANCE		8,900

EXERCISE 4-2

1. From a quick review of the account, it is obvious that the bookkeeper made many mistakes in recording the transactions, and it will be necessary to review all the accounts in the library's accounting system. The corrected Craft Supplies

account is shown below. The $300 transfer to the Regional History Collection is an acceptable transfer out of the Craft Supplies account. In fact, it may be necessary to make other transfers from one account to another during the library's fiscal year. As long as these are not taken from budgetary control points established by the Board, these transfers among budget lines are acceptable. The transfer should be shown as a reduction of the year's appropriation because it is not an expenditure in the Craft Supplies appropriation.

The returned supplies on August 1 should be considered a reduction of a previous expenditure and therefore an increase in the unencumbered balance. The bookkeeper incorrectly recorded all invoice amounts in the accounts as no check was made between the amount on the original purchase order and the final invoice. All accounts in the system need to be reviewed because of the bookkeeper's mistakes.

2. A number of solutions are acceptable for this problem, as long as the personnel salaries are recorded at the proper amounts and the total estimated revenues are computed correctly. The investment income is not given, but it can be calculated. The amount appropriated for the various expenditures must sum to $206,400. The credit to the Fund Balance is $6,600; as a result the amount of Estimated Revenues is $213,000. Once the Estimated Revenues is determined, the earned revenues are equal to $94,200 and subtracting from the Estimated Revenues leaves the amount of $118,800 estimated to be earned in investment income.

The dollar allocations to appropriations, other than personnel salaries, can vary from one answer to another. The major purpose of this exercise is to develop an understanding of the relationships between Estimated Revenues, Appropriations, and the Fund Balance, as well as attempting to set up the budget entry.

ESTIMATED REVENUES	213,000		
Investment Income	118,800		
Tuition Fees—Craft Ed.	57,000		
Ticket Revenues—Plays	25,000		
Ticket Revenues—Bus Trips	12,200		
APPROPRIATIONS		206,400	
Bookkeeping		7,500	
Personnel			6,700
Supplies			800
Administration—Director		50,800	
Personnel			41,000
Publicity			2,200
Telephone			2,100
Staff Development			800
Professional Fees			4,700
Trip Coordination		5,500	
Personnel			4,000
Reservation Deposits			1,000
Supplies			500

APPROPRIATION-EXPENDITURE LEDGER
Account No.: 72-734
Account Title: Craft Supplies
Appropriation: $975

Year: 20x2–20x3
Fund: General Fund

Date	Description	PR	Purchase Order No.	Encumbrances			Expenditures	Unencumbered Balance
				Issued	Liquidated	Outstanding Balance		
July 1	Appropriation							$975
July 15	Craft Supplies		15	$185		$185		$790
July 25	Invoice Received		15		$185	—	$200	$775
Aug 1	Returned Damaged Goods/ Reduced Appropriation		15			—	$ (25)	$800
Sept 5	$300 transferred to Regional History Fund					—		$500
Sept 9	Supplies		25	$225		$225		$275
Oct 3	Invoice Received		7		$225	—	$250	$250

	Children's Activities	56,500	
	Personnel		32,500
	Set Production Labor		11,000
	Set Production Supplies		9,000
	Costumes		4,000
	Art Exhibits	22,100	
	Personnel		15,100
	Showing Rentals		7,000
	Crafts Education	64,000	
	Personnel		6,500
	Supplies		2,500
	Faculty Salaries		55,000
FUND BALANCE		6,600	

CHAPTER 5

EXERCISE 5-1

a. June 30

FUND BALANCE	2,500	
APPROPRIATIONS	120,000	
RESERVE FOR ENCUMBRANCES	5,000	
EXPENSES		122,500
ENCUMBRANCES		5,000

In this case, the Fund Balance is reduced because expenses are more than appropriations.

June 30

FUND BALANCE	2,000	
REVENUES	118,000	
ESTIMATED REVENUES		120,000

Again, the Fund Balance is reduced. This time it is reduced because all the estimated revenues did not materialize through collections.

b. June 30

FUND BALANCE	7,500	
APPROPRIATIONS	115,000	
EXPENSES		122,500

In this entry, the Reserve for Encumbrances and Encumbrances are not closed because they are nonlapsing. Also, $5,000 is left in the Appropriations account.

June 30

FUND BALANCE	2,000	
REVENUES	118,000	
ESTIMATED REVENUES		120,000

c. The accounts payable would not be equal to the encumbrances because encumbrances only become accounts payable after the sales invoice is received and approved for payment. At that point, the original encumbrance is reversed out of the accounts and an account payable may be recognized. Any equality is only a chance occurrence.

d. **Lapsing**

HERCHAL PUBLIC LIBRARY
Balance Sheet
June 30, 20x3

Assets		Liabilities and Fund Balance	
Cash	$ 15,000	Liabilities:	
Grants Receivable	18,000	Accounts Payable	$ 25,700
Inventory	2,200		
Investments	125,000	Fund Balance[1]	132,300
		Res. for Inventory	2,200
		Total Liabilities	
Total Assets	$160,200	and Fund Balance	$160,200

Nonlapsing

HERCHAL PUBLIC LIBRARY
Balance Sheet
June 30, 20x3
Assets

Cash		$ 15,000
Grants Receivable		18,000
Inventory		2,200
Investments		125,000
Total Assets		$160,200
Liabilities, Appropriations and Fund Balance		
Liabilities:		
Accounts Payable		$ 25,700
Appropriations	$5,000	
Less: Encumbrances	5,000	—
Fund Balance:		
Unreserved[2]		127,300
Reserved for: Encumbrances		5,000
Inventory		2,200
Total Fund Balance		$134,500
Total Liabilities, Appropriations & Fund Balance		$160,200

---

1. The beginning balance in the Fund Balance needs to be adjusted for the total of the debit entries in the closing entries in (a). In a lapsing appropriation, the unexpended appropriation ($5,000), which is currently part of the Fund Balance, will be returned to the agency that granted the spending authority. The year-end Fund Balance is computed as follows:

Beginning Balance in Fund Balance	$136,800
Less: Adjustments ($2,500 + $2,000)	4,500
End of Fiscal Year Balance in Fund Balance	$132,300

2. The beginning balance in the Fund Balance is adjusted for the total of the debit entries in the closing journal entry in (b).

Beginning Balance in Fund Balance[2]	$136,800
Loss: Adjustments to Fund Balance for	
Debits in Closing Entries	9,500
End of Fiscal Year Balance in Fund Balance	$127,300

e. The similary between the two statements is that the total assets and total liabilities and fund balance amounts are equal at $160,200. The differences relate to the recording of the outstanding Appropriations, Reserve for Encumbrances, and the Encumbrances.

   The Encumbrance cannot be considered an asset because it does not provide a future benefit. Therefore, it is not listed with the assets. Instead, it is shown as a reduction of an outstanding appropriation. The effect of the encumbrance once it is reversed and the invoice is paid is a decrease of the appropriation. The appropriation and the encumbrance cancel one another.

   The Reserve for Encumbrances account is a reserve of the Fund Balance, indicating the entire Fund Balance is not available for spending. This reserve account performs the same function as a Reserve for the Inventory of Supplies. Notice the total of the Fund Balance is the same in the lapsing and nonlapsing financial statements. In addition, the amount available for spending is equal in both cases.

f. The difference is equal to ($120,000 − $118,000) $2,000. This amount is probably not a serious difference if it is spread over all the revenue sources, but if it is related to only one revenue source, it may be a serious difference. In that case, a reevaluation of this particular revenue source may be necessary so that projections will be more accurate in the future.

EXERCISE 5-2

1. a. July 1,

19x1	ENCUMBRANCES, 20x1	12,700	
	ENCUMBRANCES (old)		12,700
	RESERVE FOR ENCUMBRANCES (old)	12,700	
	RESERVE FOR ENCUMBRANCES, 19x1		12,700
	APPROPRIATIONS (old)	12,700	
	APPROPRIATIONS, 20x1		12,700

The new accounts opened on July 1 are Encumbrances, 20x1; Reserve for Encumbrances, 20x1; and Appropriations, 20x1. The purpose of this procedure is to ensure that these encumbrances and appropriations are associated with the proper year—the period ending June 30, 20x1—and the old Encumbrance, Reserve for Encumbrances, and Appropriations accounts are closed.

b. July 15,

20x1	RESERVE FOR ENCUMBRANCES, 20x1	12,700	
	ENCUMBRANCES, 20x1		12,700
	EXPENSES, 20x1	13,200	
	CASH		13,200

c. June 30,

20x2	FUND BALANCE	500	
	APPROPRIATIONS, 20x1	12,700	
	EXPENSES, 20x1		13,200

2. a. July 21,   RESERVE FOR ENCUMBRANCES, 20x1   7,100
      20x1   ENCUMBRANCES, 20x1   7,100
               Reversing the encumbrances

               EXPENSES, 20x1   7,100
                  CASH   7,100
               Recognizing the expense

   b. At the cutoff date, August 31, the remaining outstanding encumbrances for
      which no invoices have been received ($400) are canceled.
      Aug. 31,   RESERVE FOR ENCUMBRANCES, 20x1   400
      20x1   ENCUMBRANCES, 20x1   400
               Reversing the encumbrances

               APPROPRIATIONS, 20x1   400
                  FUND BALANCE   400
               Closing the Appropriations account to the Fund Balance

   c. June 30,   APPROPRIATIONS, 20x1   7,100
      20x2   EXPENSES, 20x1   7,100
               Closing entries

3. a. July 1,   RESERVE FOR ENCUMBRANCES (old)   7,300
      20x2   RESERVE FOR ENCUMBRANCES, 20x2   7,300
               ENCUMBRANCES, 20x2   7,300
                  ENCUMBRANCES (old)   7,300
               APPROPRIATIONS (old)   7,300
                  APPROPRIATIONS, 20x2   7,300

   b. July 16,   RESERVE FOR ENCUMBRANCES, 20x2   1,250
      20x2   ENCUMBRANCES, 20x2   1,250
               Reversing the encumbrances

               EXPENSES, 20x2   1,200
                  CASH   1,200
               Recognizing the expense

      July 31,   RESERVE FOR ENCUMBRANCES, 20x2   525
      20x2   ENCUMBRANCES, 20x2   525

               Reversing the encumbrances
               APPROPRIATIONS, 20x2   525
                  FUND BALANCE   525
               Closing unused appropriation to Fund Balance[1]

Aug. 10, 20x2	RESERVE FOR ENCUMBRANCES, 20x2	5,175	
	ENCUMBRANCES, 20x2		5,175

Reversing the encumbrances

	EXPENSES, 20x2	5,500	
	CASH		5,500

Recognizing the expense

Aug. 31, 20x2	RESERVE FOR ENCUMBRANCES, 20x2	350	
	ENCUMBRANCES, 20x2		350

Canceling amount remaining in encumbrance account

	APPROPRIATIONS, 20x2	350	
	FUND BALANCE		350

Closing balance of unfilled encumbrances on Aug. 31 into Fund Balance

c. June 30, 20x3	FUND BALANCE	275	
	APPROPRIATIONS, 20x2	6,425	
	EXPENSES, 20x2		6,700

Closing expenses for 20x2 to Appropriations account and Fund Balance

---

1. This entry could be made at the end of the year on June 30, 20x3, but the effect on the Fund Balance should be recorded as soon as possible.

CHAPTER 6

EXERCISE 6-1

1. a. Statement of Revenues, Expenditures and Changes in Fund Balance

   b. Balance Sheet

   c. Statement of Revenues, Expenditures, and Changes in Fund Balance—Budget and Actual

2. The General Fund records the accounting transactions for the daily operations of the organization. The unrestricted transactions of the organization are recorded in the General Fund.

3. Although the same amount of cash may be received by both the General and Special Revenue Fund, the amount received by the Special Revenue Fund is restricted to a specific use and cannot be expended for the general daily operations of the organization.

4. Discretionary board restrictions in the Fund Balance relate to the unreserved portion of the Fund Balance. A board restriction of the Fund Balance is a reserve of a portion of the Fund Balance for a specific use. Once this restriction has been made by the board, this portion of the Fund Balance is called "designated." The board may establish this portion of the Fund Balance for some future activity. In any case, it is a discretionary reservation which means the board can remove the designation as they see fit.

5. Both events (a) and (b) represent potential liabilities to the organizations and as such are considered contingencies. There are three different ways that contingencies can be handled. They can be (1) ignored in the financial statements; (2) disclosed in the notes; or (3) disclosed in the notes and journalized in the ledgers.

   A journal entry is required if it is very likely that the event will occur. There are two types of journal entries that could be made. The first type would reserve a portion of the Fund Balance for the potential liability which might occur. The second type recognizes a loss as a debit entry and establishes a liability with a credit entry. In the case of a lawsuit, this latter entry would not be made unless the court had already decided the amount of the damage settlement against the organization. To recognize a loss and a liability prior to the damage award being settled is to admit guilt in the case; therefore, this entry would only be made after the amount of the damage settlement had been determined.

   A reserve of the Fund Balance would not likely be considered an admission of guilt, and if it appeared that the organization would lose its case, this type of entry would be acceptable. When the possibility of a loss is disclosed in the notes, the range of the loss, if it is estimable, should be disclosed.

   To summarize, an entry should be made if it is likely that the organization will lose its court case. Disclosure should be made if there is a reasonable possibility of a potential obligation occurring out of the litigation. If the suit is a nuisance suit and there are not likely to be any damages awarded, disclosure does not have to be made in the notes. The disclosure in the notes should disclose the circumstances of the case, and, if estimable, the possible loss or a range of loss.

   a. The event of a loss of $75,000 is likely for the Pole Town Library. Therefore, disclosure should be made and a journal entry recorded. As the case has not been settled, it is likely that the entry to reserve a portion of the Fund Balance would be appropriate. This entry follows:

FUND BALANCE—UNDESIGNATED	75,000	
FUND BALANCE—DESIGNATED BY BOARD		75,000

   Reserving portion of Fund Balance for potential contingency in lawsuit

In addition to the entry, the circumstances of the case should be disclosed in the notes in the following manner:

Litigation: During October 20x0, a civil action was filed against the Library by the estate of the late Mr. _____ alleging the violation of an agreement whereby $75,000 was contributed to the Library. The suit asks for the return of the $75,000.

The Library has engaged its attorney to vigorously contest this action. The Board, after taking into consideration information furnished by counsel, has established a reserve in the Fund Balance.

b. The potential of a $125,000 loss for the Mason-Dixon Library is unlikely in this lawsuit, and if any loss occurs, it is likely to be in the range of $1,000 to $3,000. As the occurrence of a loss is unlikely, no journalization is necessary. Disclosure is necessary, but the amount of any settlement is so small it will not be disclosed. The note follows:

Litigation: During October, 20x1, a civil action was filed against the Library by a patron alleging that negligence on the part of the Library resulted in injury to the plaintiff. The suit asks for damages of $125,000.

The Library has engaged its attorney to vigorously contest this action and has denied the allegations set forth therein. The Board, after taking into consideration information furnished by counsel, is of the opinion that the outcome of this matter will not materially affect the financial position or operations of the Library.

6. The distinction between earned revenue and contributions is related to the manner in which they are generated. *Revenues* usually are generated through providing something of value, i.e., service, product, to a third party in return for the receipt of revenues. Examples are membership dues. In NFOs revenue can also be generated from fines such as overdue book fines. This source of revenue is derived from the sovereign authority of governments. *Contributions* are provided without any expectation of some benefit or service being received in return. Typical examples are grants, gifts, and bequests.

7. Mr. Thomas should not be rewarded as he overexpended his budget by $5,000. To see this, the adjusted budget of $90,000 should be the reference point ($100,000 − $10,000) not the original budget appropriation of $100,000. Second, the comparison should be with $95,000 (encumbrances outstanding and the expenditures) not $80,000 of expenditures, alone. (Of course, if Mr. Thomas can convince the Director that encumbrances are not a current budget issue, he will be rewarded even for overexpending his budget.)

8. Depreciation is the allocation of the purchase cost of an asset to the service periods during which it provided benefits to the organization.

CHAPTER 7

EXERCISE 7-1

1. a.   ENCUMBRANCES—Prior Year   15,200
                  FUND BALANCE—Undesignated   15,200

   Reversal of prior year's encumbrances

       RESERVE FOR ENCUMBRANCES—Prior Year   14,000
           ENCUMBRANCES—Prior Year   14,000

   Canceling prior year encumbrances

       EXPENDITURES—Prior Year   14,700
           CASH   14,700

   Payment of actual amounts owed on prior year encumbrances

       RESERVE FOR ENCUMBRANCES—Prior Year   1,200
           ENCUMBRANCES—Prior Year   1,200

   Canceling outstanding encumbrances

       APPROPRIATIONS   1,200
           FUND BALANCE—Undesignated   1,200

   Reversing the unfilled or canceled encumbrances from the prior year and returning the unexpended funds to the undesignated fund balance at end of fiscal year

   b. June 30 EXPENDITURES   315
              CASH SHORTAGE   10
                 CASH   325

   Replenishing Petty Cash Fund and recognizing the shortage [The shortage should be recognized as part of Miscellaneous Expenditure on the financial statements.]

   c. Seven months have passed since this lease was signed. Therefore, seven months are an expenditure (3,600/12 = 300) × 7 = 2,100; remaining $1,500

   June 30 FUND BALANCE—Undesignated   1,500
              RESERVE FOR LEASES   1,500

   Recognize a reserve in the fund balance for the unexpired rent on the lease

   d. June 30 PLEDGES RECEIVABLE   7,500
              PLEDGE REVENUE   7,125
              ESTIMATED UNCOLLECTIBLE PLEDGES   375

   Recognizing pledges receivable, revenues, and estimated uncollectible pledges

    ESTIMATED UNCOLLECTIBLE PLEDGES   120
        PLEDGES RECEIVABLE   120
    Writing off uncollectible pledges

e. June 30 FUND BALANCE—Undesignated   9,000
          FUND BALANCE—Designated   9,000
          Recording transfer from undesignated to the designated portion of
          the Fund Balance

EXERCISE 7-2

1. General Fund:

June 10   EXPENSES   500
              Regional History   500
                  CASH   500
          Recognizing expenses made in anticipation of a federal grant

June 30   DUE FROM THE SPECIAL REVENUE
          FUND—Regional History   500
          EXPENSES   500
              Regional History   500
          Recognizing the amount due from the Special Revenue Fund for
          expenditures made by the General Fund for the Special Revenue
          Fund in advance of the receipt of the grant

Special Revenue Fund—Regional History:

June 30   EXPENSES   500
              Federal Grant   500
                  DUE TO THE GENERAL FUND   500
          Recognition of expenditures paid by the General Fund for the
          Special Revenue Fund. [The expenditures need to be recognized in
          the fund for which they were incurred.]

2. The trial balance for the H. K. Fines Special Revenue Fund follows. It is prepared prior to the completion of the financial statements as shown in the Appendix to chapter 7.

Special Revenue Fund
Trial Balance
For the Year Ended June 30, 20x1

Cash	$29,700	—
Deferred Revenue	—	$22,200
Expenditures	7,500	—
Revenue Support	—	7,500
Due to General Fund	—	7,500
Total	$37,200	$37,200

CHAPTER 8

EXERCISE 8-1

1. The Change of Order form is an organized and legal method for making changes in the monies budgeted for construction-in-progress. Although all attempts are made to stay within set construction guidelines, circumstances may develop that require revisions in the construction project. At that time, a Change of Order is issued to the contractor describing the change and the cost of the change.

2. Progress payments are those payments that are made to a contractor over the life of a long-term construction project. These payments are made in installments that mirror the stages of completion on the project.

3. Progress payments should be retained in three cases. First, if the construction contract states that a specified percentage of the payment will be retained until the building is completed and accepted. Second, payments should be retained for materials that have been purchased by the contractor but are not physically in place in the construction. These materials can be stolen so payment should be withheld until they are actually part of the construction-in-progress. Third, if the progress payments are requested long in advance of the stage of construction actually completed. For example, a progress payment should be retained if it would result in 70 percent of all payments transferred to the contractor when actual construction is only 30 percent completed.

4. The CPF is different from the General Fund in that the CPF resources are used for one purpose: the construction of a physical facility. General Fund monies can be used for a variety of general operating purposes; hence it is not clear how the fund's remaining unexpended appropriations will be used. In order to exercise closer control over governmental resources, the General Fund usually returns its unexpended appropriations.

EXERCISE 8-2

1. The director is correct in wanting to establish an asset replacement policy by setting aside monies for the purchase of fixed assets. There is no assurance that monies will be available for future purchases of new fixed assets when they are needed. Yet, it is unlikely that the board will provide appropriations for the set aside of monies for future replacements. Frequently, the replacement policy for an NFO's fixed asset begins when the old asset has become so dilapidated that it cannot be used. The director might be more successful in establishing a fixed asset maintenance policy with the board to ensure that the assets already in use are properly maintained.

2. The renewal should be recorded in the GFAAG as follows:

LIBRARY BUILDING	11,000	
INVESTMENT IN GENERAL FIXED ASSETS—State Grant		11,000
Loading Dock		11,000

Recording a renewal as an addition to the library building

3. It is difficult to determine an accurate value for inexhaustible collections. They may be priceless. For this reason, they are not recorded at any value in the GFAAG. Disclosures are provided in the notes as to their estimated range in value. Exhaustible collections, represented by the circulating collection, are recorded at a base stock valuation. This valuation is an estimate representing a viable collection of circulating books for the patrons in that library. This estimated valuation may change as the needs of the library patrons change.

4. Land is an inexhaustible asset like inexhaustible collections. Unlike inexhaustible collections, however, the value of land is easily determinable through appraisals. Therefore, the value of the land is recorded on the books, but the value of the inexhaustible collection is not recorded, mainly because its value is so difficult to determine.

5. GFAAG:

> INVESTMENT IN GFA—General Fund   7,500
>> Office Equipment   7,500
>
> Write-off of office equipment

General Fund:

> Cash   1,800
>> Revenues   1,800
>
> Recording the receipt of cash sale

6. Depreciation is the allocation of the value of an asset to the time periods it provides benefits to the organization. The recording of depreciation is optional under current GAAP for NFOs and, as a result, it is usually not recorded. There is no reason to record depreciation in NFOs. Depreciation is not a funds flow, i.e., depreciation expense is not paid to anyone. Further, the recording of depreciation will not ensure that a fixed asset is properly maintained.

CHAPTER 9

EXERCISE 9-1

1. a. Capital additions are increases in the Fund Balance of an endowment. Capital additions can arise from three main sources. These sources are gifts, net realized gains, or net investment income. If these amounts are contributing to increases in the principal of an endowment, they should not be recognized as revenues or as other types of income because they are permanently restricted for use once they become part of the endowment's principal, whereas revenues are not restricted in this manner.

  b. The total-return concept has developed as a definition of the return that is expendable. Under the total-return concept, the return is considered to be the net realized gains of the endowment as well as the investment income. In some cases, even the net unrealized gains are part of the total return. When the total-return concept is not adopted, the return on an endowment is considered to be the investment income earned only.

c. Quasi endowments are established by the NFO rather than by an outside donor. As it was established by the NFO, such an endowment operates as a discretionary endowment, which can be closed at the discretion of the board.

d. The spending rate is established as part of the total-return concept. It is the percentage of the total return that is available for spending. It is a rate that is established by the board.

e. An investment pool is formed by merging the assets of a group of endowments into one portfolio. The group shares the income and the net realized gains in the investment pool. The main advantages of this type of arrangement arise from sharing the risk of investing, increases in the efficiency of investment decisions, and the possibility of lower commission charges.

EXERCISE 9-2

1. *Cross Trust*: (These entries record the transfer of cash between the two funds and the recognition of a capital addition in the nonexpendable endowment.)

June 30	GAIN ON SALE OF INVESTMENTS	27,000	
	CAPITAL ADDITIONS—Net Realized Gain		27,000

Recognizing capital addition equal to net gains on the investment. [Gains on the sale of investments are initially recorded as credit to the Gain on Sale of Investments account until they are later transferred into the Capital Additions account as shown here.]

June 30	TRANSFERS-OUT: FORTH TRUST	30,000	
	CASH		30,000

Recording transfer of cash to the Forth Trust

Forth Trust:

June 30	CASH	30,000	
	TRANSFERS-IN: CROSS TRUST		30,000

Recognizing cash received from Cross Trust

2. *Carrie Trust*:

Oct. 1	CASH	6,000	
	TRUST REVENUES		6,000

Recording net income received by endowment on its investments

Oct. 1	CASH	35,000	
	GAIN ON SALE OF INVESTMENTS		5,000
	INVESTMENTS		30,000

Recording realized gains on sale of investments

| Oct. 1 | TRANSFERS-OUT: CARRIE TRUST | 11,000 | |
| | CASH | | 11,000 |

Recording the amount transferred to the expendable trust

Moe Trust:

| Oct. 1 | CASH | 11,000 | |
| | TRANSFERS-IN: CARRIE TRUST | | 11,000 |

Recording transfers-in from the nonexpendable trust

3. *Ross Trust*:

| July 1 | TRANSFERS-OUT: LOWE TRUST | 25,000 | |
| | CASH | | 25,000 |

Forwarding cash to the Lowe Trust equal to a spending rate of 10 percent.[1]

Lowe Trust:

| July 1 | CASH | 25,000 | |
| | TRANSFERS-IN: ROSS TRUST | | 25,000 |

Recording receipt of cash from the Ross Trust [This entry does not disclose that realized and unrealized gains account for 28 percent of the cash transferred to the Lowe Trust.]

---

1. The amount available to the General Fund is determined by multiplying the total cost value of the securities, $250,000, by the spending rate of 10 percent. This computation makes $25,000 available to the Lowe Trust. Of this amount $18,000 is available in net income, and the rest comes from realized gains of $2,000 and unrealized gains of $5,000.

EXERCISE 9-3

1. a.

	Shares	Computation
Endowment X	1,467	110,000/75
Endowment Y	960	(15,000 + 57,000)/75
Total	2,427	

b. $17,000 + $20,000 = $37,000/2,427 = $15.245 per share

Endowment X 1,467 × $15.245 = $22,364.42
Endowment Y   960 × $15.245 = $14,635.20
                              $36,999.62

2. a. *Investment pool's books*:

| | FUND BALANCE—NFO | 59,000 | |
| | CASH | | 59,000 |

Recording the transfer of the NFO's trust at the market value of the assets to the NFO

b. *NFO's books*:

INVESTMENTS	9,000	
FUND BALANCE IN TRUST		9,000

Updating the investments to their market value [The NFO had recorded its investments on a cost basis so it must update those values to their market values of $59,000.]

FUND BALANCE IN TRUST	59,000	
INVESTMENTS		59,000

Recording withdrawal from the investment pool [After the fund balance and investments are adjusted to the market value of the investments, the withdrawal is shown as a reduction in the fund balance and investments. This entry records the liquidation of $59,000 of the NFO's investments in the investment pool.]

CASH	59,000	
TRANSFER-IN: INVESTMENT POOL		59,000

Recording the transfer of cash from the investment pool to the NFO

3. Unrealized gains and losses are automatically recorded when market value is used to value a security because the change from one market value to another *is* the unrealized gain or loss.

CHAPTER 10

EXERCISE 10-1

1. A consolidated financial statement eliminates all interrelated liabilities, receivables, or other similar interrelated accounts that exist between two or more separate organizational or accounting groups within one organization. This method views the whole organization as being of primary importance, and its parts of secondary importance. The combined approach regards the parts to be of equal importance within the overall organization. Combined financial statements do not eliminate the interrelated accounts. The balances in these interrelated accounts are added together to arrive at the organization's totals in the combined financial statements. These totals are called memorandum totals. NFOs generally use the combined approach, but only when separate subdivisions of a specific fund exist, the consolidated approach may be used to eliminate interrelated receivable and payables.

2. The CAFR contains three sections: introductory, financial, and statistical. The introductory section may include a transmittal letter from the chief executive of the organization. The purpose of the introductory section is to familiarize read-

ers with the organization, its operating environment, and the services it provides. The transmittal letter discusses the financial environment now and in the future, and it may describe some of the organization's accomplishments. Within the financial material are the combined financial statements, notes to the financial statements, combining financial statements, account group reports, and the auditor's opinion. The statistical section includes data such as listing of grant dollars received, patron usage statistics, and other nonfinancial data. This section is not covered by the audit opinion.

The GPFS are sometimes called "liftable" financial statements. They may be issued separately from the CAFR to readers who do not need the detailed information in the CAFR. The GPFS consist of the combined financial statements, the accompanying notes, and a GPFS audit opinion.

The combined statements provide a broad view of the financial position of the NFO. Although the combined statements do not present account reports, the notes to the combined statements do present information contained in the account groups as for example with the general fixed assets. The combining statements show information in more detail by providing financial data about each governmental fund. Thus, the combining statements provide the less aggregated fund information that supports the combined fund balances.

EXERCISE 10-2

1. Percentage of Mandated Expenditures and Transfers:

$$\frac{\$247,568 + 0}{\$1,098,275} = 25\%$$

Discretionary Fund Balance Changes:

$$\frac{\$12,055 + \$65,950}{\$203,450 + \$7,000 + \$500 + \$4,945 + \$12,055 + \$65,950} = 26.5\%$$

Fund Balance Ratio:

$$\frac{\$12,055 + \$65,950}{\$437,600} = 17.8\%$$

Spending Ratio:

$$\frac{\$385,800 + \$750,000 + \$113,800}{\$1,098,275 + 0} = 1.14$$

Excess/Deficiency Ratio (General Fund):

$$\frac{\$12,525}{\$178,300} = 7.02\%$$

Government Support:

$$\frac{\$173,500 + \$7,500 + \$100,000 + \$100,000 + \$750,000}{\$385,800 + \$750,000 + \$113,800} = 90.5\%$$

Rate of Return on Investments:

$$\frac{\$29,000 + \$33,000}{\$1,010,500} = 6.1\%$$

Deferred Maintenance Ratio:

$$\frac{\$250,000}{\$7,395,000 \times .05} = 67.6\%$$

Cash Turnover:

$$\frac{\$1,098,275 + 0}{(\$376,550 + \$376,050)/2} = 2.92$$

2. a. (1) A large percentage of the library's expenses and transfers are mandated.
        This affects the library's ability to respond to changes by financially support-
        ing new initiatives. (2) There has been an increase from the previous year in
        the amount of discretionary fund balances available. This indicates that the
        library has surplus resources available for spending. (3) It is difficult to inter-
        pret anything from this ratio without additional information. (4) The library's
        expenditures and mandatory transfers are less than its revenue and support.
        This is probably the reason for the increase in the discretionary Fund
        Balance. (5) This ratio shows that the General Fund had an excess during the
        20x3 fiscal year equal to 1% of the total revenue and support. It would be
        useful to have more information on this ratio from previous years so that
        additional conclusions could be made. (6) Governmental support makes up
        the largest portion of the revenue and support received by the library. (7) The
        rate of return on investments is equal to 6 percent. These are short-term
        investments and their rate of return should be at least close to other types of
        short-term investments such as U.S. Treasury bills. (8) This ratio indicates
        that maintenance expenditures on the library's fiscal facilities are presently 40
        percent below what is needed to properly maintain the library's fixed assets.
        (9) Comparative data from previous years need to be available to interpret
        this ratio.

    b. In this analysis, it would be helpful to have financial data from the previous
        two years so that a three-year comparison of the ratios could be made. It
        would also be helpful to have some performance (or benchmark) information
        from other sources such as the market rate of returns on short-term invest-
        ments.

3. The percentage of mandated expenses and transfers over the three-year period
has been decreasing as a percentage of total revenue and support (6). This
decrease in mandated expenses and transfers is probably related to the decreased
level of government support over the same three-year period. The cash turnover
ratio (9) has increased over the three-year period, indicating that the library is
attempting to maintain the minimum cash balance on hand. This may allow the
organization to keep more of its cash invested. This fact by itself may not
increase the Rate of Return on Investments (7), but it may affect the type of
investments that are made as well as reducing commission costs. (It is assumed
that this library is managing its own investment portfolio.) At any rate, the
return on investments has doubled over the three-year period.

The discretionary part of the Fund Balance (2) has decreased along with the
dollar amount of the Fund Balance (3) as a percentage of total assets. This trend
reversed itself in 20x3 when both percentages increased. Both these ratios may
be affected by the Spending Ratio (4) and the Excess/Deficiency Ratio (5).
These ratios both showed deterioration in 20x1 and 20x2, meaning that the
library was having difficulties keeping its expenditures and transfers within the
amount of revenues and support it received. In 20x1, there was a negative
Excess/Deficiency Ratio, which shows more was spent by the General Fund
than was received. This trend is also indicated in the Deferred Maintenance
Ratio which has shown a deterioration over the three years as library management has cut maintenance expenditures in order to transfer those monies to
other uses.

The library appears to be in sound financial condition at the present time.
When 20x3 expenditures and transfers are compared with revenue and support,
excesses have been reduced. This trend is more apparent in 20x3 than in the previous two years. There are no major financial recommendations for the library.
The library has a high level of government support, without which it would
experience difficulty in meeting program goals. The percentages of mandated
expenditures and transfers have been decreasing, along with governmental
support. Even with decreasing government support, the library is still able to
keep expenditures and transfers within revenue and support levels. This is an
indication of an attempt at fiscal responsibility. Unfortunately, the library has
succeeded at matching inflows and outflows by curtailing maintenance expenditures. In 20x3, the library is making only half of the expenditures necessary to
maintain its fixed assets. This is likely to result in higher costs in the future
through the premature replacement of fixed assets that have not been properly
maintained. Library management should be advised of the consequences of this
policy.

4. a. Rate of Return on Investments: In a cash system, the amount of investment
income is recognized as the cash flows into the organization and not when it
is actually earned, as occurs in modified accrual accounting under nonexpendable endowments. The rate of return under a cash system is very likely to be
different than under modified accrual-based accounting. Depending on market
conditions, this rate may be either higher or lower in a cash system than in a
modified accrual basis.

b. Spending Ratio: The ratio is affected by differences in the timing of revenue, support, and expense/expenditure recognition between the cash and modified accrual methods. The effect on the ratio is uncertain.

c. Deferred Maintenance Ratio: The timing of the maintenance expenditures is likely to be consistent in the cash and modified accrual bases so long as these costs are handled internally and not by an external service company used by the library. If maintenance costs are outsourced to a service company, then there would be some timing differences between the cash system and the modified accrual method. Otherwise, the ratio should be the same under both methods.

EXERCISE 10-3

1. The answers to this question will vary a great deal.

a. One performance measure would be the following:

$$\text{percent of increase or decrease} = 1 - \frac{\text{Current Year's Pledges Received}}{\text{Last Year's Pledges Received}}$$

This measure would determine the amount of percentage increase or decrease in pledge collections from the previous year. The organization would do well to establish a goal of increasing the percentage of pledges collected from one year to the next.

b. The percentage of uncollectible pledges could be determined based on the total pledges made. A goal could be established to reduce this percentage from previous years. To evaluate the effectiveness of collection efforts, the relationship between the amount of late pledges collected and specific collection efforts, e.g., number of letters or telephone calls, should be evaluated.

c. The expenses for the year could be divided into the revenue and support received from governmental sources. The total expenses also could be divided into the pledges collected. These measures show the contribution toward expenses by both sources of revenue and support. It would be hoped that as the percentage of governmental support decreased, the percentage contributed by pledges would increase. In this manner, the ratios will show whether the decrease in governmental support is being replaced through the pledges received.

2. Behavioral problems can develop from the use of performance measures when only one measure is used. Usually personnel whose activities are going to be evaluated will try to achieve the goals set under the performance measure regardless of possible detrimental consequences for the organization. In such cases, the individual's goals may be achieved, but at the same time, the organization's goals will not be reached. In the case of the Custodial Department, the goal of cost reduction was met, to the overall detriment of the organization. Repair and maintenance costs were reduced to the point where the structure of the building was damaged. If the only goal is to cut costs, the Custodial Depart-

ment needs only to stop using materials and supplies. If the goal is to cut costs *and* maintain the building, other performance measures have to be instituted, such as the number of hours per employee spent on repair, cost per repair project, and the number of repair jobs completed. Using one performance measure will always distort the behavior of evaluated personnel, especially when a great deal of emphasis is placed on that measure.

3. Several factors need to be considered before any action is taken against Mr. Jones. First, the question should be answered as to why Ms. Wilson never exceeded her budget. To begin with, the budget may have been excessive, and the resources allocated to Circulation were more than was needed. Therefore, the budget adopted by Mr. Jones in his first year as department head was more realistic than those under Ms. Wilson. Perhaps Ms. Wilson had neglected certain types of repairs that had to be corrected by Mr. Jones in his first year as head of Circulation. Before any action is taken, these questions should be answered. It may be that the budget recommended by Mr. Jones and adopted by the board was a more honest budget than the ones recommended and adopted under Ms. Wilson. Ms. Wilson's actual spending may never have exceeded her budget because the amounts she managed to get into the budget were more than she needed in the first place.

GLOSSARY

accounting cycle   The accounting cycle outlines the sequence of accounting procedures in the order they should be performed in a fund accounting system. Performance of these accounting steps in this sequence ensures the proper recording and functioning of the fund accounting system.

accounting equation   The concept that the assets of the organization are equal to its liabilities and fund balance. When this occurs, the accounts are in balance. Sometimes called the *bookkeeping equation.*

accrual method   An accounting method that focuses primarily on the passage of time to recognize revenues and expenses rather than on the flow of resources or cash.

adjusting entries   Journal entries made at the end of the year and as part of the accounting cycle to update or provide a "catch-up" on changes due to the passage of time rather than the occurrence of an actual business transaction. For example, recording interest that has been earned but not yet received.

agency fund   This fund accounts for monies that are passed through the NFO to another NFO or government. The monies are only temporarily held by the NFO until they are passed on to the agency that will spend the monies. A government can have several agency funds.

allotments   Allotments are spending restrictions on annual appropriations that set dollar limits for each quarter to ensure that annual appropriations are not entirely spent before the end of the year. As a result, tighter control is exercised over the expenditure process.

American Institute of Certified Public Accountants (AICPA)   The body that represents certified public accountants in the United States and has responsibility for preparing auditing standards to be followed by the profession.

amortized cost   This is the cost of a debt security adjusted for the premium or discount at which it was purchased and the time period that has lapsed since the purchase occurred.

appropriations   An appropriation is a legal authorization for making expenditures set by amount, time period, and purpose.

arm's-length transaction   A business transaction in which the parties involved are independent of one another. The transaction is based around market forces and no one party to the transaction has a business advantage over the other party that would allow an unfair exchange to occur.

assets   Items with a determinable future value to an organization that are owned by the organization.

audit   The procedures that are followed by the CPA in reviewing the financial statements prepared by management. Audit practices are used to ascertain that management has followed GAAP methods in preparing the financial statements and that needed disclosures have been made to inform the public about the NFO's significant financial circumstances.

audit opinion   A statement in the annual report indicating whether management has prepared the financial statements in accordance with generally accepted accounting principles.

availability criteria   At the end of the fiscal year, collections within 60 days of the year-end are recognized as revenues of the current year under the principles of modified accrual accounting. This criterion is not used under accrual or cash accounting.

Balance Sheet   A financial statement that reports on the balances in asset, liability, and Fund Balance accounts as of the last day of the fiscal year.

betterment   An expenditure that extends the life of a fixed asset is capitalized and considered to be a betterment and not a repair expense.

book value   The book value of an asset is the net value that the asset is listed at in the accounts of the organization. Many times the book value is compared with the market value or market price of an asset.

budget   A guide and forecast for a future period, usually a year, of the type of expenditures and revenues that are expected to be made and received, respectively. Some NFOs may be legally required to prepare the budget on a basis other than GAAP.

budgetary accounts   These are accounts that are expected to be realized at the amounts that are shown in them in the beginning of the year when the budget is recorded. They are estimates, not actual dollar amounts. In governmental accounting, these estimates are recorded in the journals and ledgers as if they had actually occurred. They include Appropriations, Estimated Revenues, Encumbrances, and Reserve for Encumbrances. *See* proprietary accounts.

capital maintenance   The accrual method of accounting uses capital maintenance concepts. *See* resource flows.

Capital Projects Fund (CPF)   Capital projects funds record the appropriations used in constructing a new physical facility such as a new building or annex. All appropriations and other funding available for the construction project are accounted for in the CPF. It would be acceptable to have one Capital Projects Fund for each construction project.

capitalization   When incurred costs are considered to have a future value, and thus recorded as assets in the books rather than as expenditures, they are *capitalized.*

cash method   This method of accounting records business transactions when a cash exchange has actually taken place. Its emphasis is on the flow of cash rather than the passage of time or the flow of resources.

certified public accountant (CPA)   A certified public accountant is someone who has passed a nationally standardized examination developed by the AICPA and administered by state CPA societies. CPAs must meet other conditions for certification as required under the laws of the certifying state, such as experience requirements.

Change of Order   This form records an agreed-upon change in a construction project, detailing the specific change and the cost of the change. It is made between the contractor and client paying for the construction.

closing entries   The closing entries are journalized at the end of the year. They close all revenues and expenditure/expense accounts into the Fund Balance. These entries are made at the end of every year so that in the new year all revenues and expenditures can be freshly recorded. Thus, revenues and expenditures are related to an annual period, unlike the accumulation of assets and unpaid liabilities.

combined financial statement   A combined financial statement aggregates each individual fund and account group into a separate major fund grouping for each fund type as well as reporting on memo totals. For example, it does not show separate financial reports for each separate special revenue fund, but combines all the special revenue funds into one financial report for all special revenue funds.

combining financial statements   Combining financial statements report on each separate fund individually. For example, all special revenue funds are shown separately and not combined in one special revenue report.

commercial paper   An investment vehicle used by some NFOs. Commercial paper is based on the good name of the organization issuing the notes and is not backed or secured by collateral.

component unit   Component units are governmental entities that are part of a larger governmental unit. Although legally separate, the larger governmental unit has primary control over the component unit. Most libraries and many other NFOs are component units of other governmental organizations.

Comprehensive Annual Financial Report (CAFR) This annual financial report covers all funds and account groups of the reporting government; it includes an introductory section, combined, combining, and individual fund statements as well as notes to the financial statements, schedules, narrative descriptions, and any statistical tables.

consolidations Consolidated financial reports require that cross-fund accounts be removed from all completed financial statements. Under governmental accounting, consolidation is done between similar fund groups, such as among special revenue funds, but is not done between dissimilar fund groups, such as the general fund and the special revenue fund.

construction-in-progress Large construction projects that are uncompleted as of the reporting date are reported as construction-in-progress. After their completion, their completed cost is removed from the construction-in-progress account and recorded as a completed asset, i.e., building, annex, parking lot.

consumption method Inventory accounting used under modified accrual and accrual methods where the annual cost of inventory is equal to the amount used rather than the amount purchased during the year. *See* purchases method.

cost of capital This is the interest rate (cost) for borrowing long-term financing (capital resource). If no long-term debt is issued by the NFO, it should be the rate (cost) incurred on the monies transfer to the NFO by the city, county, or state. This is also referred to as a discount rate.

deferred maintenance If maintenance expenditures are not made on a routine basis to keep the fixed asset in proper working order, the maintenance has been deferred. As a result, the service potential of the asset has been reduced. The gap between the maintenance performed and maintenance required to keep the asset in working order can be measured and recorded to prevent the passing of this cost, unrecognized, on to later time periods.

deficit A loss arising from expenses/expenditures in excess of revenues during the current period.

depreciation The allocation of the value (purchase price or construction cost) of a long-term fixed asset to the time periods to which the asset provides benefits. Depreciation is the accounting recognition of the usage or obsolescence of the asset. It is recorded as an expense, but unlike other expenses, it does not create a cash or resource outflow.

dollar-for-dollar accountability This concept is used in budgeting to assign accountability for each budget dollar that is expended.

"Due from" accounts   These accounts represent monies receivable from other governments. They are assets. *See* "Due to" accounts.

"Due to" accounts   These accounts represent monies owed to other governmental units. They are liabilities. *See* "Due from" accounts.

encumbrance   An encumbrance discloses a commitment of budgetary monies for an anticipated purchase. It is recorded at the time the purchase order is issued by the NFO. An encumbrance is not a liability.

Endowment Fund   An endowment, or trust, fund is used to account for donor-contributed gifts and other contributed items of value. In some cases, the assets may be designated by the board as an endowment. *See* expendable endowment and nonexpendable endowment.

entity concept   This concept defines the boundaries of the accounting reporting focus. In governmental accounting, the fund is recognized as the major focus for transaction occurrence and reporting. In accrual or corporate accounting, the corporation as a whole is recognized as the reporting entity around which accounting transactions occur. This difference results in changes in the amount of consolidation and aggregation of reporting information. More aggregation occurs in corporate reporting.

estimated revenues   The amount of revenues that are projected to be received at the beginning of the year. Estimated revenues are part of the legally adopted budget. They represent the amount expected to be collected and allocated for use as budget appropriations during the year.

excess   This residual occurs when revenues are more than expenses/expenditures during the current period.

expendable endowment   The resources generated through investment earnings or contributions to an endowment that can be spent. Spending may be restricted to a specific purpose or spending may be for general operations depending on the wishes of the donor or the board.

expenditure   Expended resource outflows during the current period. Expenditures include most expenses.

expense   Expiration of resources, or the incurrence of a liability recognized by the passage of time, or the incurrence of the actual expenditure used to generate revenues and provide services in the current period.

fair market value   *See* market value.

fiduciary fund   *See* agency fund.

Financial Accounting Standards Board (FASB)   This is the body that sets the accounting principles, rules, and standards that are to be followed by corporations and governmental nonprofits based on accrual accounting methods.

financial statements   The three basic financial statements for an NFO such as a library are the Balance Sheet and the Statement of Revenues, Expenditures and Changes in Fund Balance on both a GAAP basis (SREF) and a budgetary basis (SREF2). In some cases, these reports are referred to as the "financials."

fiscal period   A twelve-month accounting period used in tabulating comparable financial statements for the entity. A calendar period is from January to December, but a fiscal period may be any twelve-month time period. Most governmental organizations use a fiscal period from July to June.

fixed asset   Any asset with a life longer than one year such as land, a building, or equipment.

fund   A fund is a self-balancing set of accounts with monies set aside for a specific purpose. A fund is an accounting division used in NFO accounting to show how monies whose use is restricted in purpose are expended.

Fund Balance   A residual account, it develops because of the difference between assets and liabilities. The Fund Balance functions as both a residual between the assets and liabilities and the account where the summarization of each year's difference between the inflows of revenues and expenditure outflows occurs. For most funds, the balance in the Fund Balance indicates an available source for additional appropriations or spending.

gain   A gain or realized gain occurs when an investment is actually sold for more than it was purchased. The market price is higher than the investment's cost. *See* unrealized gain.

general fixed asset account group (GFAAG)   A self-balancing set of accounts that keeps a record of the fixed assets owned by the NFO. A common characteristic of account groups is that they do not record the inflow and outflow of resources within the NFO.

General Fund   The General Fund accounts for those appropriations or tax receipts that can be used for the general operations of the government and are not specifically designated to be used for a particular governmental activity. An NFO has only one General Fund.

general purpose financial statements (GPFS)   The general purpose financial statements are part of the comprehensive annual financial report (CAFR) and consist of the combined financial statements. The GPFS are sometimes called "liftable" because they represent the minimum portion of the financial statements that can be distributed to those readers who do not need the CAFR.

generally accepted accounting principles (GAAP)   The principles, standards, and interpretations that are followed, used, and accepted in preparing the financial statements of large publicly owned firms, nonprofit organizations, and governments.

Government Accounting Standards Board (GASB) This is the accounting body that sets the accounting principles, rules, and standards that are to be followed by state and local governments as well as most libraries. The standards are based on modified accrual accounting methods.

Government Finance Officers Association (GFOA) The GFOA is a group composed of state and local government officials who are responsible for various aspects of the finances of these organizations. The GFOA at one time was the single most important authority in setting accounting guidelines for state and local governments. This role is still apparent today with the 1994 edition of the "blue book." The blue book, also known as *Governmental Accounting, Auditing and Financial Reporting* (GAAFR), provides practical guidance on accounting practices for state and local government.

investment pool The invested assets of a number of different organizations or separate endowments may be combined for investment purposes as well as to reduce the overall risk of the portfolio. Such a grouping is called an investment pool.

journal A listing of transactions in debit and credit format by date of occurance.

journalization The recording of debits and credits in the journal book (now a computerized journal file) usually called the general journal. The journalization of a transaction is its entry point into the accounting system.

lapsing appropriation An appropriation that does not continue into the new budget year and must be returned to the government providing the funding. Under various statutes, it may be considered lapsing if it is (1) unencumbered (has no encumbrance); or (2) unexpended even if it is encumbered (committed under an encumbrance).

ledger A summarized listing of each account such as Cash, Equipment, etc., showing current balances or amounts in each account. The debit and credit balances in the ledger accounts are equal. In this book, only the general ledger is used.

liabilities Liabilities are the amounts owed to others outside the specific organization or to another specific fund. Liabilities exist as legitimate claims against the assets of an entity.

market-unit method A method of distributing investment pool earnings among the endowments or governments forming the investment pool. It is based on the change in market value of the pool's investments and the number of shares held by each member in the pool.

market value This refers to the price at which an asset, security, or other item of value will sell for in an open market. With securities, this is reported on a daily basis. With other assets, it may be more difficult to determine an accurate market value. Also called fair market value.

modified accrual method (MAM)   This accounting method uses a combination of accrual and cash-based accounting methods, and it strongly focuses on the flow of resources through funds rather than the passage of time to recognize business transactions. MAM is the recommended method of accounting for governmental NFOs.

Net Assets   Used with nongovernmental NFOs. Net assets represent the difference between assets and liabilities, like the Fund Balance, but this residual is divided into unrestricted, temporarily restricted, and permanently restricted amounts. Those net assets that have a donor-related stipulation restricting the donated resources from being used and allow only the income earned on the resources to be used are permanently restricted net assets. Those net assets that can be used for spending after the expiration of a stipulation or actions of the NFO are classified as temporarily restricted. The remaining net assets are defined as unrestricted. *See* Fund Balance.

nonexpendable endowment   The amounts contributed to the NFO whose principal must be maintained into perpetuity. When donors contribute such assets to a trust fund, their intention is that the assets will be maintained intact by the organization.

nonlapsing appropriation   An appropriation that does not expire at the end of the budget year. The NFO can use this appropriation for spending in the next year.

not-for-profit organization (NFO)   This is the acronym used throughout the book when discussing libraries. NFOs can be either governmental or nongovernmental, as explained in chapter 1.

operating transfer   This monetary transfer is a regularly recurring transfer between funds in a governmental organization.

Other Financing Sources   This account appears on the Statement of Revenues, Expenditures, and Changes in Fund Balance and is used to record operating transfers into the organization. It is considered a subdivision of revenues.

outstanding encumbrance   A purchase commitment to which appropriations have been assigned before the purchased item has been received. Outstanding encumbrances therefore remain as outstanding commitments at the year-end.

petty cash   Instead of paying for small miscellaneous items, such as delivery charges, by check, organizations place cash into a petty cash account maintained in the office and under the control of one person. The person responsible for the petty cash makes cash payments and collects receipts as small miscellaneous payments occur. Periodically, the petty cash must be reconciled and replenished.

posting   The process of copying the entries in the journal into the ledger accounts.

prepaid assets   A prepaid asset is an expense that has been paid for before the organization uses it; common examples include the prepayment of rent, insurance, or supplies. As time passes, the asset becomes an expense and the "prepaid asset" is reduced to a zero value.

proprietary accounts   Those accounts that record the actual business transactions in the organization rather than the estimated budgetary events. All accounts that relate to actual business events, as in corporate accounting. *See* budgetary accounts.

purchases method   Inventory accounting accepted under modified accrual methods where the annual cost of inventory is equal to the amount purchased during the year whether or not the inventory is entirely used during the year. *See* consumption method.

qualified audit opinion   A qualified audit opinion indicates that the entity's financial statements are less than satisfactory in some regard as generally accepted accounting principles have not been followed. *See* unqualified audit opinion.

repairs   Expenditures on fixed assets to maintain them in proper working order that do not increase their lives. *See* betterment.

repurchase agreements   Repurchase agreements are purchased from a bank by the NFO for short-term investments of cash that otherwise would be idle. In a traditional repurchase agreement, the NFO provides cash to a broker or bank. In return, the broker or bank transfers securities to the NFO as collateral. At the maturity date of the transaction, the same securities are returned to the broker and the NFO receives its cash back along with an interest payment.

reserve for encumbrances   This account is used to recognize the commitment or encumberment of appropriations for purchases that have not yet been received. With nonlapsing appropriations, it appears as a reserve of the Fund Balance at the year-end.

residual   This term can be applied in many different ways. Generally, it refers to some dollar amount that is left over at the completion of a transaction process. For example, the residual transfer occurs when a fund is closed and its remaining resources are transferred to another fund. The equity or fund balance itself is a residual of the difference between liabilities and assets. Even the book value of an asset or the excess are considered to be residuals.

residual equity transfer   A nonrecurring or one-time transfer that transfers the remaining monetary resources in one fund to another fund.

resource flows   Under modified accrual accounting, the measurement focus is on the flow of appropriations into and out of the organization's funds during the fiscal year. Under accrual accounting, the focus is on the effect of accrued expenses and revenues on the capital of the organization during the fiscal year. This latter method is called *capital maintenance*.

retainage   This is the dollar amount withheld from requested contractor payments on construction-in-progress to ensure the satisfactory completion of the project. Once the project has been inspected and approved, all retained monies are paid to the contractor.

revenues   Amounts that are realized, or owed as earned, or available. The definition of "earned" varies with the method of accounting being used.

reverse repurchase agreements   Reverse repurchase agreements occur when the NFO gives its securities as collateral for a loan and promises to repay cash and interest at the maturity date of the loan or repurchase date. Reverse repurchase agreements create a liability for the NFO whereas repurchase agreements are an asset. *See* repurchase agreements.

Special Revenue Fund   The Special Revenue Fund accounts for those appropriations or tax receipts that are specifically designated to be used for a special governmental activity. A special revenue fund should be established for each source of designated revenues.

spending rate   The percentage of the total return on investments that can be spent. The return is measured in terms of interest, gains, and possibly unrealized gains. This rate is set by the board, and it may result in the spending of unrealized gains.

Statement   Statements and Interpretations issued by the GASB or FASB represent enforceable GAAP accounting standards to be followed in preparing financial statements. *See also* financial statements.

Statement of Cash Flows   For funds based on the accrual method, this statement provides information about cash flows that would not otherwise be disclosed on other financial statements prepared under that method.

Statement of Position   A source of AICPA guidance in accounting reporting that does not represent enforceable standards to be followed.

Statement of Revenues, Expenditures, and Changes in Fund Balance (SREF)   This financial report discloses the results of operations related to revenues, other financing sources, and expenditures as well as changes in the fund balance occurring during the year.

Statement of Revenues, Expenditures, and Changes in Fund Balance—Budget and Actual (SREF2) In this statement, the results of operations related to revenues, other financing sources, and expenditures as well as changes in the fund balance are compared with those amounts budgeted for at the beginning of the year. Variances from budgeted amounts are shown and thus available for additional investigation as to the reason for the variance.

subsidiary ledger Subsidiary ledgers are subdivisions of a general ledger providing detailed information about general ledger accounts. Sometimes the general ledger account is considered to exercise control over the subsidiary ledger account. Using subsidiary ledgers makes it unnecessary to include detailed information related to general ledger accounts in the general ledger.

total-return concept Under the total-return concept, the spendable return is considered to be the net realized gains of the endowment as well as the investment income. In some cases, even the unrealized gains and losses (net) are considered part of the total return. By using this method, it is possible to increase the spendable resources available from the endowment.

transfers Monetary transfers occur between various governmental funds. They can be considered transfers-in or transfers-out. *See* operating transfer and residual equity transfer.

trial balance The trial balance is a summation of all the balances in the accounts contained in the ledger to ensure that the debits are equal to the credits. It is prepared prior to the preparation of financial statements but after the closing entries are entered in the books.

transmittal letter A letter accompanying the CAFR written by the director of the NFO and addressed to the public and the board of directors. The letter highlights the financial environment facing the NFO, indicates management responsibility for the financial statements, and describes any significant financial events.

Trust Fund *See* Endowment Fund.

unqualified audit opinion An unqualified audit opinion indicates that the entity's financial statements appear to be correctly compiled in line with GAAP. *See* qualified audit opinion.

unrealized gain An unrealized gain occurs when an investment's book value is higher than its cost. The investment has not been sold; therefore, this is a paper or unrealized profit. *See* gain.

variance As used in accounting, variances are the difference between budgeted dollars and the actual dollar levels of spending. The reporting of variances shows how closely actual spending conformed with budgeted projections and thus can serve as a performance measure.

voucher Documentation showing that a transaction has been approved and the accounts to which the debits and credits should be made in the journal. This document is used in manual accounting systems, sometimes with a voucher register.

INDEX

G. Stevenson Smith, PhD, CPA, CMA, CCA, is a professor of accounting at West Virginia University. He is the author of *Managerial Accounting for Libraries and Other Not-for-Profit Organizations* (American Library Association, 1991) as well as an earlier edition of this book. His published research has appeared in the *Journal of Accounting and Public Policy, Library Trends* (*Festschrift* edition), the *International Journal of Accounting, Journal of Accounting Education,* and *Issues in Accounting Education* as well as numerous other scholarly journals. In addition, he has conducted seminars on nonprofit accounting issues as well as provided consulting services for governmental organizations. His e-mail address is figure_man@hotmail.com.